冯汉骥全集 ❽

图书馆学卷

冯汉骥 著　　张勋燎　白　彬 主编

巴蜀书社

目录

汉和图书
分类法

Committees on Far Eastern Studies,

American Council of Learned

Societies, 1943

漢和圖書分類法

A CLASSIFICATION SCHEME

FOR

CHINESE AND JAPANESE BOOKS

BY

A. K'AI-MING CH'IU 裘開明

LIBRARIAN OF THE HARVARD–YENCHING INSTITUTE AT HARVARD UNIVERSITY

*Formerly Librarian of Amoy University, Member of the Supervisory Board
and Chairman of the Cataloging Committee of the
Library Association of China*

WITH THE ASSISTANCE OF

H. Y. FÊNG 馮漢驥

*Professor of Archaeology and Ethnology
National University of Szechuan
Formerly Director of the Provincial Library of Hupeh*

ZUNVAIR YUE 于震寰

*Chief of the Cataloging Department, National Central
Library of China, Formerly Office Manager
of the Library Association of China*

COMMITTEES ON FAR EASTERN STUDIES
AMERICAN COUNCIL OF LEARNED SOCIETIES
1219 16TH STREET, N. W., WASHINGTON, D. C.

Preliminary Lithoprint Edition, 1943

目　　次　　CONTENTS

自　序

僕畢業于大學時值吾國新文化運動初興，研究國學整理國故之聲浪彌漫國中。讀胡適之先生在北大國學季刊創刊號（民國十二年一月）提出索引式結帳式及專史式三項整理國故之步驟，心頗好之。竊思索引式之圖書整理實乃辦理圖書館者分內之事。顧當時各館部勒舊籍多仿西制，僕亦採杜威十進法試行于廈門大學圖書館。但每多扞格難通，乃變更計畫，從改良中國固有分類法入手。

民國十六年春草漢和圖書分類法大綱及署例發表于中日美三國圖書館學雜誌，並試用之于哈佛大學漢和圖書館及燕京大學圖書館。四方聞之，詢索印本者甚多。惟個人賦性迂拙，素尚實踐，施用未有成效以前，雅不欲遽然付梓以自誤誤人，僅國內外圖書館借鈔稿本數份而已。（國立北平圖書館在未擬定其舊籍十五類分類法以前曾借鈔拙法，皮高品君在發表其中國十進分類法以前曾借閱拙法，哥命比亞大學漢文圖書館曾借拙稿複本，分編其後入館書籍。）民國十九年春，燕大及哈佛兩館始將各類綱目及中西文索引油印以應館內需要，並分送數處就正專家。民國二十七年至二十九年間哈佛大學圖書館漢籍分類目錄經學類，哲學宗教類，及歷史科學類，相繼出版，蒙美國人文科學理事會遠東學術委員會（Committee on Far Eastern Studies, American Council of Learned Societies）諸君之慫德，並願由會資助印刷，不得已允將此不完全之稿本正式付印，初校排版正在中國進行中，太平洋戰事忽起，只得改用石印方法，先在美國發行。

綜計此法在孕育中十有五年，蒙前後友人同事相助者不下十餘人，僕雖訂其大綱並始終其事但本法能得稍有優點者皆益友與前賢之賜。襄助編校者，依時間先後述之有馮君漢驥，湯君吉禾，梁君思永，岩本君英夫，下山君重丸，田君洪都，房君兆楹，杜聯喆女士（房兆楹夫人），顧君廷龍，聶君崇岐，洪煨蓮教授，賈德納博士（Dr. C. S. Gardner），魏楷教授（Professor J. R. Ware），趙元任博士，葉理綏教授（Professor Serge Elisseeff），楊君聯陞及于君震寰，謹誌不忘。其中尤以馮于兩兄與僕同事最久，而對此法貢獻亦最大。又適之先生于公務百忙中為此書題簽，亦僕所深感者也。

民國三十二年春，鎮海裘開明闇輝識于美國麻省劍橋哈佛大學哈燕學社。

叙　例

考中國圖書分類法之演變，其能深切影響後世體制而可稱劃時代者凡八．

（一）漢成帝時劉向劉歆父子領校中秘典籍，首創別錄，七畧：曰輯畧，曰六藝畧，曰諸子畧，曰詩賦畧，曰兵書畧，曰術數畧，曰方技畧．（註一）後班固依七畧而作漢書藝文志，是為目錄學之鼻祖，歷兩漢三國，所有官私目錄大都採用取則．

（二）魏秘書郎鄭默就七畧改制中經．晉初秘書監荀勖又因中經更著新簿．荀氏總括羣籍，分為四部：曰甲部，紀六藝小學等書，曰乙部，統古今諸子兵家術數，曰丙部，有史記皇覽簿雜事，曰丁部，納詩賦圖贊汲冢書．

（三）東晉惠懷之亂，圖籍喪亡，著作郎李充重分四部遺書，因荀氏之法而易其乙丙之次．後世沿用甲經乙史丙子丁集之序，至此始定．

（四）唐貞觀間長孫無忌等撰修隋書，經籍一志，亦依四部分類，惟部目不標甲乙丙丁而直稱經史子集，末附道佛之書．每部分若干類，部類後各有結論，以計圖書總數並述各部類典籍之源流與興廢．其體制頗為後世諸史藝文志所效法．（註二）

（五）南宋之初鄭樵作通志二十畧，其中藝文一畧，不拘七畧四部之成例而別出心裁，重創新法，分古今書籍為十二類：曰經類，曰禮類，曰樂類，曰小學類，曰史類，曰諸子類，曰天文類，曰五行類，曰藝術類，曰醫方類，曰類書類，曰文類．類下各分數家，家之下又分數種，綱舉目張，有條不紊．自序云「學術之苟且，由源流之不分，書籍之散亡，由編次之失紀」又曰，「學術不專者，為書之不明，書之不明者，為類例之不分也」故鄭氏對于圖書分類主依義細分．其法在當時雖未為世重，然其影響于後世之創分類法者則甚大也．

（六）元明二代，圖書分類多法四部，無足稱述．降及遜清，大興文教．高宗朝所編四庫全書總目二百卷，實集千餘年來四部分類法之大成．雖多仍舊貫，而類目之釐訂，創見不少：計經部十，史部十五，子部十四，集部五，凡類四十又四；類下各別為屬，凡為屬六十六．四部法之子目至此始臻完備．又每部冠以總叙，類各冠以小序，以撮述學術源流，論斷羣書得失，尤為治學之門徑．以後四庫制遂成一代分類法之典型，二百年來所有官私書目以及清人所補前朝史志，大都奉為圭臬，引為楷證．觀其體例亦多參差牴牾之處，（註三）雖有帝王之威權以維持，而不足盡服學者；因是另立體系重創新法者，相繼而起．

註一　姚振宗七畧別錄佚文（師石山房叢書本）叙云：「七畧首一篇，阮氏云，即六篇之總最，故以輯畧為名．顏藝文志注亦云，輯與集同，謂諸書之總要，蓋六畧分門別類之總要也．」又胡應麟經籍會通云：「劉歆七畧，一曰六藝，一曰諸子，一曰詩賦，一曰兵書，一曰術數，一曰方技；而首之輯畧以總集諸書之要，分列品題．實六畧耳．」

註二　如後晉劉昫等所撰之舊唐書經籍志，其取材雖以唐開元四部書目為準，然其分門別類亦多本之隋志，合用四部書目及隋志四類總稱，曰甲部經錄，乙部史錄，丙部子錄，丁部集錄，為書目中用「甲經，乙史，丙子，丁集」各目之最初者．歐陽修謂四部之制始于唐蓋指此．

註三　近人言四庫分類弊病者，以劉國鈞四庫分類法之研究（圖書館學季刊第一卷第三期）為最詳．

　　（七）最初離四庫而出之新法為乾隆末年孫星衍所編之孫氏祠堂書目，其書分十二類：一經學，二小學，三諸子，四天文，五地理，六醫律，七史學，八金石，九類賦，十叢書，十一書畫，十二小說。類各有條釋述其源流。孫氏受知于乾嘉大師，歷官要職，引退後復主鐘山書院有年。其分類法之影響，遞及于中國第一任國立圖書館館長繆荃孫，與今日最完備之國學書目（江蘇省立國學圖書館圖書總目），至為顯明。

　　（八）繼孫氏而出之書目，在晚近七八十年吾國學界最有聲望者，則推張之洞繆荃孫合撰之書目答問。其分類雖仍遵四部之體，然其分析子目實較四庫為合理。其別立叢書于四部之末，更闢吾國分類法有總類之先河。（註四）故葉德輝郋園讀書志云「此目前後屢經刪補改刻，故世間傳本不同，雖仍四部之舊，與四庫分類出入多有異同。大致本之孫星衍祠書目參以隋志崇文總目，不背于古，不戾于今，大體最為詳慎。」宜其為士子書賈所重，人手一編耳。

　　鼎革以還，新書迭出，舊有部類，頗難統攝，摹襲西制之分類法遂應運而生，所謂仿杜威，補杜威，改杜威，十進，世界，中外，形形色色，不一而足，要皆以強學術本位不同之舊籍，就西洋體製類目號碼為能事。施之實際，不免削足適履。僕不敏，敢師孫繆等先賢之意，本吾國舊有書志之類目，另擬一法，以部勒漢文新舊圖書及同文鄰邦之典籍。茲將其大綱，畧述于後。

　　一、本分類法以中法為經，西法為緯。大綱則根據魏荀勖新簿甲乙丙丁四部之次序及清張之洞繆荃孫書目答問別立叢書于四部末之例，擴充為中國經學，哲學宗教，歷史科學，社會科學，語言文學，美術遊藝，自然科學，農業工藝，總錄書志等九類。每類子目關于人文科學者則參酌吾國舊有分類成法，關于自然科學及近世工藝者則依據中外多數專門分類法定訂之。

　　二、中國經學類。經學定名，由來久矣，且已蔚成專門學術，著作載籍，浩如煙海。今之倡言廢經者，姑無論其在學理上已否得普遍之公認，就實際分類言，至今確無一適當途徑。蓋經學為我國學術之淵源，包羅萬象，脈絡相關，折入他類，殊非易事，故本法仍存經學一類。

　　四庫經類各書排比一以時代為次，不分體裁，于研究者頗為不便。今從鄭樵通志藝文畧例，各經下畧依體裁分為經本，經注經說經義，及專篇專題考證等數種，每種之內仍以撰者時代為次。

　　小學歷代為經學之附庸，雖為研究經學之門徑，然究係語言文字之學，故入語言文學類。樂類中之樂經早亡，後之撰著與近世音樂無別，以之入美術中之音樂類，似較存諸經部為妥。

　　各經先後一仍四庫次序，惟于各經之前冠以羣經合刻，諸經目錄，經學辭典，諸經總義，經學歷史，等新立合類。舊有五經總義，今改稱諸經總義。

註四　　近人有謂劉氏輯畧即西洋分類法中之總類者，其實輯畧乃劉氏分類法之敘例也。見註一。鄭樵藝文畧及孫星衍祠堂書目，雖亦將叢書提出，另列一大類，然此所謂類書，乃近日學校所稱之參考書中用國書多為有系統之編著，而非叢錄雜著之屬，故書目答問仍列之于子部，別立叢書部以收彙集叢錄之書。中國書目至此始有近似西洋分類法中之總類焉。

三、哲學宗教類。歷來論子部者有廣義狹義二派,而以荀勖為二者之樞紐,荀勖以前皆取狹義,故子之範圍甚為單純。自荀勖創立四部,合諸子兵書術數而一之,唐以後之四庫子部遂包羅至十餘類之多,殊與古人異。今從古人狹義例,擇諸子中之純屬哲學者,如儒家,墨家,道家,名家,等入此類。其他各家則按其性質入下列各類:

兵家入軍事學類。 法家及縱橫家入政法類。
農家入農林類。 醫家入醫學類。
術數與今之神祕學相近,故入宗教類。 藝術分入美術及工藝類。
譜錄按其性質分入各類。
雜家按其性質分入各類,不能分類者入總錄之雜著。
類書入總錄之類書及百科全書類。
小說家或入文學中之小說,或入總類中之雜著,視其內容酌定之。

宗教與哲學關係密切,故合為一大類。道家與道教截然二事,前者多純粹哲理,後者多迷信神仙,故劉氏七畧道之學與神仙各自為錄。今依歷代著錄家分道家與神仙家之義,以道家入哲學而以道教入宗教。

舊有著錄于諸子分類頗不一致,如管子漢志入道家,隋志則入法家,淮南子有入道家者有入雜家者。諸如此類,不勝枚舉。雖古人稱子者必持之有故言之成理卓然成一家之言,然一家之言往往受外家之影響。如宋儒理學,有儒學亦有禪學,全列儒學似乎欠妥。至如晚清譚嗣同仁學受西洋哲學影響,更為顯著,則其應入何家有更難決。今師明黃虞稷千頃堂書目及清四庫總目併名臺縱橫為一家(雜家)例,將諸子之闡涉宇宙及人生哲學者一律著者朝代及其可考生卒年代排列。至哲人年代之斷定多取決于專家之考訂,少有出入,識者諒之。

四、歷史科學類。史地之書四庫總目以體裁分,杜威十進法及美國國會圖書館則先分史地為兩大類,然後再以國分。兩者均欠妥當,蓋前者不能將論某一時代之各種史籍彙集一處,後者則將一國史地之書割裂兩處,殊屬不便。今仿美國哈佛大學圖書館成例,史地之書先以國分,再以年代分。如是則不但一國之史地齊集一處,即時代之史籍,一方域之史志亦同列一架矣。

考古金石民族學,傳記及家譜,為史學之原料,故併入史地而冠該類之首。合傳不專屬一科者入普通傳記類,專屬一科者各入其類。

五、社會科學類。四庫史部之職官政書多載歷代典章制度,包含近世所謂政治法律社會經濟教育等書。今統名曰社會科學,自成一類。又因此類與史地有密切關係,故使與歷史科學蟬聯。

六、語言文學類。文字文學,關係至切,故合為一類。先以語系分,每語系下再分語言文學二種。中國語言學又根據文字之義形聲分為訓詁字書及音韻,兼三者而有之者,如文字通論等書則置諸三者之前,文典,方言字典辭書等,則殿于三者之後。

中國文學分類先諸體總集(如文選,唐文粹,宋文鑑,元文類,等),次諸體別集(即詩文別集或個人全集),再次則各體之細分,如詞曲,戲劇,小說,書牘及雜著等類。每類又分作法,歷史評論,總集專集等項。排列一依著者時代為次。

七、美術游藝類。即操合四庫子部藝術類及近世所謂建築遊藝運動等項。藝術與文學關係頗密,且琴棋書畫為中日文人學士所通習,今以美術類置于文學類之後,即本斯旨。

八、自然科學類．概照美國國會分類法分類，以此分類法科學部分之價值已為世所公認也．舊有子部天文算法草木鳥獸等類，今各按其性質入自然科學．

九、農業工藝類．此類亦稱應用科學．凡四庫史部之考工及子部之雜技皆依內容性質，分入此類．

十、總錄書志類．吾國書目之分類大概採先分後合之旨，西洋則多用先合後分之法．旨意雖異，邏輯則同．今仿書目答問于四部後另加叢書部之意，以總類列于諸類之末，包羅叢書，雜著，期刊，類書，書志，圖書館學及新聞學等類．

納入總錄類之叢書以俱普通性質者為限．分多人叢書及個人叢書二大類．多人叢書又分彙刻郡邑與族姓三種．叢書依彙刻年代排次，但個人叢書則以著者年代為次，因此類書籍乃含有個性寓有時代之作品也．

雜著一律以著者時代排列，不用雜學雜考雜述雜纂等名目分類，蓋一書內容及體裁既雜，無可分類，復何學考述纂之可言耶？

普通書目及藏書志為各種學術之指南，故入總錄類．專類書目（如小學考經義考）則按其性質分入各類．

十一、本分類法以分類本身為研究之對象，不斤斤于符號之出入．因符號不過為類目之一種速寫代表，不能以符號之數目限分類綱目之多寡，故本法所採用之符號為純一阿拉伯數字，隨類目之多少分配，不泥于十進法之形式，求其便于識寫而已．

　　　　　　　民國十六年春初稿，　民國三十二年春重訂．

INTRODUCTION

CLASSIFICATION IN CHINA

The earliest known Chinese general bibliography was the Pieh Lu 別錄
compiled between B.C. 26 and B.C. 8 by Liu Hsiang 劉向 (B.C. 79-8)
under imperial commission from Emperor Ch'êng Ti 成帝 . When Liu Hsiang
died, his son Hsin 歆 (? - 23 A.D.) succeeded him in this task. They classified all the books then present in the imperial library to form an inventory
entitled the "Seven Epitomes" or Ch'i Lüeh 七畧:

1. Ch'i lüeh or General Introduction
2. Liu i lüeh or Classics
3. Chu tzŭ lüeh or Philosophical Works
4. Shih fu lüeh or Poetical Works
5. Ping shu lüeh or Military Science
6. Shu shu lüeh or Astronomy, Occultism, etc.
7. Fang chi lüeh or Medicine

In 58-75 A.D. Pan Ku 班固 (32-92) compiled the Han shu i wên chih 漢
書藝文志(the "Bibliographic Essay" in the "Standard History of the Former
Han Dynasty"). He reproduced the contents of the Ch'i Lüeh and used its classification scheme but reduced the number of divisions to six by distributing
the preliminary materials from Liu's general introduction among the other six
categories.

Now the Ch'i Lüeh as an independent work was lost at about the end of
the T'ang Dynasty (cir. 906 A.D.). Though scholars under the Ch'ing Dynasty
like Yen K'o-chün 嚴可均 (1762-1843), Ma Kuo-han 馬國翰(1794-1857),
Hung I-hsüan 洪頤煊 (1765-?), Chang Tsung-yüan 章宗源 (1752?-1800)
and Yao Chên-tsung 姚振宗 (1842-1906), tried to reconstruct the Ch'i Lüeh
by compiling fragments preserved in other books, yet the present generation
would never be able to see the whole of it except through Pan Ku's Han shu i
wên chih whose classification is now a landmark in the history of Chinese
bibliographic classification systems.

Between 220 and 265 A.D. the famous four-fold classification scheme gradually came into being. Hsün Hsü 荀勖 , basing his work upon Chêng Mo's 鄭默 Chung Ching 中經 , compiled a catalogue of the books in the Wei imperial library under his charge and gave it the name Hsin Pu 新簿. Hsün's four divisions comprised: 1. Classics and Philology; 2. Philosophy, military science, mathematics and divination; 3. History, anecdotes, state documents and miscellaneous records; and 4. Poetry, eulogies and treatises found in the old Wei tombs. Between 317 and 408 Li Ch'ung 李充 compiled another catalogue of the books in the imperial library of the Eastern Chin Dynasty. He adopted Hsün's four-fold scheme but reversed the position of the second and the third classes. His order of 1. Classics, 2. Histories, 3. Philosophers and 4. Belles-lettres was followed by most later bibliographers and librarians without change until the end of the Ch'ing Dynasty in 1912.

Both Hsün Hsü and Li Ch'ung, however, were content to mark the divisions of their catalogues with the first four characters of the Ten Celestial Stems 天干, i.e. Chia 甲, I 乙, Ping 丙 and Ting 丁 , as Western librarians use the letters of the alphabet as notation for their classification schemes. The modern terms for the four divisions: Ching 經 (Classics), Shih 史 (Histories), Tzû 子 (Philosophers) and Chi 集 (Belles-lettres) were first adopted in 628-656 by the compilers of the Sui shu ching chi chih 隋書經籍志 (the "Bibliographic Essay" in the "Standard History of the Sui Dynasty"), who combined certain features from both the Ssû-pu (four fold) and the Ch'i lüeh (seven epitomes) systems. In addition to the four divisions which were given the names of Ching, shih, tzû and chi without the celestial stem characters chia, i, ping and ting, the Sui Chih 隋志 ("Sui Essay") has also two added classes, namely, Tao 道 (Taoism) and Fo 佛 (Buddhism). Therefore, strictly speaking, the system adopted in the Sui Chih could not well be called "four-fold."

It is not until the Chiu T'ang shu ching chi chih 舊唐書經籍志 (the "Bibliographic Essay" in the "Old Standard History of the T'ang Dynasty"), completed cir. 940, that the combination of the stem characters and the names of the divisions first appears in Chinese bibliography, i.e., chia: ching, i: shih, ping: tzû, and ting: chi. Now the source for the Chiu T'ang shu ching chi chih was the K'ai-yüan ssû pu shu mu 開元四部書目 (the four-fold catalogue of the K'ai-yüan period compiled in 713-721). That is the reason why Ou-yang Hsiu 歐陽修 (1007-1072), co-author of the Hsin T'ang Shu 新唐書 ("New Standard History of the T'ang Dynasty"), declares that the four-fold system of book classification originated in T'ang times. Actually, as we have seen, the rudiments of the four-fold system are traceable to the third century.

Summing up, we may conclude that the four-fold bibliographic classification system was begun in a rudimentary form by Chêng Mo and Hsün Hsü in the middle of the third century A.D. and that it developed into its present form at the beginning of the eighth century. As compared with the more ancient system of the Ch'i Lüeh it emphasizes the form rather than the subject as basis for classification.

Next may be mentioned the chief dissenters who deviated from the ssû-pu (Four-fold) system in bibliographies and catalogues which have been considered important in Chinese intellectual history. Between the first appearance of the four-fold system in Hsün Hsü's Hsin Pu and its final establishment in the T'ang dynasty, though most catalogues were compiled according to that scheme, yet the Ch'i Lüeh classification of the two Lius was not forgotten. Several important pre-T'ang catalogues used it, with certain modifications. Among these were the following:

473 A.D. - Wang Chien's <u>Ch'i Chih</u> 王儉 七志 which was classified into seven divisions plus two appendices: 1. Classics; 2. Philosophers; 3. Belles-lettres; 4. Military Science; 5. Occultism; 6. Medicine and Miscellaneous Arts; 7. Geography and Maps; appendix 1, Taoism; appendix 2, Buddhism.

520-526 A.D. - Juan Hsiao-hsü's <u>Ch'i Lu</u> 阮孝緒七錄 which had these seven divisions: (1) Classics; (2) Histories; (3) Philosophers; (4) Belles-lettres; (5) Science and Technology; (6) Buddhism; (7) Taoism.

In the Sung dynasty (960-1279) dissatisfaction with the <u>ssû-pu</u> (four-fold) system still existed among the scholars. Thus the great historian Chêng Ch'iao 鄭樵 (1104-1162) strongly criticized it as absurd, and compiled his monograph on bibliography, the <u>I wên lüeh</u> 藝文畧 , according to a scheme of twelve divisions: (1) Classics, (2) Rituals, (3) Music, (4) Linguistics, (5) Histories, (6) Philosophers, (7) Astronomy, (8) Numerology, (9) Fine Arts, (10) Medicine, (11) Encyclopedias, and (12) Belles-lettres. Subsequent scholars regard Chêng's classification system as logical, detailed and well-defined. Furthermore, the books listed under each heading were minutely classified and conveniently referred back and forth by cross-references.

However, in spite of many criticisms leveled against it, the four-fold system was followed with slight change in the official bibliographies of the Sung, Yüan and Ming Dynasties -- a period of nearly seven hundred years (960-1644). In 1773-1781 when Emperor Kao Tsung (Ch'ien-lung) ordered the compilation of the select imperial library, <u>Ssû k'u ch'üan shu</u> 四庫全書 and an annotated catalogue of it, the compilers carefully studied the development of the four-fold system of classification and remedied many of its defects in a rearrangement of the subdivisions in the four main classes. This may be called the neo-classical step in the reconstruction and perfection of the

ssû-pu system. Notwithstanding the many improvements then made and the great
weight of imperial patronage, the scheme still did not receive uniform and
unchallenged approval from scholars. Before long important dissenters again
arose, among whom the following were the most prominent.

In 1800 the great critical scholar and archaeologist Sun Hsing-yen 孫星衍
(1743-1818) completed the catalogue of the books in the Clan Memorial Hall of
his family, entitled Sun shih tz'u t'ang shu mu 孫氏祠堂書目 in which
he created a new classification of 12 divisions as follows: (1) Classics,
(2) Linguistics, (3) Philosophers, (4) Astronomy and Mathematics, (5) Geography, (6) Medicine and Law, (7) History, (8) Archaeology, (9) Encyclopedias,
(10) Belles-lettres, (11) Calligraphy and Painting, and (12) Fiction. This
catalogue was not printed until 1883.

Shortly afterwards Miao Ch'üan-sun 繆荃孫 (1844-1919), initial director
of the first modern national library in China and co-author of the most widely
circulated Chinese bibliography, followed Sun's footsteps in discarding the
ssù-pu system. He used Sun's scheme with slight modifications in his I feng
t'ang ts'ang shu chi 藝風堂藏書記 a critical catalogue of books in his
library, which was printed in 1900. The two important changes introduced by
Miao were (1) reduction in the number of the main classes to ten by omitting
the fourth and sixth (Astronomy and Mathematics, Medicine and Law), which he
placed under the division of Philosophers, and (2) transfer of the subdivision
of Bibliography from the division of Encyclopedias to that of Archaeology. His
ten classes are (1) Classics, (2) Linguistics, (3) Philosophers, (4) Geography,
(5) History, (6) Archaeology and Bibliography, (7) Encyclopedias, (8) Belles-
lettres, (9) Calligraphy and Painting, and (10) Fiction.

The most widely used bibliography mentioned above is the Shu mu ta wên
書目答問 ("Catechism on Bibliography"), which was initiated by Chang

Chih-tung 張之洞 (1837-1909) and completed in 1875 by Miao Ch'üan-sun.
Though the Shu mu ta wên follows the Ssû k'u ch'üan shu ts'ung mu 總目,
the "General Catalogue" of the Ch'ien-lung library, in having the traditional
four-fold divisions, yet it differs from it in many respects.　First, it ends
with a "Generalia Class", which was an innovation in the history of Chinese
classifications, after the four usual divisions.　Second, the subdivisions
in each of the four major classes have all been improved and made more logical
than those in Ch'ien-lung's Ssû-k'u catalogue.　That is the reason why it has
held such undisputed sway among Chinese scholars and book-collectors during
the last seventy years.　It is still being reverently studied and memorized
by dealers in the Chinese book trade.　Western sinologists are often astonished
by the consequent knowledge of old Chinese books revealed by young apprentices
in the bookstores of Liu-li ch'ang 琉璃廠 and Lung-fu szû 隆福寺,
Peiping.

　　After contact with Western intellectual influences, Chinese scholarship
has undergone considerable changes.　The reorganization of old libraries for
modern uses is one of those changes.　The story of the development of modern
library classification systems (including the present one) in China has been
ably reviewed by K. T. Wu 吳光清 in his "Ten Years of Classification
and Cataloging in China" in Libraries in China, Peiping, Library Association
of China, 1935, pp. 19-58; readers who are interested in this subject are
hereby referred to that scholarly paper.

CLASSIFICATION IN JAPAN

The earliest Japanese general bibliographic classification is to be found in Fujiwara Sukeyo's (?-898) <u>Nihonkoku Genzaisho Mokuroku</u> 藤原佐世 日本國見在書目錄 compiled during the period 889-897 A.D. and first printed in 1850. This bibliography records about 1579 Chinese works then existing in Japan. Its system of classification is modelled after that of the <u>Sui shu ching chi chih</u> 隋書經籍志 (The "Bibliographical Essay" in the "Standard History of the Sui Dynasty"). It is divided into forty subdivisions in the regular Chinese order of Classics, History, Philosophy and Belles-lettres, but without the names of the last three main divisions being listed.

During the Muromachi Period Kiyowara Naritada 清原業忠 was commissioned by the then ruling Shōgun Ashikaga Yoshinori 足利義教 (1394-1441) to compile a catalogue of the Japanese books at his court. This catalogue, completed about 1440, is known to posterity by several names: <u>Honchō shoseki mokuroku</u> 本朝書籍目錄 ("Catalogue of Books of the Present Dynasty"), <u>Ninna ji shoseki mokuroku</u> 仁和寺書籍目錄 ("Catalogue of Books at the Ninna Temple "), <u>Omuro Washo mokuroku</u> 御室和書目錄 ("Catalogue of Japanese Books in the Imperial Palace"), and <u>Nihon shoseki sō mokuroku</u> 日本書籍總目錄 ("General Catalogue of Japanese Books"). This catalogue, first printed in 1671, includes about 500 works by Japanese authors, which were classified in 20 divisions as follows:

(1) Shinto; (2) Imperial biographies; (3) Rituals; (4) Law; (5) Genealogy; (6) Geography; (7) Encyclopedias, etc.; (8) Dictionaries; (9) Literary collections of Chinese prose and poetry; (10) Miscellaneous literary works; (11) <u>Waka</u> 和歌 (Japanese Songs); (12) <u>Wa-Kan rōei</u> 和漢朗詠 (Chinese

and Japanese poetic quotations); (13) Music; (14) Medicine; (15) Occultism;
(16) Biographies; (17) Records of official appointments and civil lists;
(18) Imperial rescripts and maxims; (19) Miscellaneous books; (20) Monogatari
物語 (Japanese Fiction).

The third general classified bibliography of Japanese books printed in
1791 is the Kokuchō shomoku 國朝書目 ("Catalogue of National Books")
by the great archaeologist Fujiwara Teikan 藤原貞幹 (1722-1789). Building
upon the foregoing catalogue he greatly increased the number of admitted works,
which were marked with his own special sign. The books were classified in 41
divisions as follows:

(1) Standard histories; (2) Annals; (3) Miscellaneous histories;
(4) Imperial writings and chronologies; (5) Other chronologies, diaries and
travels; (6) Government and Law; (7) Rituals; (8) Official appointments;
(9) Genealogies; (10) Biographies; (11) Astronomy; (12) Geography; (13) Palaces
and temples; (14) Furniture; (15) Costumes; (16) Foods; (17) Moral precepts;
(18) Social antiquities; (19) Cyclopedias and bibliography; (20) Linguistics;
(21) Calligraphy; (22) Painting; (23) Music; (24) Medicine; (25) Sports -
Outing and hunting; (26) Sports - Ball-games; (27) Amusements - Incense-
burning; (28-31) Shinto; (32-33) Buddhism; (34) Miscellanies; (35) Anthologies
of Chinese prose; (36) Anthologies of Chinese poetry; (37) Collected literary
works of individual authors; (38) General works on literature (Rhetoric,
prosody, etc.); (39) Waka; (40) Renga 連歌 (Japanese "chain" poems);
(41) Monogatari.

The fourth work of this class is the descriptive catalogue of the great
Japanese sōsho 叢書 (series or collections of reprints) entitled Gunsho Ruijū
群書類從 compiled by Hanawa Hokiichi 塙保己一 (1746-1821) and

published during the period 1779-1820. The separate catalogue volume contains a description of all the works admitted with a further index of titles by kana. This great collection contains 1,270 works in the first series and 2,103 works in the supplement (Zoku). All the books are classified under 25 divisions as follows:

(1) Shinto; (2) Works on Emperors; (3) Official appointments; (4) Genealogies; (5) Biographies; (6) Government; (7) Law; (8) Rituals; (9) Costumes; (10) Literature; (11) Letters; (12) Waka; (13) Renga; (14) Monogatari; (15) Diaries; (16) Travel; (17) Music; (18) Sports - Ball games; (19) Sports - Hunting and outing; (20) Amusements; (21) Foods; (22) Military arts; (23) Buke 武家 (Feudal Barons) institutions; (24) Buddhism; (25) Miscellanies.

The fifth general classification scheme for Japanese books is to be found in an annotated catalogue by an Osaka book-dealer by the name of Ozaki Masayoshi 尾崎雅嘉 (1755-1827) who spent some thirty years in compiling and publishing in 1802 a general review of all books, entitled Gunsho ichiran 群書一覧. He classified about 2000 books by Japanese authors (1700 printed editions and 300 manuscripts) in 34 divisions as follows:

(1) National histories; (2) Shinto; (3) Miscellaneous historical works; (4) Rituals; (5) Government and Law; (6) Genealogy; (7) Linguistics; (8) Letters; (9) Calligraphy; (10) Monogatari; (11) Sōshi 草子 (Vernacular or popular stories); (12) Diaries; (13) Japanese prose; (14) Travel; (15) Waka - Collections compiled by Imperial order; (16) Waka - Collections privately compiled; (17) Waka - Collections of individual authors; (18) Waka - Uta-awase 歌合 (capping verses); (19) Waka - Selections of 100 poems; (20) Waka - Selections of 1000 poems; (21) Waka - Classified collections; (22) Waka - Miscellaneous; (23) Waka - Selections of poets of genius; (24) Waka - Prosody; (25) Literary

works in Chinese; (26) Medicine; (27) Practical ethics; (28) Buddhism; (29) Music; (30) Geography; (31) Places of interest; (32) Personal notes; (33) Polygraphic and miscellaneous works; (34) Sō-sho.

This bibliography has no index and it is hard to find a book in one of the 34 divisions. Moreover, there is no indication of editions. Pronunciation of titles is marked only for difficult characters.

In 1892 Nishimura Kanebumi 西村兼文 compiled a supplement to Ozaki's catalogue and called it Zoku gunsho ichiran 續群書一覽 ("Supplementary General Review of All Books"), which may be considered as the sixth in our series. He remedied the salient defect of Ozaki's work by supplying two indices of titles - one by kana and the other by a classified list of subjects. He included 1446 books and arrayed them in a new classification of his own as follows:

(1) National histories; (2) Shinto; (3) Miscellaneous historical works; (4) Government and law; (5) Rituals; (6) Biographies; (7) Genealogy; (8) Official appointments; (9) Inscriptions; (10) Geography; (11) Literary works in Chinese; (12) Waka - General collections; (13) Waka - Classified collections; (14) Waka - Uta-awase; (15) Waka - Selections of 100 poems; (16) Waka - Collections of individual authors; (17) Waka - Prosody; (18) Waka - Miscellaneous; (19) Travel; (20) Illustration-scrolls; (21) Buddhist tales; (22) Medicine; (23) Music; (24) Practical ethics or moral precepts; (25) Linguistics; (26) Calligraphy; (27) Personal notes; (28) Buddhism; (29) Polygraphic and miscellaneous works.

Editions of works admitted are indicated, but pronunciation of titles is not. There is no biography of authors in the descriptive notes.

The seventh, last and most important general bibliography of pre-Meiji Japanese works is the monumental annotated catalogue, entitled Kokusho kaidai 國書解題 ("Annotated Bibliography of National Books") by Samura Hachirō

xvi

佐村八郎 (1865-1914) who spent the major part of his life in compiling
this most outstanding bibliography ever produced in Japan. The first edition
was published in 1900 and the third enlarged edition by his son, Toshio 敏郎
in two volumes, was issued in 1926 by Rikugōkan 六合館 a publishing house
in Tokyo. This bibliography includes about 27,000 Japanese works from antiquity
to the third year of Keiō 慶應 (1867), the year before the accession of
Emperor Meiji. Each book is described concisely as to its contents with a
brief biography of its author. The reading of each title is indicated in
kana, which is a great help to non-Japanese users, and even to the Japanese
themselves. The most readily available edition of each work is also mentioned.
If a book is available only in manuscript, that fact is indicated. The main
body of the catalogue is arranged alphabetically by the kana-reading of titles.
The appendix includes (1) author-index by kana; (2) a subject index by a very
logical system of classification; and (3) in the third edition, also a title
index by the count of strokes in the first character.

The distinctive feature of Samura's general catalogue is his comprehensive
scheme for classifying Japanese books. He divides the whole field of knowledge
into eleven main divisions and fifty-five subdivisions as follows:

I. General Works

    1. Bibliography -- Brief Lists
    2. Bibliography -- Descriptive Catalogues
    3. Encyclopedias
    4. Collections or Sōsho   5. Dictionaries

II. Religion and Philosophy

    6. Shinto
    7. Buddhism
    8. Christianity
    9. Confucianism (Confucian Classics and Studies)
    10. Other Chinese Philosophical Schools
    11. Ethics

III. Government and Law

    12. Law and Government
    13. Rituals

IV. History

    14. Historical Essays
    15. Chronological Tables
    16. Standard Histories
    17. Miscellaneous Histories
    18. Annals
    19. Biographies
    20. Genealogies
    21. Miscellaneous (Archaeology included here)

V. Geography

    22. Topography and Geography
    23. Maps and Atlases
    24. Travel

VI. Languages

    25. General Works
    26. Phonology
    27. Etymology
    28. Grammar

VII. Literature

    29. Japanese Prose
    30. Chinese Prose
    31. Chinese Poetry
    32. Japanese Poetry or _Waka_
    33. Drama
    34. Fiction

VIII. Fine and Recreative Arts

    35. Music
    36. Calligraphy and Painting
    37. Architecture
    38. Amusements
    39. Sports

IX. Useful (Technical) Arts

    40. Military Tactics
    41. Military Sports and Physical Training
    42. Medicine
    43. Productive Arts (Fishing, etc.)
    44. Agriculture
    45. Industries
    46. Commerce
    47. Domestic Science (Foods and Clothing)

X. Pure Science

    48. Mathematics
    49. Astronomy
    50. Physics and Chemistry
    51. Zoology
    52. Botany
    53. Geology

XI. Miscellanies

    54. Personal Notes
    55. Miscellaneous and Polygraphic Works

Since the Meiji Restoration in 1868, the organization and management of Japanese libraries have been much influenced by Western systems, especially the ones devised by American librarians like Dewey, Cutter, and their contemporaries. The two most influential schemes now current in Japan are the Classification System of the Imperial Library at Tokyo and the Japanese Decimal Classification Scheme devised by Mori Kiyoshi 森清 in 1929 under the auspices of the Japanese League of Young Librarians. Information about the development of these and other modern Japanese library classification systems is readily available in the articles by Murajima Yasuo 村島靖雄 "Contemporary Japanese Classification Schemes" (in Japanese) in Toshokan Zasshi 圖書館雑誌 ("Journal of the Japanese Library Association"), no. 48, February, 1922, and by Mamiya Fujio 間宮不二雄, "Dr. M. Dewey and his Decimal Classification influenced upon Japanese Libraries" (in English) in Toshokan Kenkyū 圖研究 ("Studies in Library Science" -- a quarterly publication of the League of Young Librarians, volume 6, September, 1933.)

GENESIS OF THE HARVARD-YENCHING SYSTEM

At the time when the present scheme of classification was devised toward
the end of 1926 there was no comprehensive and generally accepted system available in China nor in Japan. It was a period of transition during which three
tendencies were dominant. The first was to stick tenaciously to the old
Ssû-ku classification of the late 18th century. The second, diametrically
opposed to it, was to abandon old systems completely and to adopt some Western
scheme. Dewey's Decimal Classification, because of its simple notation and
numerous mnemonic features and on account of its high international standing
(it was adopted by the Institut International de Bibliographie in 1895), was
frequently followed in both China and Japan. The third tendency was to
divide old and new books into two water-tight compartments, using the Ssû-ku
scheme for the old books and adopting some modern system (generally D. C.
or some modification of it) for the new books.*

The Harvard-Yenching scheme was one of the early attempts at a com-
promise between the old and the new. Its main outline is based upon the
initial Chinese ssû-pu or four-fold schedule of Classics, Philosophy, History
and Belles-lettres as evolved by Hsün Hsü in the third century. The very
broad definition of "philosophy" as used in the four-fold system after the
T'ang Dynasty, to make it include in one class, all works on moral and natural
philosophy, art and life, and other miscellaneous compilations, has been
abandoned. Instead, the Tzû or Philosophy class has been restricted to its
original meaning as employed by Liu Hsiang, Liu Hsin and Pan Ku in their

---

* The great Sinological Library at the Academy of Oriental Culture (Tōhō-
Bunka-Gakuin), Kyoto and the Library of the National Chiao-t'ung University
(Nan Yang College), Shanghai and several others in China and Japan still
follow such a practice.

system of the "Seven Epitomes". Accordingly, therefore, all works on art, science and technology, and other miscellaneous compilations have been separated from the Tzŭ Class, leaving therein only works on Philosophy proper and Religion. This has necessitated the setting up of three new classes, namely, Fine Arts, Natural Sciences, Agriculture and Technology, to accommodate works thus separated from the Philosophy class.

The position of works on Linguistics, which has always been placed as an appendix to the division of Classics, has been shifted and put at the head of the Belles-lettres class; thus, Language and Literature stand together in this system. The idea of a Generalia class at the end, which was first initiated by Chang Chih-tung and Miao Ch'üan-sun in their Shu mu ta wên, has been followed. Into this Generalia class not only collective series or ts'ung-shu, but also general periodicals, general encyclopedias, bibliography, works on library science, journalism and many miscellaneous compilations have been placed.

The division of "History" in the old four-fold system includes not only historical, geographical, archaeological and biographical works, but also those on social and political institutions, such as economics, government, law and education. These latter works have all been grouped together to form a separate class entitled Social Sciences, which is placed immediately after the division of Historical Sciences.

The system has as a consequence altogether nine main classes or divisions, namely, Chinese Classics, Philosophy and Religion, Historical Sciences, Social Sciences, Language and Literature, Fine and Recreative Arts, Natural Sciences, Agriculture and Technology, Generalia and Bibliography. In the construction of subdivisions within each main class old Chinese and Japanese classification

systems have furnished many headings for the humanities and social sciences,
but for the natural sciences, technology and agriculture, the Library of
Congress Classification System and the Classification Scheme of the International Institute of Agriculture at Rome have been drawn upon rather heavily.

In devising this system and in daring to deviate from the venerable
ssŭ-ku or four-fold scheme, the compiler is under the inspiration of Sun
Hsing-yen and Miao Ch'üan-sun who early saw the necessity of change and
reform in the traditional book classification system of China. For general
principles and mnemonic devices, no modern librarian can be free from the
influence of such American pioneers as Cutter, Dewey and others. For help
in various special subjects the compiler is indebted to the following friends
and colleagues, arranged in chronological order: -- Messrs. H. Y. Feng,
T. F. Currier, E. C. Tang, S. Y. Liang, Hideo Kishimoto, Shigemaru Shimoyama,
H. T. Tien, C. Y. Fang (and Mrs. Fang), T. L. Ku, C. C. Nieh, Professors
William Hung, C. S. Gardner, J. R. Ware, Y. R. Chao, and Serge Elisseéff,
Mr. L. S. Yang and Mr. Zunvair Yue. Professors Elisseéff and Gardner have
been of particular help in final proof-reading. Dr. Feng and Mr. Yue have
contributed so much to the system that they are almost co-compilers. Hence,
their names are placed on the title page. Last of all, the compiler wishes
to extend his sincere thanks to the Cataloging Committee of the Committees
on Far Eastern Studies of the American Council of Learned Societies, and to
Mr. Mortimer Graves, Administrative Secretary of the Council, for their
encouragement and interest in having the book first published in the United
States, because the partially set-up type pages in China have to be abandoned
on account of the Pacific War.

APPLICATION OF THE SYSTEM

The notation for this scheme consists in straight arabic numerals of three or four digits (three figures for Classics and four figures for each of the other classes) without any decimal connotation. For subjects peculiar to sinological and japanological studies, the subdivisions have been made rather minute, so that a necessity for inserting new topics may not frequently arise. In science and technology many subjects will be found unrepresented in the tables. In such cases any new or other subject may be intercalated at any point by adding to the relevant main number decimal numbers from .0 to .9 as may be found necessary. By this means ten entirely new places can be found between any two existing main numbers, in addition to the large number of spaces purposely left blank all through the classification.

For numbering different books having the same class number any system may be used. The system used for Chinese and Japanese books at Harvard and Yenching Universities and many libraries in China is based upon Wong's "Four-corner Numeral System," and is quite simple to apply in actual operation. It has been presented in the appendix, pp. 354-357. A warning may not be amiss here. That is, the "Cutter-Sanborn Author Table" devised for Western names, is entirely unsuitable for Chinese and Japanese names in romanized transliteration.

Unified or parallel collections: In China and Japan most libraries put Chinese and Japanese books in one unified collection and Western books (English, French, German, etc.) in another unified collection. In such a case, there is no need to put any distinctive mark on Chinese or Japanese books. But, if it is desired to separate Chinese and Japanese books into two parallel collections (as is done at Harvard but not at Yenching), it will be necessary to put a distinctive mark on either the Chinese books (generally C or Ch) or the Japanese books (generally J or Jap). The distinctive letter should be placed before the call numbers for books only in the smaller collection, in order to reduce the necessity of writing it to a minimum. In libraries where Western books on China and Japan are also classified by this system (as is done in the Harvard-Yenching Library) a letter "W" may be placed before the call number for a Western book.

A. K. Chiu

Cambridge, Massachusetts
April, 1943.

分類 總目　　　　TABLE OF MAIN CLASSES

100-999　　中國經學類　　CHINESE CLASSICS

1000-1999　哲學宗教類　　PHILOSOPHY AND RELIGION

2000-3999　歷史科學類　　HISTORICAL SCIENCES

4000-4999　社會科學類　　SOCIAL SCIENCES

5000-5999　語言文學類　　LANGUAGE AND LITERATURE

6000-6999　美術游藝類　　FINE AND RECREATIVE ARTS

7000-7999　自然科學類　　NATURAL SCIENCES

8000-8999　農業工藝類　　AGRICULTURE AND TECHNOLOGY

9000-9999　總錄書志類　　GENERALIA AND BIBLIOGRAPHY

各類綱目　SUMMARY TABLE OF MAIN CLASSES

100-999		中國經學類	CHINESE CLASSICS
100-999	羣經		GENERAL
200-299	易經		I CHING (BOOK OF CHANGES)
300-399	書經		SHU CHING (BOOK OF DOCUMENTS)
400-499	詩經		SHIH CHING (BOOK OF POETRY)
500-599	三禮		SAN LI (RITUALS)
520-549		周禮	CHOW LI (CHOW RITUAL)
550-579		儀禮	I LI (DECORUM RITUAL)
580-639		禮記	LI CHI (BOOK OF RITES)
640-669		三禮總義	GENERAL TREATISES ON RITUALS
680-779	春秋		CH'UN CH'IU (SPRING AND AUTUMN ANNALS)
682-709		總義	GENERAL TREATISES
710-739		左傳	TSO CHUAN
740-769		公羊傳	KUNG-YANG CHUAN
770-789		穀梁傳	KU-LIANG CHUAN
800-849	孝經		HSIAO CHING (BOOK OF FILIAL PIETY)
850-999	四書		SSŬ SHU (THE FOUR BOOKS)
850-899		總義	GENERAL TREATISES
890-909		大學	TA HSÜEH (THE GREAT LEARNING)
910-929		中庸	CHUNG YUNG (THE DOCTRINE OF THE MEAN)
930-959		論語	LUN YÜ (CONFUCIAN ANALECTS)
960-999		孟子	MÉNG TZŬ (THE WORKS OF MENCIUS)

2

1000-1999　哲學宗教類　PHILOSOPHY AND RELIGION

1000-1008　哲學總論　　PHILOSOPHY IN GENERAL

1009.1-1009.9　東方哲學　ORIENTAL PHILOSOPHY

1010-1429　中國哲學　CHINESE PHILOSOPHY

1430-1469　日本哲學　JAPANESE PHILOSOPHY

1470-1499　印度哲學　HINDU PHILOSOPHY

1500-1539　西洋哲學　OCCIDENTAL PHILOSOPHY

1540-1569　哲學問題與系統　PHILOSOPHICAL PROBLEMS AND SYSTEMS

1570-1609　論理學　LOGIC

1610-1649　形而上學　METAPHYSICS

1650-1699　倫理學　ETHICS

1700-1729　宗教總論　RELIGION IN GENERAL

1730-1738　神話　MYTHOLOGY

1739-1749　神秘學 術數　OCCULTISM NUMEROLOGY

1750-1779　宗教通史　HISTORY OF RELIGIONS

1780-1799　中國國家祀典　CHINESE STATE CULTS

1800-1919　佛教　BUDDHISM

1920-1939　道教　TAOISM

1940-1974　神道　SHINTOISM

1975-1987　基督教　CHRISTIANITY

1988-1999　其他宗教　OTHER RELIGIONS

2000-3999　歷史科學類 HISTORICAL SCIENCES

2000-2199　考古學,金石學 ARCHAEOLOGY, ANTIQUITIES

　　2000-2049　總錄　　　　GENERAL

　　　　　　　各國考古 ARCHAEOLOGY OF VARIOUS COUNTRIES

　　2050-2194　　亞洲　　　ASIA

　　　　2060-2159　中國　　　　CHINA

　　　　2160-2184　日本　　　　JAPAN

　　　　2185-2187　高麗　　　　KOREA

　　　　2188-2194　其他亞洲諸國 OTHER COUNTRIES

　　　2195　　　歐洲　　　EUROPE

　　　2196-2197　美洲　　　AMERICA

　　　2198　　　非洲　　　AFRICA

　　　2199　　　海洋洲,兩極 OCEANIA AND POLAR REGIONS

2200-2249　民族學,民族志 ETHNOLOGY, ETHNOGRAPHY

2250-2256　家譜　　　　GENEALOGY AND HERALDRY

2257-2299　傳記　　　　BIOGRAPHY

2300-3999　史地　　　　HISTORY AND GEOGRAPHY

　　2300-2399　世界　　　WORLD

　　2400-2449　亞洲　　　ASIA

　　2450-3299　中國　　　CHINA

　　3300-3479　日本　　　JAPAN

　　3480-3499　高麗　　　KOREA

　　3500-3599　其他亞洲諸國　OTHER COUNTRIES

　　3600-3799　歐洲　　　EUROPE

3800-3899	美洲	AMERICA
3900-3949	非洲	AFRICA
3950-3999	海洋洲及兩極	OCEANIA AND POLAR REGIONS

4000-4999	社會科學類	SOCIAL SCIENCES
4000-4019	總錄	GENERAL
4020-4099	統計	STATISTICS
4100-4299	社會	SOCIOLOGY
4300-4599	經濟	ECONOMICS
4600-4899	政法	POLITICS AND LAW
4900-4999	教育	EDUCATION

5000-5999	語言文學類	LANGUAGE AND LITERATURE
5000-5039	語言學總論	LINGUISTICS IN GENERAL, COMPARATIVE PHILOLOGY
5040-5059	文學總論	LITERATURE IN GENERAL, COMPARATIVE LITERATURE
5060-5199	中國語言文字學	CHINESE LANGUAGE
5061-5069	總錄	GENERAL
5070-5089	訓詁	SEMANTIC STUDIES
5090-5119	字書	GRAPHIC STUDIES
5120-5139	音韻	PHONOLOGICAL STUDIES
5140-5149	文法	GRAMMAR
5150-5159	方言	DIALECTS
5160-5169	蒙求教本及其他	TEXTS FOR LEARNING THE LANGUAGE AND OTHER MISCELLANEOUS TOPICS

5170-5199	字典辭書	LEXICOGRAPHY DICTIONARIES
5200-5799	中國文學	CHINESE LITERATURE
5100-5209	總錄	GENERAL
5210-5217	詩文評	LITERARY CRITICISM
5218-5229	史傳	HISTORY AND BIOGRAPHY
5230-5235	專集彙刊	COLLECTIONS OF COMPLETE WORKS
5236-5241	總集	GENERAL ANTHOLOGY
5242-5569	別集 (詩文)	COLLECTED LITERARY WORKS OF INDIVIDUAL AUTHORS
5570-5649	詞	TZ'Ŭ
5650-5730	曲及戲劇	LYRICAL WORKS AND DRAMA
5731-5769	小說	FICTION
5770-5779	書牘	LETTERS
5780-5799	雜著	MISCELLANY
5800-5809	中國特種語文	MINOR LANGUAGES IN CHINA
5810-5859	日本語訣字學	JAPANESE LANGUAGE
5810	總錄	GENERAL
5811-5813	音韻	PHONOLOGY
5814-5815	漢字	CHINESE CHARACTERS
5816-5825	假名遣	KANA AND SPELLING
5827	語原學	ETYMOLOGY
5828-5845	辭書	DICTIONARIES
5846-5854	文法	GRAMMAR
5855-5857	方言	DIALECTS
5858	課本	INSTRUCTION BOOKS

5860-5969	日本文學	JAPANESE LITERATURE
5861-5867	總錄	GENERAL
5868-5879	史傳	HISTORY AND BIOGRAPHY
5880-5889	文集	COLLECTED WORKS
5890-5909	詩歌	POETRY
5910-5919	戲曲	DRAMA
5921-5939	小説	FICTION
5940-5959	散文	PROSE
5960-5969	雜著	MISCELLANIES
5970-5872	日本特種語文	MINOR LANGUAGES IN JAPAN
5973	朝鮮語言文學	KOREAN LANGUAGE AND LITERATURE
5975-5993	印歐語言文學	INDO-EUROPEAN LANGUAGES AND LITERATURES
5994-5999	其他語言文學	OTHER LANGUAGES AND LITERATURES
6000-6999	美術游藝類	FINE AND RECREATIVE ARTS
6000-6019	總錄	GENERAL
6020-6019	美學	AESTHETICS
6030-6059	美術史	HISTORY OF ARTS
6070-6299	書畫	CALLIGRAPHY AND PAINTING
6070-6189	中國書畫	CHINESE CALLIGRAPHY AND PAINTING
6190-6289	日本書畫	JAPANESE CALLIGRAPHY AND PAINTING
6290-6299	文房	MATERIALS AND INSTRUMENTS
6300-6349	西洋畫	WESTERN PAINTING

6350-6359	版畫集	ENGRAVINGS　PRINTS
6360-6399	攝影	PHOTOGRAPHY
6400-6499	雕刻	SCULPTURE
6500-6599	建築	ARCHITECTURE
6600-6669	工藝美術	INDUSTRIAL ARTS
6700-6799	音樂	MUSIC
6800-6899	游藝娛樂	AMUSEMENTS AND GAMES
6900-6999	體育運動	PHYSICAL TRAINING AND SPORTS

7000-7999	自然科學類	NATURAL SCIENCES
7000-7019	總錄	GENERAL
7020-7099	算學(數學)	MATHEMATICS
7100-7199	天文學	ASTRONOMY
7200-7299	物理學	PHYSICS
7300-7399	化學	CHEMISTRY
7400-7499	地學	GEOLOGICAL SCIENCES
7500-7599	生物學	BIOLOGY
7600-7699	植物學	BOTANY
7700-7799	動物學	ZOOLOGY
7800-7869	人類學	ANTHROPOLOGY (PHYSICAL)

人類分布學人體比較(ANTHROPOGRAPHY, SOMATOLOGY,
學,人體解剖學,生理學. ANATOMY AND PHYSIOLOGY)

7870-7899	心理學	PSYCHOLOGY
7900-7999	醫學	MEDICAL SCIENCE

8000-8999	農業工藝類	AGRICULTURE AND TECHNOLOGY
8020-8239	農業	AGRICULTURE
8240-8269	家政	HOME ECONOMICS (DOMESTIC SCIENCE)
8300-8349	手工業	HANDICRAFTS AND ARTISAN TRADES
8400-8499	機製工業	MANUFACTURES
8500-8599	化學工業	CHEMICAL TECHNOLOGY
8600-8699	礦業冶金	MINING AND METALLURGY
8700-8899	工程	ENGINEERING
8900-8999	軍事學	MILITARY AND NAVAL SCIENCE

9000-9999	總錄書志類	GENERALIA AND BIBLIOGRAPHY
9100-9120	中國普通叢書	CHINESE GENERAL SERIES (TS'UNG-SHU)
9100	彙刻叢書	OF A COMPOSITE NATURE
9101-9109	特種叢書	OF A SPECIAL TYPE
9110	地方叢書	OF A PARTICULAR LOCALITY
9111	族姓叢書	OF A PARTICULAR FAMILY
9112-9120	個人叢書	OF INDIVIDUAL AUTHORS
9130-9163	中國雜著隨筆	CHINESE INDIVIDUAL POLYGRAPHIC BOOKS
9165-9179	日本普通叢書	JAPANESE GENERAL SERIES (SŌSHU)
9180-9189	日本雜著隨筆	JAPANESE INDIVIDUAL POLYGRAPHIC BOOKS
9200-9229	普通雜誌社刊	GENERAL PERIODICALS AND SOCIETY PUBLICATIONS
9230-9289	普通會議,博物院	GENERAL CONGRESSES AND MUSEUMS
9290-9339	普通類書	GENERAL ENCYCLOPEDIAS AND REFERENCE BOOKS

9

9400-9699 書志學（目錄學）　BIBLIOGRAPHY
　9401-9409 總錄　　　　　　GENERAL
　9410-9499 圖書學　　　　　BIBLIOLOGY
　9500-9519 專科書目　　　　SUBJECT BIBLIOGRAPHIES
　　　　　各國書目　　BIBLIOGRAPHIES OF VARIOUS COUNTRIES
　9520-9639 中國書目　　CHINESE BIBLIOGRAPHIES
　　9520-9529 書目叢刻　　　COLLECTIVE BIBLIOGRAPHIES
　　9530-9539 歷代史志　　　BIBLIOGRAPHICAL SECTIONS
　　　　　　　　　　　　　　IN DYNASTIC HISTORIES
　　9540-9549 一般書目　　　OTHER GENERAL BIBLIOG-
　　　　　　　　　　　　　　RAPHIES
　　9550-9559 治學書目　　　READING LIST AND BEST BOOKS
　　9560-9561 雜志論文目錄及索引 PERIODICAL INDEXES
　　9562-9569 特種書目　　　SPECIAL BIBLIOGRAPHIES
　　9570-9579 題跋書評　　　BOOK REVIEWS
　　9580-9589 地方書目　　　LOCAL BIBLIOGRAPHIES
　　9590-9599 族姓及個人書目 FAMILY AND PERSONAL
　　　　　　　　　　　　　　BIBLIOGRAPHIES
　　9600-9629 藏書目錄　　　LIBRARY CATALOGUES
　　9630-9639 書業目錄　　　DEALERS' AND PUBLISHERS'
　　　　　　　　　　　　　　CATALOGUES
　9640-9679 日本書目　　JAPANESE BIBLIOGRAPHIES
　9680-9689 朝鮮書目　　KOREAN BIBLIOGRAPHIES
　9690-9699 其他各國書目 OTHER COUNTRIES
9700-9939 圖書館學　　LIBRARIANSHIP (LIBRARY SCIENCE)
9940-9999 報學（新聞學）JOURNALISM NEWSPAPERS

10

100-999 中國經學類 CHINESE CLASSICS

100-199 羣經 GENERAL

110	羣經合刻	COLLECTIONS
120	經學書目	BIBLIOGRAPHY
130	經學辭典	DICTIONARIES, ETC.
140-159	諸經總義	GENERAL TREATISES
141	漢	Han Dynasty (B. C. 206-220 A. D.)
143	三國	The Three Kingdoms (220-280)
144	晉	Chin Dynasty (265-420)
145	南北朝	Epoch of Southern and Northern Dynasties (420-589)
146	隋	Sui Dynasty (589-618)
147	唐	T'ang Dynasty (618-907)
148	五代	The Five Dynasties (907-960)
149	宋	Sung Dynasty (960-1279)
151	元	Yüan Dynasty (1279-1368)
152	明	Ming Dynasty (1368-1644)
154	清	Ch'ing Dynasty (1644-1912)
156	民國	The Republic (1912-)
157	外國著者	Non-Chinese Authors
158	羣經緯	APOCRYPHAL WORKS
160	經學史傳	HISTORY AND BIOGRAPHY (Subdivide chronologically by Table III
180	諸經校勘	TEXTUAL CRITICISM (Subdivide chronologically by Table III

先依書籍內容之時代
次依著者之時代分用附表三。

依著者時代分用附表三。

11

190	石經	STONE INSCRIPTIONS OF CLASSICS
191	總錄	General
192	易經	I Ching
193	書經	Shu Ching
194	詩經	Shih Ching
195	禮經	Li Ching
196	春秋	Ch'un Ch'iu
197	孝經	Hsiao Ching
198	四書	Ssŭ Shu
	爾雅　見5071	Er-yah　see 5071

<u>200-299</u>　易經　BOOK OF CHANGES

220-239 白文,注疏,論說　TEXTS, COMMENTARIES AND TREATIES

221	白文 其他各經白文仿此分	Texts (Similar treatment to be followed for the other Classics)
222	古易 連山,歸藏.	Antiquity
223	西漢	Western Han (B. C. 206-25 A. D.)
224	東漢	Eastern Han (25-220)
225	三國	The Three Kingdoms (220-280)
226	晉	Ch'in Dynasty (265-420)
227	南北朝	Epoch of Southern and Northern Dynasties (420-589)
228	隋	Sui Dynasty (589-618)
229	唐	T'ang Dynasty (618-907)
230	五代	The Five Dynasties (907-960)
231	宋	Sung Dynasty (960-1279)
233	元	Yüan Dynasty (1279-1368)

12

白文注疏論説(續) TEXTS, COMMENTARIES AND TREATIES (Cont.)

234	明	Ming Dynasty (1368-1644)
235	清	Ch'ing Dynasty (1644-1912)
238	民國	The Republic (1912-　　)
239	外國著者	Non-Chinese Authors
240-269	篇章研究	SPECIAL CHAPTERS OR SECTIONS
270-289	專題研究 見表甲	SPECIAL TOPICS.　See Table A.
290	易緯	APOCRYPHAL WORKS
	占筮見術數：易卜	For Divination see 1740

300-399　　書經　BOOK OF DOCUMENTS

白文注疏論説 TEXTS, COMMENTARIES AND TREATIES

323	西漢	Western Han Dynasty (B. C. 206-25 A. D.)
324	東漢	Eastern Han Dynasty (25-220)
325	三國	The Three Kingdoms (220-280)
326	晉	Ch'in Dynasty (265-420)
327	南北朝	Epoch of Southern and Northern Dynasties (420-589)
328	隋	Sui Dynasty (589-618)
329	唐	T'ang Dynasty (618-907)
330	五代	The Five Dynasties (907-960)
331	宋	Sung Dynasty (960-1279)
333	元	Yüan Dynasty (1279-1368)
334	明	Ming Dynasty (1368-1644)
335	清	Ch'ing Dynasty (1644-1912)
338	民國	The Republic (1912-　　)
339	外國著者	Non-Chinese Authors

BOOK OF DOCUMENTS (Cont.)

340-369	篇章研究	SPECIAL CHAPTERS
345	禹貢	Yü-kung
362	洪範	Hung-fan
370-389	專題研究 見表甲	SPECIAL TOPICS　See Table A
390	書緯	APOCRYPHAL WORKS

400-499　詩經　BOOK OF POETRY

410-419	三家詩	THE DIFFERENT TEXTS OF SHIH CHING
410	魯詩	Text of Lu
411	齊詩	Text of Ch'i
412	韓詩	Text of Han
413	三家詩合論	Three Texts Compared
421-439	毛詩 白文注疏論說	MAO SHIH: TEXTS, COMMENTARIES AND TREATIES
423	西漢	Western Han Dynasty (B. C. 206-25 A.D.)
424	東漢	Eastern Han Dynasty (25-220)
425	三國	The Three Kingdoms (220-280)
426	晉	Chin Dynasty (265-420)
427	南北朝	Epoch of Southern and Northern Dynasties (420-589)
428	隋	Sui Dynasty (589-618)
429	唐	T'ang Dynasty (618-907)
430	五代	The Five Dynasties (907-960)
431	宋	Sung Dynasty (960-1279)
433	元	Yüan Dynasty (1279-1368)

14

毛詩
白文注疏論說(續) MAO SHIH: TEXTS, COMMENTARIES AND
            TREATIES (Cont.)

434	明	Ming Dynasty (1368-1644)
435	清	Ch'ing Dynasty (1644-1912)
438	民國	The Republic (1912-)
439	外國著者	Non-Chinese Authors
440-469	篇章研究	SPECIAL CHAPTERS
470-489	專題研究 見表甲	SPECIAL TOPICS See Table A
490	詩緯	APOCRYPHAL WORKS

500-599 三禮 RITUALS

520-549	周禮	CHOU RITUAL
521-529	白文注疏論說 依作者時代分用表三	TEXTS AND COMMENTARIES (Subdivide chronologically by authors like Table III)
530-539	篇章研究	SPECIAL CHAPTERS
535	考工記	K'ao-kung-chi
537	輪輿	Lun-yü
540-549	專題研究 見表甲	SPECIAL TOPICS See Table A
550-579	儀禮	DECORUM RITUAL
550-559	白文注疏論說 依作者時代分用表三	TEXTS AND COMMENTARIES (Subdivide chronologically by authors like Table III)
560-579	專題研究	SPECIAL TOPICS
560	饗禮	The Sacrificial Ceremony
561	冠禮婚禮	Capping and Marriage Ceremonies
562	喪禮	The Mourning Ceremony

15

儀禮
專題研究（續）

DECORUM RITUALS (Cont.)

563　喪服　Mourning Garments

565

566

567　宮室　Palaces

568　冕服　Costumes

569　索引　Indexes

禮記 LI CHI　　　　　(BOOKS OF RITES)

580-619　小戴禮記 HSIAO TAI LI CHI

白文,注疏,論說TEXTS AND COMMENTARIES (Subdivide
依著者時代分,用表三. chronologically by authors like Table III)

590-609　篇章研究　SPECIAL CHAPTERS

591

592　檀弓　T'an-kung

593　王制　Wang-chih

594　月令　Yüeh-ling

595

596　禮運　Li-yün

597　坊記,表記,緇衣Fang-chi; Piao-chi and Tzŭ-i

598　深衣　Shēn-i

599　其他　Other Chapters

610-619　專題研究　SPECIAL TOPICS　See Table A
見表甲

620-639　大戴禮記 TA TAI LI CHI

621-619　白文,注疏,論說TEXTS AND COMMENTARIES (Subdivide
依著者時代分,用表三. chronologically by authors like Table III)

16

大戴禮記(續)TA TAI LI CHI (Cont.)

630-639	篇章研究	SPECIAL CHAPTERS
632		
633	夏小正	Hsia-hsiao-chêng
635		
638	• 其他	Other Chapters
639	專題研究	SPECIAL TOPICS See Table A

見表甲.

640-669	三禮總義	GENERAL TREATISES ON RITUALS
641-649	注疏,論說	TREATISES AND COMMENTARIES (Subdivide

依作者時代分,用表三. chronologically by authors like Table III)

651-659	專題研究	SPECIAL TOPICS
651	宮廟	Palaces and Temples
653	宗法	Patriarchal Family System
655	郊禘	State Sacrifices and Worship
657		
659		
660-668	雜禮	MISCELLANEOUS CEREMONIES
669	禮緯	APOCRYPHAL WORKS

680-809	春秋	SPRING AND AUTUMN ANNALS
681-709	春秋總義	GENERAL TREATISES ON THE ANNALS
682	西漢	Western Han Dynasty (B. C. 206-25 A. D.)
683	東漢	Eastern Han Dynasty (25-220)
684	三國	The Three Kingdoms (220-280)
685	晉	Chin Dynasty (265-420)

17

春秋總義 (續)　　　　　SPRING AND AUTUMN ANNALS (Cont.)

686　南北朝　　Epoch of Southern and Northern Dynasties (420-589)

687　隋　　Sui Dynasty (589-618)

688　唐　　T'ang Dynasty (618-907)

689　五代　　The Five Dynasties (907-960)

690　宋　　Sung Dynasty (960-1279)

691　元　　Yüan Dynasty (1279-1368)

693　明　　Ming Dynasty (1368-1644)

695　清　　Ch'ing Dynasty (1644-1912)

697　民國　　The Republic (1912-   )

698　外國蓍者　　Non-Chinese Authors

700　專題研究　　SPECIAL TOPICS

701　年表　　Historical Tables and Charts

702　世族名號　　Feudal Genealogy

703　地理　　Geography

704　職官　　Officials

705　禮儀　　Etiquette and Ceremonial

706　文藝　　Literature and Arts

708　曆書　　Chronology

710-739　左傳　　TSO CHUAN

710-719　白文注疏論說　TEXTS, COMMENTARIES AND TREATISES (Sub-
依作者時代分,用表三.　divide by Table III)

720-729　篇章研究　　SPECIAL CHAPTERS

730-739　專題研究　　SPECIAL TOPICS　See Table A
見表甲.

740-769 公羊傳　　KUNG-YANG CHUAN

740-749　白文 注疏 論說 TEXTS, COMMENTARIES AND TREATISES
依作者時代分,用表三. (Subdivide by Table III)

750-759　篇章研究　　SPECIAL CHAPTERS

760-769　專題研究　　SPECIAL TOPICS　See Table A
見表甲.

770-799 穀梁傳　KU-LIANG CHUAN

770-779　白文 注疏 論說 TEXTS, COMMENTARIES AND TREATISES
依作者時代分,用表三. (Subdivide by Table III)

780-789　篇章研究　　SPECIAL CHAPTERS

790-799　專題研究　　SPECIAL TOPICS　See Table A
見表甲.

800-809 春秋緯　APOCRYPHAL WORKS ON THE ANNALS (Sub-
依作者時代分,用表三. divide chronologically by authors like Table III)

810-849　孝經　　BOOK OF FILIAL PIETY

810-820 白文 注疏 論說 TEXTS, COMMENTARIES AND TREATISES (Sub-
依作者時代分,用表三. divide chronologically by authors like Table III)

821-829 篇章研究　SPECIAL CHAPTERS OR SECTIONS

830-839 專題研究　SPECIAL TOPICS　See Table A
見表甲.

840-849 孝經緯　APOCRYPHAL WORKS

850-999　四書　THE FOUR BOOKS

850-859 四書總義　GENERAL TREATISES

853　　宋　　　　Sung Dynasty (960-1279)

854　　元　　　　Yüan Dynasty (1279-1368)

855　　明　　　　Ming Dynasty (1368-1644)

856　　清　　　　Ch'ing Dynasty (1644-1912)

858　　民國　　　The Republic (1912-　　)

859　　外國著者　　Non-Chinese Authors

19

四書總義（續）　　　　　THE FOUR BOOKS (Cont.)

860-889　專題研究　SPECIAL TOPICS　See Table A
　　　　　見表甲、

890-909　　大學　　THE GREAT LEARNING

895-900　白文 注疏 論説 TEXTS, COMMENTARIES AND TREATISES (Sub-
　　　　　依作者時代分,見表三 divide chronologically by authors like Table III)

901-909　專題研究　SPECIAL TOPICS　See Table A
　　　　　見表甲

910-929　　中庸　　THE DOCTRINE OF THE MEAN

910-919　白文 注疏 論説 TEXTS, COMMENTARIES AND TREATISES (Sub-
　　　　　依作者時代分,見表三 divide chronologically by authors like Table III)

920-929　專題研究　SPECIAL TOPICS　See Table A
　　　　　見表甲.

930-959　　論語　　ANALECTS OF CONFUCIUS

930-940　白文 注疏 論説 TEXTS, COMMENTARIES AND TREATISES (Sub-
　　　　　依作者時代分,見表甲 divide chronologically by authors like Table III)
　　　　　　　用三

941-949　篇章研究　SPECIAL CHAPTERS

950-958　專題研究　SPECIAL TOPICS　See Table A
　　　　　見表甲

959　　論語緯　APOCRYPHAL WORKS

960-990　　孟子　　THE WORKS OF MENCIUS

960-970　白文 注疏 論説 TEXTS, COMMENTARIES AND TREATISES (Sub-
　　　　　依作者時代分,用表三 divide chronologically by authors like Table III)

971-979　篇章研究　SPECIAL CHAPTERS OR SECTIONS

980-998　專題研究　SPECIAL TOPICS　See Table A
　　　　　見表甲.

999　　孟子外書　OTHER WORKS ON MENCIUS

1000-1999 哲學宗教類 PHILOSOPHY AND RELIGION

1000-1008 哲學總論 PHILOSOPHY IN GENERAL

1000-1008 總錄　　　GENERAL (Subdivide by form like Table I)
依體裁分,用表一.

1009-1499 東方哲學 ORIENTAL PHILOSOPHY

1009.1-.9 總錄　　　GENERAL (Subdivide by form like Table I)
依體裁分,用表一.

1010-1429 中國哲學 CHINESE PHILOSOPHY

1010.1-.9 總錄　　　GENERAL (Subdivide by form like Table I)
依體裁分,用表一.

1011-1130 中國哲學史 HISTORY OF CHINESE PHILOSOPHY

1012	古代	Ancient (Earliest to 206 B. C.)
1014	中世	Mediaeval (B. C. 206-960 A. D.)
1015	漢	Han Dynasty (B. C. 206-218 A. D.)
1017	魏晉六朝	Wei, Chin and the Six Dynasties (218-589)
1019	隋唐五代	Sui, T'ang and the Five Dynasties (589-960)
1020	近世	Modern (960-1911)
1022	宋	Sung Dynasty (960-1279)
1024	元	Yüan Dynasty (1279-1368)
1025	明	Ming Dynasty (1368-1644)
1027	清	Ch'ing Dynasty (1644-1912)
1030		The Republic (1912-　　)

1035　　諸子通論　GENERAL TREATISES

1040-1059 宗派　　SCHOOLS
專論一家之書入
此,個人創作入
個人哲學專著.
　　(Only special treatises on particular schools are classified here. Works of individual authors are placed in 1065-1429)

宗派 (續)　SCHOOLS (Cont.)

1042　儒家　Confucianism

1044　道家　Taoism

1046　墨家　Mohism

名家
見論理學　Logicians.　See 1610　Logic

法家
見經濟理論
政治理論
法理學　Political and Legal Philosophers.　See 4310
Economic Theory; 4614
Political Theory; 4870
Jurisprudence

1060-1069　諸子合刻
哲學叢書　SERIES (Collected works of more than two philosophers)

1065-1429　個人哲學專著　THE INDIVIDUAL PHILOSOPHERS (Works by
依哲人時代排.凡
個人創作及他人討
論其著述之書均入
此.於每人下依表乙排
列之.　them and works about them, arranged chronologically by philosophers; and under each philosopher all the books may be arranged by Table B.)

古代
Ancient Period　(Earliest to B. C. 206)

1067　陰符經　Yin Fu Ching

1068

1069　鬻子　Yü Tzû

1070

1071　老子　Lao Tzû　(B. C. ? - 590?)

1072

1073

1074　關尹子　Kuan Yin Tzû

1075　孔子　K'ung Tzû (Confucius B. C. 551-479)

1076

1077

1078　子華子　Tzû Hua Tzû (B. C. ? - 550?)

古代（續）
Ancient Period (Earliest to B. C. 206) Cont.

1079	晏子	Yen Tzû
1080	顏子	Yen Tzû (B. C. 521-481)
1081	漆雕子	Ch'i Tiao Tzû (B. C. 540-450?)
1082	曾子	Tsêng Tzû (B.C. 505-436)
1083	孔伋 子思	K'ung Chi (B.C. 492-431?)
1084	墨子	Mo Tzû (B. C. 480-390?)
1085		
1086		
1087	文子	Wên Tzû
1088	列子	Lieh Tzû (B. C. 450-375?)
1089	甯越	Ning Yüeh (B. C. 445-381?)
1090		
1091	鬼谷子	Kuei Ku Tzû
1092		
1093	鶡冠子	Ho Kuan Tzû
1094		
1095	楊朱	Yang Chu (B. C. 395-335?)
1096		
1097	尸佼	Shih Chiao (B. C. 390-330?)
1098	惠施	Hui Shih (B. C. 380-300?)
1099		
1110		
1111	莊子	Chuang Tzû (B. C. 365-290?)

古代 (續)
Ancient Period (Earliest to B. C. 206) Cont.

1112		
1113		
1114		
1115	宋子	Sung Tzû (B. C. 360-290?)
1116	陳仲子	Ch'ên Chung Tzû (B. C. 350-260?)
1117	田駢	T'ien P'ien (B. C. 350-275?)
1118	尹文	Yin Wên (B. C. 350-285?)
1119	慎到	Shên Tao (B. C. 350-175?)
1120	荀子	Hsün Tzû (B. C. 340-245?)
1121		
1122		
1123		
1124	公孫龍子	Kung Sun Lung Tzû (B. C. 320-250?)
1125		
1126	呂不韋	Lü Pu-wei (B. C. 290-235?)
1127		
1128	其他古代諸子 Other Ancient Philosophers	

漢,三國
Han Dynasty and the Three Kingdoms 206 B. C.-265 A. D.

1130	孔鮒	K'ung Fu
1131	陸賈	Lu Chia
1134	其他同時作者 Other Contemporary Writers	
1135	賈誼	Chia I (B. C. 200-168)
1138	其他同時作者 Other Contemporary Writers	

漢.三國 (續)
Han Dynasty and the Three Kingdoms 206 B. C.- 265 A. D. (Cont.)

1140	劉安 淮南子	Liu An (? - B. C. 122)
1143	其他同時作者	Other Contemporary Writers
1145	劉向	Liu Hsiang (B. C. 77-6)
1148	其他同時作者	Other Contemporary Writers
1150	揚雄	Yang Hsiung (B. C. 52-18)
1156	其他同時作者	Other Contemporary Writers
1158	馬融	Ma Jung (79-166 A. D.)
1159	其他同時作者	Other Contemporary Writers
1160	王充	Wang Ch'ung (29-109)
1161	其他同時作者	Other Contemporary Writers
1162	荀悅	Hsün Yüeh (148-209)
1163	其他同時作者	Other Contemporary Writers
1164	王符	Wang Fu (cir. 80-160?)
1165	其他同時作者	Other Contemporary Writers
1166	徐幹	Hsü Kan (170-217)

晉至隋
Chin Dynasty to Sui Dynasty [265-618]

1180	劉邵以前作者	Other Writers before Liu Shao
1182	劉邵	Liu Shao (cir. 210)
1183	其他同時作者	Other Contemporary Writers
1185	傅玄	Fu Hsüan (217-278)
1196	其他同時作者	Other Contemporary Writers
1187	葛洪	Ko Hung (234-305)
1189	其他同時作者	Other Contemporary Writers
1190	王通	Wang T'ung (584-618)

唐.五代
T'ang Dynasty and the Five Dynasties (618-960)

1191	孫思邈	Sun Ssû-mo (581-682)
1192	其他同時作者	Other Contemporary Writers
1193	林慎思	Lin Shên-ssû
1194	其他同時作者	Other Contemporary Writers
1195	韓愈	Han Yü (768-824)
1196	李翶羽	Li Ao (chin shih 798)
1197-8	其他同時作者	Other Contemporary Writers
1199	譚峭	T'an Ch'iao
1200	其他同時作者	Other Contemporary Writers

宋
Sung Dynasty (960-1279)

1201	周敦頤前作者	Other Writers before Chou Tun-i
1202	周敦頤	Chou Tun-i (1017-1073)
1204	其他同時作者	Other Contemporary Writers
1205	邵雍	Shao Yung (1011-1077)
1206	其他同時作者	Other Contemporary Writers
1207	張載 横渠	Chang Tsai (1020-1077)
1208	其他同時作者	Other Contemporary Writers
1209	程頤 二程入此	Ch'êng I (1033-1107)
1210	程顥	Ch'êng Hao (1032-1085)
1211	王開祖	Wang K'ai-tsu
1212	其他同時作者	Other Contemporary Writers
1214	謝良佐	Hsieh Liang-tso (1050-1103)
1215	其他同時作者	Other Contemporary Writers

宋（續）
Sung Dynasty (960-1279) Cont.

1217	楊時	Yang Shih (1053-1135)
1219	其他同時作者	Other Contemporary Writers
1221	邵伯温	Shao Po-wên (1057-1134)
1223	其他同時作者	Other Contemporary Writers
1224	胡宏	Hu Hung (? -1155)
1226	其他同時作者	Other Contemporary Writers
1227	羅從彦	Lo Tsung-yen (1072-1135)
1229	其他同時作者	Other Contemporary Writers
1231	李侗	Li T'ung (1088-1158)
1233	其他同時作者	Other Contemporary Writers
1234	張栻	Chang Shih (1133-1180)
1236	其他同時作者	Other Contemporary Writers
1237	朱熹	Chu Hsi (1130-1200)
1239	其他同時作者	Other Contemporary Writers
1241	蔡元定	Ts'ai Yüan-ting (1135-1198)
1243	其他同時作者	Other Contemporary Writers
1244	蔡沈	Ts'ai Ch'ên (1167-1230)
1246	其他同時作者	Other Contemporary Writers
1247	黄榦	Huang Kan (1152-1221)
1249	其他同時作者	Other Contemporary Writers
1251	陳淳	Ch'ên Shun (1151-1216)
1253	其他同時作者	Other Contemporary Writers
1254	陸九淵	Lu Chiu-yüan (1140-1192)
1256	其他同時作者	Other Contemporary Writers

宋 (續)
Sung Dynasty (960-1279)　Cont.

1257	楊簡	Yang Chien (1140-1225)
1259	其他同時作者	Other Contemporary Writers
1261	袁燮	Yüan Hsieh (1144-1224)
1263	其他同時作者	Other Contemporary Writers
1264	呂祖謙	Lü Tsu-Ch'ien (1137-1181)
1266	其他同時作者	Other Contemporary Writers
1267	項安世	Hsiang An-shih (? -1208)
1269	其他同時作者	Other Contemporary Writers
1271	葉適	Yeh Shih (1150-1223)
1273	其他同時作者	Other Contemporary Writers
1274	魏了翁	Wei Liao-wêng (1178-1239)
1276	其他同時作者	Other Contemporary Writers
1278	真德秀	Chên Tê-hsiu (1178-1235)
1279	其他同時作者	Other Contemporary Writers

元
Yüan Dynasty (1279-1368)

1281	許衡	Hsü Hêng (1209-1281)
1282	其他同時作者	Other Contemporary Writers
1283	劉因	Liu Yin (1241-1293)
1284	其他同時作者	Other Contemporary Writers
1285	吳澄	Wu Chên (1247-1331)
1286	其他同時作者	Other Contemporary Writers
1287	鄭玉	Chêng Yü (1298-1358)
1289	其他同時作者	Other Contemporary Writers

		明　　Ming Dynasty (1365-1644)
1290	劉基	Liu Chi (1311-1375)
1291	吳與弼	Wu Yü-pi (1391-1469)
1293	其他同時作者	Other Contemporary Writers
1294	薛瑄	Hsieh Hsüan (1392-1464)
1296	其他同時作者	Other Contemporary Writers
1297	曹端	Tsao Tuan (1376-1437)
1299	其他同時作者	Other Contemporary Writers
1301	胡居仁	Hu Chü-jên (1434-1484)
1303	其他同時作者	Other Contemporary Writers
1304	陳獻章	Ch'ên Hsien-chang (1428-1500)
1306	其他同時作者	Other Contemporary Writers
1307	王守仁	Wang Shou-jên (1472-1528)
1309	其他同時作者	Other Contemporary Writers
1311	湛若水	Chan Jo-shui (1464-1560)
1313	其他同時作者	Other Contemporary Writers
1314	羅欽順	Lo Ch'in-shun (1465-1547)
1316	其他同時作者	Other Contemporary Writers
1317	王畿	Wang Chi (1498-1582)
1318	王艮	Wang Kên (1483-1540)
1319	其他同時作者	Other Contemporary Writers
1321	劉宗周	Lui Tsung-chou (1578-1646)
1323	其他同時作者	Other Contemporary Writers

清　　Ch'ing Dynasty (1644-1912)

1330	孫奇逢以前作者	Other Writers before Sun Ch'i-fêng
1331	孫奇逢	Sun Ch'i-fêng (1583-1675)
1332	其他同時作者	Other Contemporary Writers
1333	黃宗羲	Huang Tsung-hsi (1610-1695)
1334	顧炎武	Ku Yen-wu (1613-1681)
1335	其他同時作者	Other Contemporary Writers 133
1336	李顒	Li Yung (1630-1705)
1336.9	湯斌	T'ang Pin (1627-1687)
1337	陸世儀	Lu Shih-i (1611-1672)
1338	陸隴其	Lu Lung-ch'i (1630-1692)
1339	其他同時作者	Other Contemporary Writers
1340	顏元	Yen Yüan (1635-1704)
1341	李塨	Li Kung (1659-1733)
1342	張伯行	Chang Po-hsing (1651-1725)
1343	戴震	Tai Chên (1722-1777)
1344	其他同時作者	Other Contemporary Writers
1345		
1346		
1347		
1348		
1349		
1350		

民國　　The Republic (1912-　　)

1371

1372

1373

1374

1375

1376

1377

1378

1379

1380

1381

1382

1383

1384

1385

1386

1430-1469 日本哲學 JAPANESE PHILOSOPHY

1430-1439 總錄 GENERAL (Subdivide by form like Table I)

　　　　　依體裁分用表一.

1440-1449 宗派 SCHOOLS

1442-1443 儒學 Confucianism (All works on Confucianism

　　　　　凡日人儒學著作皆入此 by Japanese are classed here)

1442 概說及歷史 General Treatises and Histories

1442.9 總集 General Collections

	宗派 (續)	SCHOOLS (Cont.)
1443	儒學流派	Systems and Sects
.2	漢學	Conservative Schools
.3	宋學	Rationalism
.31	理學	Materialism
.36	朱子學	Chuhsiism
.41	京學 聖堂派	Kyōto Chuhsiism Hayashi School
.45	南學	Southern Chuhsiism
.47	闇齋學派	Yamazaki Ansai School
.49	大阪朱子學	Ōsaka Chuhsiism
.5	心學	Idealism
.52	陽明學	Subjective School, Wang Yangming School
.6	日本心學	Japanese Moralism
.62	獨立學	Independent School
.64	條理學	Systematicism
.65	報德教	Hōtoku kyō
.66	水戸學	Chu Shunshui School
.7	古學	Classicism
.72	堀河學派	Kyōto School, Itō Jinsai School
.74	護園學派	Edo School, Ogyū Sorai School
.76	折衷學	Eclecticism
.8	考證學	School for Textual Criticism
.9	其他	Others
1448	日本主義 日本精神, 大和魂	Japanism Yamatoism
1449	日本學, 國學	Japanology

日本哲學（續）　　　JAPANESE PHILOSOPHY (Cont.)

1450-1459　個人哲學專著 THE INDIVIDUAL PHILOSOPHERS

1456　　荷田春滿　　Kada no Azumamaro, 1669-1736

1457　　賀茂真淵　　Kamo Mabuchi, 1697-1769

1458　　本居宣長　　Matori Norinaga, 1730-1801

1459　　平田篤胤　　Hirata Atsuta, 1776-1843

1470-1489 印度哲學 HINDU PHILOSOPHY

1470-1479　總錄　　　GENERAL (Subdivide by form like Table D
　　　　依體裁分, 用表一.

1480-1486　宗派　　　SYSTEMS AND SCHOOLS

1481　　聲論派　　　Pūrva-mīmānsā
　　　　彌曼蹉派.

1482　　吠檀多派　　Vedānta (Uttara-mīmānsā)
　　　　後彌曼蹉派

1483　　數論派　　　Sānkhya
　　　　僧佉耶派

1484　　瑜珈派　　　Yoga

1485　　勝論派　　　Vaiséṣika
　　　　吠世師迦派.

1486　　正理派　　　Nyāya
　　　因明見佛教哲學
　　　　　　For Hetu-vidyā see 1813.8

1487-1489　個人哲學專著 THE INDIVIDUAL PHILOSOPHERS (Arrange
　　　　　　　chronologically by philosophers)

1490-1499 其他東方哲學家 OTHER ORIENTAL PHILOSOPHERS

1492　　埃及　　　EGYPTIAN

1493　　猶太　　　JEWISH

1494　　波斯　　　PERSIAN

1495　　加爾底亞　CHALDAEAN

1496　　腓尼基　　PHENICIAN

1497-99　其他　　　OTHERS

33

1500-1539　西洋哲學　OCCIDENTAL PHILOSOPHY

哲學史及 History and Works of Individual Philosophers
個人哲學專集

1501	概論	General Treatise
1502	通史	General History
1504	古代 — 希臘	Ancient Greece
1505	蘇格拉底	Socrates
1507	伯拉圖	Plato
1509	亞里士多德	Aristotle
1511	其他	Others
1512	中古時代	Early Christian and Mediaeval
1516-1519	文藝復興時代	Renaissance
1520	近代	Modern

各國哲學 Division by Countries: General Treatises and
Works of Individual Philosophers

	美國	American
1521	通論	General
1522	個人哲學專著	Individual Philosophers
	英國	British
1523	通論	General
1524	個人哲學專著	Individual Philosophers
	法國	France
1525	通論	General
1526	個人哲學專著	Individual Philosophers
	德國	Germany
1527	通論	General
1528	個人哲學專著	Individual Philosophers

各國哲學 (續) Division by Countries (Cont.)

意國　　Italy

1529　　通論　　　General

1530　　個人哲學專著 Individual Philosophers

荷蘭　　　Netherlands

1531　　通論　　　General

1532　　個人哲學專著 Individual Philosophers

俄國其他斯拉 Russia and Other Slavic Countries
夫諸國　　General

1533　　通論

1534　　個人哲學專著 Individual Philosophers

西班牙,葡萄牙 Spain and Portugal

1535　　通論　　　General

1536　　個人哲學專著 Individual Philosophers

斯堪地那威亞 Scandinavia

1537　　通論　　　General

1538　　個人哲學專著 Individual Philosophers

1539　　其他諸國　Other Countries

1540-1569 哲學問題及系統 PHILOSOPHICAL PROBLEMS AND SYSTEMS

1541　　不可知論　　Agnosticism

1542　　批評論　　　Criticism

1543　　獨斷論　　　Dogmatism

1544　　二元論　　　Dualism

1545　　折衷論　　　Electicism

1546　　經驗論　　　Empiricism (Associationalism)

1547　　進化論　　　Evolution

1548　　人文主義人本論 Humanism (New-humanism)

哲學問題及系統(續) PHILOSOPHICAL PROBLEMS AND SYSTEMS (Cont.)

1549	命運論	Fatalism
1551	唯心論	Idealism
1553	唯物論	Materialism
1554	一元論	Monism
1555	神秘論	Mysticism
1556	虛無論	Nihilism
1557	積極論,改善論	Optimism Meliorism
1558	消極論	Pessimism
1559	實證論	Positivism
1560	實用主義,工具論	Pragmatism Instrumentalism
1561	唯理論	Rationalism
1562	唯實論	Realism
1563	懷疑論	Scepticism
1565	經典派	Scholasticism
1566	精神論	Spiritualism
	超絕論 見唯心論	Transcendentalism see Idealism
1567	功利主義	Utilitarianism
1568	生機論	Vitalism

1570-1609 論理學(名學) LOGIC

1570	總錄	GENERAL
1571	期刊	Periodicals
1572	會社	Societies
1573	叢集	Collections

論理學總錄 GENERAL (Cont.)
(續)

1574	參考書目	Bibliography
1575	辭書,類書	Encyclopedias
1578	歷史	History

1580-1589 中國名家通論 TREATISES ON CHINESE LOGICIANS

專論名家之書入
此. 古代名家創作 Works of ancient Chinese logicians are
入中國哲學個人 classed in 1065-1429. However, if a
哲學專著.但如顧 library wishes to classify those works
將古代名家專著列此 here, 1581-1589 may be used.
者,可利用此諸號碼細分.

1590	總論	GENERAL TREATISES
1591	演繹法	Deductive logic
1592	歸納法	Inductive and Empirical Logic
1593	進化論理學	Genetic and Evolutionary Logic
1594	數理論理學	Mathematical and Algebraic Logic (Symbolic)
1595	機械邏輯法	Mechanical Logical Methods & Systems
1596	幾率論,或然論	Logic of Chance. Probability
1600	各論	SPECIAL TOPICS
1601		
1602		
1603		

1610-1649 形而上學(玄學) METAPHYSICS

1610-1619	總錄	GENERAL (Subdivide by form like Table I)
	依體裁分,用表一.	
1620	知識論	EPISTEMOLOGY. THEORY OF KNOWLEDGE
1628	方法論	METHODOLOGY
1630	本體論	ONTOLOGY
1640	宇宙論	COSMOLOGY

形而上學(續)　　　METAPHYSICS (Cont.)

1647	價值論	THEORY OF VALUE
1649	形而上學各論	SPECIAL TOPICS

1650-1699　倫理　ETHICS

	總錄	GENERAL
1651	期刊	Periodicals
1652	會社	Societies
1653	叢雜	Miscellany
1654	書目	Bibliographies
1655	教學	Study and Teaching
1656	辭典	Dictionaries
1657	撮要	Compends
1658	歷史	HISTORY
1658.1	中國	China
.4	日本	Japan
.5	印度	India
.6	西洋	Occident
	概論	GENERAL TREATISES
	中國著作	Chinese
1660	總集	Collective
1661-1669	別集	Individual
	依著者時代分 用表三.	(Divide by dates of authors like Table III)
	日本著作	Japanese
1670	總集	Collective

38

倫理概論 (續) GENERAL TREATISES (Cont.)

	日本著作	
1671-1674	別集	Individual
1671	上代	Nara-Heian Period, 700-1186
1672	近古	Kamakura-moromachi Period, 1186-1603
1673	近世	Tokukawa Period, 1603-1911
1674	現代	Present Age, 1912-　date
	印度著作	Indian
1676	總集	Collective
1677	別集	Individual
	西洋著作	Occidental
1678	總集	Collective
1679	別集	Individual
	各論	SPECIAL TOPICS
1681	個人倫理	Personal Ethics
	普通修身壹懿行錄入此. 格言等入文學雜著.	Class here common moral precepts and anecdotes of good conduct. Maxims, mottoes etc., are entered in 5787　Literary Miscellany
1682	家庭倫理	Family Ethics
	家訓入此	Class here family rules and precepts
.1	家庭生活	Home Life
.2	親子	Duties of Parents and Children
.3	父	Fathers
.4	母 (慈)	Mothers
.5	子女 (孝)	Sons and Daughters
.6	兄弟姊妹	Duties of Brothers and Sisters
.7	夫婦	Duties of Husbands and Wives

39

倫理各論（續）　SPECIAL TOPICS (Cont.)

1682.8	家庭倫理 主從	Duties of Masters, Mistresses and Servants
.9	其他	Other Topics
1683	性倫理	Sexual Ethics
1684	社會倫理	Social Ethics
1685	政治倫理	Political Ethics
.1	領袖	Leadership
.2	官箴	Duties of Public Officers
.3	君臣	Duties of Monarchs and Ministers
.4	君道	Monarchs
.5	臣道	Ministers
.6	國民道德	Duties of Citizens.　Patriotism
.7	武士道	Bushido (The Way of Warrior)
.8	國際道德	International Ethics
1686	敕語	Imperial Rescripts
.1-.8	中國 依時代分，用表三.	China (Subdivide by periods like Table III)
.9	日本	Japan
1687	職業倫理	Professional and Business Ethics
1688	遊藝倫理	Ethics of Amusements
1689	其他倫理問題	Other Ethical Topics

1700-1729　宗教總論 RELIGION IN GENERAL

1701-9	總錄 依體裁分，用表一.	GENERAL (Form Subdivision see Table I)
1710	宗教學	SCIENCE OF RELIGION
1712	宗教心理學	PSYCHOLOGY OF RELIGION

宗教總論（續）　　　RELIGION IN GENERAL (Cont.)

1713

1714　宗教社會學 SOCIOLOGY OF RELIGION

1715　宗教哲學　PHILOSOPHY OF RELIGION

1717　宗教與哲學 RELIGION AND PHILOSOPHY

1718　宗教與科學 RELIGION AND SCIENCE

1720　宗教發生論 ORIGIN OF RELIGIONS

1721　比較宗教　COMPARATIVE RELIGION

各國宗教
通史見1751- For history of religions in individual
1779　　　countries, see 1751-1779

1722　世界宗教　UNIVERSAL RELIGION

1723　原始宗教　PRIMITIVE RELIGIONS

　.1　民間信仰　Popular Beliefs

　.3　自然崇拜　Nature Worship

　.4　咒物崇拜　Fetishism

　.7　祖先崇拜　Ancestor Worship

1724　神秘主義　MYSTICISM

1725　有神論　　THEISM

1726　汎神論,無神論PANTHEISM AND ATHEISM

1727　信仰及得救 FAITH AND BELIEF　　SALVATION

1728　悟,解脫　 ENLIGHTENMENT　　 EMANCIPATION

1729　永生,輪廻 IMMORTALITY　　 TRANSMIGRATION

1730-1738　神話附傳說MYTHOLOGY

總錄
1731　中國神話　CHINESE

1732　中國境內小民族 OTHER RACES IN CHINA
　　　神話

	神話（續）	MYTHOLOGY (Cont.)
1733	日本神話	JAPANESE
1734	朝鮮神話	KOREAN
.8	臺灣神話	FORMOSAN
.9	琉球神話	LOOCHOO
1735	印度神話	HINDU
1736	其他東方各國神話	OTHER ORIENTAL COUNTRIES
.1	緬甸神話	Burmese
.2	暹羅神話	Siamese
.3	安南神話	Annamese
.4	菲律賓神話	Philippine
.5	馬來神話	Malayan
.6	爪哇,蘇門答臘神話	Javanese and Sumatran
1737	希臘羅馬神話	GREEK AND ROMAN
1738	其他各國神話	OTHER COUNTRIES

1739-1749 神秘學 術數 OCCULTISM NUMEROLOGY

1739	總錄	GENERAL (Popular Superstitions)
1740	易卜	DIVINATION BY THE "BOOK OF CHANGES"
1741	其他卜筮 龜卜,卦卜,測字,等.	DIVINATION BY OTHER MEANS
1742	占候	ASTROLOGY
1743	陰陽五行	DIVINATION BY THE POSITIVE AND NEGATIVE PRINCIPLES AND THE "LAW OF FIVE ELEMENTS"
1744	奇門遁甲	CH'I-MÊN—TUN-CHIA
1745	相術	PHYSIOGNOMY

神秘學術數 (續)　　　OCCULTISM NUMEROLOGY (Cont.)

1746	命書	FORTUNE-TELLING
1747	堪輿	GEOMANCY
1748	巫祝	WITCHCRAFT
1749	雜術	MISCELLANEOUS SUPERSTITIOUS ARTS

1750-1779 各國宗教通史 HISTORY OF RELIGIONS IN VARIOUS COUNTRIES

1750	世界宗教通史	GENERAL HISTORY OF WORLD RELIGIONS
1751	亞洲宗教通史	HISTORY OF RELIGIONS IN ASIA
1752	中國宗教通史	HISTORY OF RELIGIONS IN CHINA
1753	太古至漢	Earliest to Han Dynasty (? to 106 B. C.)
1754	漢魏六朝	Han Dynasty to Sui Dynasty (206 B. C.-589 A. D.)
1755	隋唐五代	Sui, T'ang and the Five Short Dynasties (589-960)
1756	宋元	Sung and Yüan Dynasties (960-1368)
1757	明	Ming Dynasty (1368-1644)
1758	清	Ch'ing Dynasty (1644-1912)
1759	民國	The Republic (1912-　　)
1760-8	日本宗教通史 用表三細分	HISTORY OF RELIGIONS IN JAPAN (Subdivided chronologically by Table III)
1769	朝鮮宗教通史	HISTORY OF RELIGIONS IN KOREA
1770	印度宗教通史	HISTORY OF RELIGIONS IN INDIA
1771	其他亞洲各國宗教通史	HISTORY OF RELIGIONS IN OTHER ASIATIC COUNTRIES
1772-9	西洋宗教通史	HISTORY OF RELIGIONS IN OCCIDENTAL COUNTRIES
1772	美國	America
1773	英	Britain

各國宗教通史 (續) HISTORY OF RELIGIONS (Cont.)

1774	法國	France
1775	德國	Germany
1776	意國	Italy
1777	西班牙	Spain
1778	俄國	Russia
1779	其他西洋各國	Other Occidental Countries

1780-1799 中國國家祀典 CHINESE STATE CULTS

| 1780-1785 | 總論 | GENERAL TREATISES |

如壇廟樂章祭祀典禮諸書以書所論之時代分.

| 1781 | 儀注 | Rituals |
| 1782 | 郊祀封禪 | Worship of Heaven and Earth (Subdivide |

依著者時代分, 用表三. chronologically by authors like Table III)

| 1783 | 城隍 | Local District Temples (Subdivide geo- |

依地域分, 用表二. graphically by Table II)

| 1784 | 宗廟 | Imperial Ancestral Temples (Subdivide |

依朝代分, 再依作者 chronologically by periods like Table III)
時代分, 用表三.

| 1786-1790 | 祀孔 | THE CULT OF CONFUCIUS |

| 1786.1 | 總錄 | General Treatises |

記祀孔掌故之書.

| 1786.2 | 史傳 | Genealogies |

如東家雜記及祖庭廣記諸書.

1786.8	儀注	Rituals
1787	曲阜孔廟	Confucian Temple in Ch'ü-fu
1788	各地文廟	Confucian Temples in Various Places (Sub-

依地域分, 用表二. divide geographically by Table II)

| 1789 | 文廟從祀諸賢 | Disciples' Tablets in Confucian Temples |
| 1790 | 孔教 | Confucianism as a Religion |

教義

1794-1796 祀關岳　　THE CULT OF KUAN AND YO

1795　　關羽　　Kuan Yü

1796　　岳飛　　Yo Fei

1798-1799 地方祀典　OTHER LOCAL CULTS
　　　　依受祀者時代分,用表三.

1800-1919 佛教　BUDDHISM

1801-1815 總錄　　GENERAL

1801　　雜誌　　Periodicals

1802　　會社刊物　Societies

1803　　叢書(藏經)　Collections.　(Tripitaka in Sets)

1804　　叢選　　Selections

1805　　中國人全集　Collected Works of Chinese Authors (Sub-
　　　照下日本人全集細分.　divide like 1806)

1806　　日本人全集　Collected Works of Japanese Authors

1806.2　　諸家著作集　　Collected Works of Several Authors

　.4　　一家著作集　　Collected Works of One Author

　.6　　諸家隨筆雜著集　Miscellaneous Writings of Several Authors

　.8　　一家隨筆雜著集　Miscellaneous Writings of One Author

1807　　書目　　Bibliography

1808　　研究法　　Study and Teaching

1809　　類書事彙　　Encyclopedias

1810　　字典辭書　　Dictionaries

1812　　概論　　Compends; General Treatises

1813　　教理 哲學　Theory. Philosophy

1813.1　　佛陀論　　Buddhology

　.3　　原始佛教哲學　Early Buddhism
　　　　因明

45

1815-1839 佛經 (細分)　　THE TRIPIṬAKA (CLASSIFIED)

1815-1826 　經及經疏　SŪTRA-PIṬAKA (Including Commentaries)

　　　　　小乘經　　　HĪNAYĀNA SŪTRA

1816　　阿含部　Āgamas

1817　　本緣部　Avadāna

　　　　大乘經　　　MAHĀYĀNA SŪTRA

1818　　般若部　Prajñâpâramitâ

1819　　法華部　Saddharmapuṇḍarika

1820　　華嚴部　Avataṁsaka

1821　　寶積部　Ratnakûta

1822　　大集部　Mahâsannipâta

1823　　涅槃部　Nirvâna

1824　　經集部　Nikāya

1825　　秘密部　Mantrayāna or Tantrayāna

1826　　僞經　　Spurious and Apocryphal Works

1827-1832　律及律疏 VINAYA-PITAKA (Including Commentaries)

1828-9　　小乘律　Hīnayāna-vinaya

1830-31　大乘律　Mahāyāna-vinaya

1832　　雜律　　Miscellaneous vinaya

1833-1839　論及論疏 ABHIDHARMA-PITAKA (Including Commentaries)

1834　　釋經部　Commentaries Expository Works on Sūtra

1835　　毗曇部　Abhidharma

1836　　中觀部　Mādhyamika

1837　　瑜伽部　Yoga

論及論疏(續)ABHIDHARMA-PITAKA (Cont.)

1838	秘密部	Mantra
1839	論集部	Çastra or Sastra
1840-1856	儀規,佛事	RITUALS AND PRACTICES
1840	總錄 行事作法	General
1841	節會 年中行事	Festivals, Calendars
1842	法會,講式	Assembly for Preaching or Worship
1843		
1844	受戒	Initiation into Discipleship
1845	願文表白起請	Prayers
1846	道場,懺法	Offering Prayers and Sacrifices to Departed Spirits
1847-1851	服具	Dresses, Furniture & Sacred Articles, etc.
1852-1853	諷誦	Hymn-chanting and Sutra-reading
1854		
1855-1856	雜儀規	Miscellaneous Buddhist Life
	佛教生活 佛教習俗	
1857-1867	護教,佈教	APOLOGETICS, MISSIONARY WORK
1857	總錄	General
1858	與婆羅門教及 印度教	Relation with Brahmanism and Hinduism
1859	與儒家	Relation with Confucianism
1860	與道教	Relation with Taoism
1861	與神道	Relation with Shintoism
1862	與基督教	Relation with Christianity
1863	與回教	Relation with Mohammedanism
1864	與其他宗教	Relation with Other Religions
1864.5	與科學	Buddhism and Science

護教佈教 (續) APOLOGETICS (Cont.)

1865	佛教團體	Buddhist Associations
1866	佛教教育	Buddhist Education
1867	其他佈教事項	Miscellaneous

諸宗　SECTS (Under each sect use Table C for subdivisions)

1868	諸宗通論	General Treatises
1869	俱舍宗	Satya-siddhi-śāstra or Ch'êng-shih sect (Kushashū)
1870	成實宗	Abhidharma-kośa-śāstra or Chü-shê sect (Jōjitsushū)
1871	三論宗	Three Śāstra or San-lung sect (Sanronshū)
1872	法相宗	Dharma-lakṣaṇa or Fa-hsiang sect (Hossōshū)
1873	天台宗	T'ien-t'ai sect (Tendaishū)
1874	華嚴宗	Avataṁsaka-sūtra or Hua-yen sect (Kegonshū)
1875	律宗	Vinaya or Lü sect (Ritsushū)
1876	真言宗	Mantra or Chên-yen sect (Shingonshū)
1877	淨土宗	Sukhāvatī or Pure-land sect (Jōdoshū)
1878	融通念佛宗, 時宗	Yūzūnembutsushū.　Jishū
1879	真宗	Shinshū
1880	禪宗	Dhyāna or Ch'an sect (Zenshū)
1881	禪宗各派	Branches of Ch'an sect
.1	臨濟宗	Lin-chi-tsung (Rinzaishū)
.2	曹洞宗	Ts'ao-tung-tsung (Sōdōshū)
.3	黄檗宗	Huang-pai-tsung (Ōbakushū)

宗派 (續)　　SECTS (Cont.)

| 1882 | 日蓮宗 | Nichiren Sect |
| 1883 | 其他各宗 | Other Sects |

史傳　　HISTORY AND BIOGRAPHY

1884	通史	General Works (History of a particular sect
	宗派史入各宗派.	with that sect)
1885	印度	India
1886	西域及南亞	Central and Southern Asia
1887	中國	China
1888	西藏蒙古	Tibet, Mongolia
1889	朝鮮	Korea
1890	日本	Japan
1891	歐美	Europe, America and Other Lands
1893	釋迦傳	Biography of Buddha (Śākyamuni)
1894	佛弟子傳	Biography of Buddha's Disciples
1895	僧尼居士傳	Collective Biography of Monks and Lay Workers
1896	印度:總傳	India: Collective Biography
1897	印度:別傳	India: Individual Biography
1898	中國:總傳	China: Collective Biography
1899	中國:別傳	China: Individual Biography
.8	靈驗傳	
.9	往生傳	
1900	西藏:總傳	Tibet: Collective Biography
1901	西藏:別傳	Tibet: Individual Biography
1902	日本:總傳	Japan: Collective Biography
1903	日本:別傳	Japan: Individual Biography

史傳(續)　　HISTORY AND BIOGRAPHY (Cont.)

1904　　其他各國　Other Countries

地誌 紀行　GEOGRAPHY AND TRAVELS

1905.1　　總記　　　General

.2　　印度　　　India

.3　　西域及南亞　Central and Southern Asia

.4　　中國　　　China

.5　　西藏　　　Tibet

.6　　朝鮮　　　Korea

.7　　日本　　　Japan

.8　　其他各國　Other Countries

寺廟　　MONASTERIES AND TEMPLES

1906　　總記　　　General

1907　　印度　　　India

1908　　西域及南亞　Central and Southern Asia

1909　　中國　　　China

1910　　西藏　　　Tibet

1911　　朝鮮　　　Korea

1912　　日本　　　Japan

1913　　其他各國　Other Countries

佛教美術　BUDDHISTIC ART

1914　　總錄　　General Treatises

1915　　佛像　　Portraits of Buddha

1916　　祖像　　Portraits of founders of Sects

1917　　圖譜　　Other Pictures

佛教美術(續) BUDDHISTIC ART (Cont.)

1918	彫塑	Iconography: Sculpture & Plastic Arts
1919	雜錄	MISCELLANY

1920-1939　道教　TAOISM

1920.1-.9	總錄 依體裁分,用表一.	GENERAL (Subdivide by form like Table I)
1921-8	道藏	COLLECTIONS OF TAOIST SCRIPTURES
	三洞三經	The Three Divisions of Classics
1922	洞真部	Tung Chen Division
.1	本文類	Canonical Works
.2	神符類	Charm
.24	玉訣類	Secrets for Understanding the Canons
.27	靈圖類	Portraits of Deities and Spirits
.3	譜錄類	Chronologies
.4	戒律類	Rules for Repentance and Abstinency
.5	威儀類	Rituals
.6	方法類	Ways of Practicing Occultism
.7	眾術類	Ways of Practicing Alchemy
.8	記傳類	Biographies
.9	讚頌類	Eulogies
.95	表奏類	Memorials to the Gods
1923	洞玄部 仿洞真部細分.	Tung Hsüan Division (Subdivide like 1922)
1924	洞神部 仿洞真部細分.	Tung Shen Division (Subdivide like 1922)
	四輔	The Four Groups of Commentaries
1925	太玄	Tai Hsüan

	道藏四輔 (續)	Four Groups (Cont.)
1926	太平	Tai P'ing
1927	太清	Tai Ch'ing
1928	正一	Cheng I
1929	儀規	RITUALS AND PRACTICES
1930	護教	APOLOGETICS
.1	道教與他教	Relation with Other Religions
.2	與儒教	With Confucianism
.3	與佛教	With Buddhism
1931	宗派	SECTS
	史傳	HISTORY AND BIOGRAPHY
1932	道教史	History
1933-4	道士傳	Biography of Famous Taoists
1935	地誌	GEOGRAPHY AND TRAVELS
1936	觀廟	MONASTERIES AND TEMPLES
1937	道教美術	TAOIST ART
1938	雜錄	MISCELLANY

1940-1974　神道　SHINTOISM

1940	總錄	GENERAL (Subdivided by form like Table I)
	依體裁分,用表一;	For history see 1970
	歷史見1970.	
1941	神道哲學	SHINTO PHILOSOPHY; SHINTO THEOLOGY
1942	國體神道	SHINTO AS NATIONAL POLITY
	參見:皇室系譜;憲	See also 2255; 4772; 4775; 3409.5
	法;皇帝;陵墓.	
1943	神器	SACRED TREASURES
	三種神器	Three Imperial Regalia
1943.2	八咫鏡	Yata (no) Kagami

神器 (續)　　　SACRED TREASURES (Cont.)

1943.3	賢所　内侍所.	Kashikodokoro (Naishidokoro)
1943.5	草薙劍	Kusangi no tsurugi
1943.7	八阪瓊曲玉　神璽.	Yasakani no magatama
1943.9	十種神寶	Tokusa no kandakara
1944	神社及諸神	SHRINES AND GODS IN GENERAL
1944.1	神祇史	History
1944.2	神名帳	Register of Gods
1944.3	神階記	Ranks of Gods
1944.4		
1944.5	神社錄	Lists of Shrines
1944.6	官國幣社　殿舍調度見後 1973.5.	Shrines Established by Imperial Government
1944.71	二十二社	Nijūni-sha
1944.73	一宮	Ichino miya
1944.75	總社	Sōsha
1944.77	招魂社, 靖國神社	Shōkonsha; Seikoku jinja
1944.8	府縣鄉村社	Local Shrines
1944.9	社領	Land of Shrines
	各神社	Individual Shrines
1945	神宮　伊勢神宮. 兩宮儀式帳, 五部書入此.	Imperial Shrine of Ise
1945.01	内宮　皇大神宮.	Shrines of Amaterasu ōmikami
1945.02	外宮　豐受大神宮	Shrines of Toyoe ōmikami
1945.031	別宮	Wakare no miya
1945.035	攝社, 末社, 所管社	Appendant Shrines

	各神社(續)	Individual Shrines (Cont.)
	神宮(續)	
1945.04	造營	Building
.041	宮域	Ground
.042	殿舍	Halls
.044	金物	Metal
.045	木材, 杣萱	Wood
.046	造營料	Expenditure
.048	橋梁	Bridges
1945.05	遷宮	Move
1945.06	祭祀, 奉幣	Divine Service.　See also 1948
1945.07	法制	Administration
.071	法令, 禁制	Laws and Prohibitions
.072	忌穢	Taboo of Foulness
.073	公文式	Documents
.075	組織	Organization
.076	神宮教	Jingūkyō
.079	神領	Property
1945.08	神官	Sacerdotal Officers
1945.082	齋宮	Saigū (Itsukinomiya)
1945.083	祭主	Saishū
1945.084	司家	Shika
1945.985	禰宜及以下	Negi & Subordinates
1945.089	師職	Shishoku
1945.09	參宮	Public Worship
.092	神拜被式	Liturgy

	各神社 (續)	Public Worship (Cont.)
	參宮 (續)	
1945.04	參宮記及案内記	Notes & Information
.06	獻物	Dedication
1945.1-.9	其他各神社	Other Individual Shrines. (Divided geo-
	依地理分用表二.	graphically by Table II)
1946	各神	Individual Gods
1947	神典	SACRED BOOKS
	姓氏錄入傳記, 風土記入地理.	
1947.1	古事記神典	Kojiki (Furukotobumi) Shinten
1947.2	日本書紀神代卷	Nihon Shoki jindai no maki
1947.3	古語拾遺	Kogo shūi
1947.4	祝詞	Norito
1947.5	祓	Harai
1947.6	壽詞	Yogotao
1947.7	宣命	Semmyō
1947.8	祭文願文	Saimon
1947.9	疑僞神典	Pseudepigrapha
1947.91	伊勢二所皇太神宮御鎮座本緣	Ise nisho kōdaijingū gochinza honen
1947.92	神皇實錄	Jinnō jitsuroku
1947.93	神道五部書	Shintō gobuno sho
	入伊勢神宮下	
1947.94	神別記	Jinbek ki
1947.95	天書記	Tensho ki
1947.96	別天神記	Bet-tenjin ki
1947.97	上記	Jōki
1947.98	先代舊事本紀	Sendai kuji honki
1948.1	祭禮	RITUALS; DIVINE SERVICE
1948.1	祭式及作法	Practice

祭禮(續)　　RITUALS (Cont.)

1948.11	祭式	Rites and Ceremonies
1948.12	行事作法	Sacriments, Ordinanances
1948.13	齋戒	Abstinence, Fasting
1948.15	音樂	Music
1948.17	祝詞	Norito
1948.18	祝詞作文	Composition of norito
1948.19	祓詞	Harai
1948.2	調度	Furnishing
1948.23	裝束,服飾	Vestment and Ornaments
1948.24	祭具	Sacred Tools
1948.26	神饌	Sacrifice
1948.28	幣帛	Paper or Silk Cuttings for Hanging
1948.3	大嘗祭	Great Thanksgiving Service after the Enthronment (Oniematsuri)
1948.31	國郡卜定	Location
1948.32	禊祓	Purification
1948.33	拔穗使	Imperial Messenger for Collecting
1948.34	由奉幣	Yoshi no hopei
1948.35	祝詞,歌舞	Prayers, Music and Dance
1948.36	調度	Furnishing
1948.37	裝束,服飾	Vestments and Ornaments
1948.38	神饌供御	Sacrifice and Supplies
1948.39	和歌,本文	Waka and Hombun
1948.4	年中行事及例祭	Ordinary Divine Service
1948.41	年中行事,例幣	Calendar; Festivals and Fasts

年中行事及例祭 Ordinary Divine Service (Cont.)
(續)

1948.42	祈年祭	Prayer for Abundant Year, Feb. 4 (Toshigoinomatsuri)
1948.43	神嘗祭	Thanksgiving, Oct. 17 (Kannamematsuri)
1948.44	新嘗祭	Harvest Festival, Nov. 23 (Niinamematsuri)
1948.45	鎮魂祭	Imperial Reguiem, Nov. 22 (Ōmitamafurinomatsuri)
1948.46	大殿祭	Prayer for the Security of Palaces (Ōtonohogai)
1948.47	四方拜	New Year Service (Shihōhai)
1948.48	大祓	Purification (Ōharae)
1948.49	追儺	Exorcism (Tsuina)
1948.5	臨時祭祀	Casual Divine Service
1948.6	祈禱,奉幣	Prayer and Offering
1948.7	葬祭	Ministry of Dead
1948.71	葬儀	Burial
1948.72	靈祭	Worship of the Dead
1948.8	占卜及禁厭	Divination and Taboo
1948.9	習俗	Customs
1949	神職	SACERDOTAL OFFICERS
1950	信仰,靈驗記	BELIEFS; TESTIMONIALS
1951	布教,傳道	APOLOGETICS; MISSIONARY WORK
1952	宗派	SECTS
1953	原始神道	Early Shintoism
1954	古典神道	Classical Schools
1954.1	佛教神道 家	Buddhist shintō

宗派（續）   SECTS (Cont.)

1954.11	天台神道 山王一實神道	Tendai shintō
1954.12	真言神道	Shingon shintō
1954.13	御流神道	Goryū shintō
1954.14	三輪神道 兩部神道	Miwa shintō
1954.15	雲傳神道	Unden shintō
1954.16	立川神道	Tatsukawa shintō
1954.17	修驗神道	Shūgen shintō
1954.173	當山派	Tōzampa
1954.176	本山派	Honzampa
1954.18	法華神道 習合神道.論本地垂跡之書入此.	Hokke shintō
1954.2	伊勢神道 度會神道,社家神道. 神宮教見神宮下.	Ise shintō Jingūkyō see 1945.076
1954.3	吉田神道 卜部神道,忌部神道.唯一神道,元本宗源神道.	Yoshida shintō
1954.35	弓矢神道 橘神道.	Yamiya shintō
1954.4	吉川神道 理學神道	Yoshikawa shintō
1954.5	垂加神道	Shidemasu (Shiga) shintō
1954.6	土御門神道 安家神道,安信神道.天社神道.	Tsuchimikado shintō
1945.7	白川神道 伯家神道	Shirakawa shintō
1954.8	復古神道	Fukko shintō
1954.9	儒家神道	Confucian shintō
1954.95	物部神道	Mononobe shintō
	井上神道 見禊教	Inoue shintō See also 1965
1954.97	梅辻神道 烏傳神道	Umetsuji shintō
1954.98	富士講	Fujikō

58

宗派 (續)　　　SECTS (Cont.)

1954.99	其他古典神道	Others (Zakka shintō, Singaku shintō, etc.)

例如雜家神道 (狷土學派),心學神道.

1955	近代神道	Modern Sects
1956	神道本局	Shintō honkyoku

大教,神道事務局.

1957	黑住教	Kurozumi-kyō
1958	神道修成派	Shintō shūseiha
1954.25	神宮教	Jingū-kyō

見神宮下.

1959	大社教	Taisha-kyō
1960	實行教	Jikkō-kyō
1961	扶桑教	Fusō-kyō
1962	大成教	Taisei-kyō
1963	神習教	Shinshū-kyō
1964	御嶽教	Ōtake-kyō
1965	禊教	Misogi-kyō
1966	天理教	Tenri-kyō
1967	神理教	Shinri-kyō
1968	金光教	Konkō-kyō
1969.3	修養團	Shiūyodan
1970	神道歷史	HISTORY OF SHINTŌISM
1971-2	神道傳記	BIOGRAPHY OF SHINTŌISTS
1973	神道美術	SHINTŌIST ARTS

神道考古學

1974	雜錄	SHINTŌIST MISCELLANY

1975-1987　基督教　CHRISTIANITY

1975.1-.9	總錄 依體裁分,用表一.	GENERAL (Form subdivision like Table I)
1977	聖經	BIBLE
.1	舊約	Old Testament
.5	新約	New Testament
.9	僞書	Apocrypha. Deuterocanonical Books
1978	神學	DOCTRINAL THEOLOGY. DOGMATICS
.1	神,三位一體	God Unity Trinity
.2	基督論	Christology
.8	信條	Creeds
.9	護教	Apologetics and Evidences
1979	儀規	RITUALS AND PRACTICES
1980	傳道,佈教	HOMILETIC, PASTORAL AND MISSIONARY WORK
1981	宗派	SECTS
.1	原始及東方教會	Primitive and Oriental Churches
.2	天主教	Roman Catholic Church
.3	聖公會	Episcopal Church
.4	美以美會	Methodist Church
.5	長老會	Presbyterian Church
.6	浸禮會	Baptist. Immersionist
.7	公理會	Unitarian *Congregations*
.9	其他	Others
1982	教史	HISTORY
.1	上古	Early
.2	中古	Mediaeval
.3	近世	Modern

基督教（續）　　　CHRISTIANITY (Cont.)

1983	傳記	BIOGRAPHIES
1984	寺院及院派	MONASTERIES AND MONASTIC ORDERS
1985	教會組織	CHURCH ORGANIZATIONS AND ASSOCIATIONS
.1	教會與國家	Church and State
.2	教會行政	Church Government, Ecclesiastical Polity
.3	教會團體	Church Associations
.4	主日學校	Sunday Schools
.5	青年會	Y. M. C. A.
1986	基督教美術	CHRISTIAN RELIGIOUS ART
1987	雜錄	MISCELLANY

1988-1900 回教（清真教天方教）MOHAMMEDANISM (ISLAM)

1988.1-.9	總錄	GENERAL (Subdivide by form like Table I)
	依體裁分，用表一.	
1989	回教經典	MOSLEM SCRIPTURES (KORAN)
	古蘭經	
.9	回教神學	MOSLEM THEOLOGY
1990.1	儀規	RITUALS AND PRACTICES
1990.2	護教，佈教	APOLOGETICS MISSIONARY WORK
1990.3	宗派	SECTS
1990.4	回教史	HISTORY
1990.5	傳記	BIOGRAPHIES
1990.6	地志，紀行	GEOGRAPHY AND TRAVELS
1990.7	清真寺	MOSQUES AND TOMBS
1990.8	回教美術	MOSLEM RELIGIOUS ART
1990.9	雜錄	MISCELLANY

1991-1999 其他宗教 OTHER RELIGIONS

1991　　犹太教　　JUDAISM

1992　　婆羅門教印度教 BRAHMANISM　　HINDUISM

1993　　波斯教祆教　PARSEEISM　　ZOROASTRIANISM
　　　　　　火神教

1994

1995

1996

1997

1998

1999

2000-3999 歷史科學類 HISTORICAL SCIENCES

2000-2149 考古學,金石學 ARCHAEOLOGY, ANTIQUITIES

2000-2049 考古學總論 ARCHAEOLOGY IN GENERAL

2000-2009	總錄 依體裁分用表一	General (Subdivide by form like Table D
2010-2019	史前遺跡 史前文化	Prehistoric Antiquities
2020-2024	舊石器時代	Paleolithic (Early Stone) Age
2025-2029	新石器時代	Neolithic (Late Stone) Age
2030-2039	青銅時代	Bronze Age
2040-2049	鐵器時代	Iron Age

各國考古 ARCHAEOLOGY OF VARIOUS COUNTRIES

2050-2194	亞洲考古學 ASIA	
2050-2059	總錄 依體裁分 用表一	GENERAL (Subdivide by form like Table D
2060-2159	中國考古學 CHINA	
2065-2085	總錄	GENERAL WORKS
2061	期刊	Periodicals
2062	會社,博物院	Societies, Museums
2063	叢書	Collections
2064	會議	Congresses
2065	展覽	Exhibitions
2066	書目	Bibliographies
2067	義例,概論	Theory, Methodology, General Treatises
2068-9	史傳	History and Biography
2070	法令	Laws, regulations, etc.
2073-9	目錄	Catalogues

中國考古學總錄(續)GENERAL WORKS (Cont.)

2080	考釋, 題跋	Commentaries. Identifications
2081		
2082	文字	Inscriptions
2083	摹拓, 圖象	Reproductions. Rubbings. Illustrations
2084	造法	Technology
2085	雜錄	Miscellanies

專類器物　　SPECIAL CLASSES OF ARCHAEOLOGICAL REMAINS

2086-2089	甲骨類	SHELLS AND BONES
2086	總錄 依體裁分, 用表丁.	General (Form subdivisions like Table D)
2089-2095	匋類	TERRA COTTA
2089	總錄 依體裁分, 用表丁.	General (Form subdivisions like Table D)
2090	瓦當	Tiles
2091	磚	Bricks
2092	封泥	Sealings
2093	明器	Mortuary Objects
2094	瓦器	Pottery
2095	其他匋器 每種器物再依表丁細分.	Others (Under each object subdivide like Table D)
2096-2104	石類	STONE OBJECTS
2096	總錄 依體裁分, 用表丁.	General (Form subdivisions like Table D)

	石類（續）	STONE OBJECTS (Cont.)
2097	墳墓	Tombs
2098	石鼓	Drums
2099	石像	Statues
2100	碑銘	Monuments and Tablets
2101	玉器	Jades
2102	石經 見中國經學類190	Stone Inscriptions of Classics, see 19 For libraries which want to class such works here 2102 may be used.
2103	其他石類 每種器物再依表丁細分	Others. (Under each object subdivide like Table D)
2105-2114	金類	METAL OBJECTS
2105	總錄 依體裁分,用表丁.	General (Form subdivisions like Table D)
2106	彝器	Sacrificial Vessels
2107	泉幣	Numismatics
2108	兵器	Armor and Weapons
2109	鏡	Mirrors
2110	鐘	Bells
2111	鼓	Drums
2113	其他金器 每種器物再依表丁細分	Others. (Under each object subdivide like Table D)
2115-2125	竹木及其他雜器類	BAMBOO, WOODEN AND OTHER MISCELLANEOUS OBJECTS
2115	總錄 依體裁分,用表丁.	General (Form subdivisions like Table D)
2116	簡牘	Document Straps
2117	符牌	Tallies

竹木及其他雜器類(續) BAMBOO, WOODEN AND OTHER
　　　　　　　　　　　MISCELLANEOUS OBJECTS (Cont.)

2119		
2120		
2121		
2122		
2123	權度	Weights and Measures
2124		
2125	其他	Others
2126-2159	地方考古及金石志 依區域分.	PARTICULAR SITES AND LOCAL ANTI-QUITIES
		(Divide by Geographical Locations)
2127	東三省	Three Eastern Provinces (Manchuria)
2128	遼寧	Liaoning
2129	吉林	Kirin
2130	黑龍江	Helungkiang
2131	河北	Hopei
2132	北平	Peiping (Peking)
2133	山東	Shantung
2134	河南	Honan
2135	山西	Shansi
2136	陝西	Shensi
2137	甘肅	Kansu
2138	西康	Hsikang
2139	四川	Szechuan
2140	湖北	Hupeh

	地方考古及金石志	PARTICULAR SITES AND LOCAL ANTI-QUITIES (Cont.)
2141	湖南	Hunan
2142	江西	Kiangsi
2143	安徽	Anhwei
2144	江蘇	Kiangsu
2145	南京	Nanking
2146	浙江	Chekiang
2147	福建	Fukien
2148	廣東	Kwangtung
2149	廣西	Kwangsi
2150	雲南	Yunnan
2151	貴州	Kweichow
2152	熱河	Jehol
2153	綏遠, 寧夏	Suiyuan and Ninghsia
2154	察哈爾	Charhar
2155	外蒙	Outer Mongolia
2156	新疆	Sinkiang
2157	青海	Chinghai (Kokonor)
2158	西藏	Tibet
2159	西北 (總)	The Northwest (General)
2160-2184	日本考古學	JAPAN
	總錄	GENERAL WORKS
2160.1	期刊	Periodicals
.2	會社	Societies

日本考古學總錄(續)GENERAL WORKS (Cont.)

2160.3	叢集	Collections
.4	博物院	Museums
.5	展覽	Exhibitions
.6	書目	Bibliographies
.7	目錄	Catalogues of Antiquities
.8	辭典	Dictionaries
.9	撮要	Compends
2161.1	歷史	History
.2	傳記	Biographies
.3	通論	General Treatises
.4	義例	Theory, Methodology
.5	考釋	Identifications
.6	文字	Inscriptions
.7	圖象	Illustrations, Rubbings
.8	造法	Technology
.9	雜錄	Miscellanies
	專類器物	SPECIAL CLASSES OF ARCHAEOLOGICAL REMAINS
2162	甲骨類	SHELLS AND BONES
	總錄 依體裁分,用表丁.	General (Subdivide like Table D)
2163.1	貝塚 依體裁分,用表丁. 掘獲器物分入其他各類.	Shell Mounds (Divide by inserted Table D)
2164	陶類 本類及以後各類所應器物下均照表丁析分.	TERRA-COTTA (Divide under this division and each of its subdivisions by inserted Table D)
2165.1	瓦	Tiles

	陶類 (續)	TERRA-COTTA (Cont.)
2165.2	磚	Bricks
.4	埴輪	Haniwa (Clay images)
.5	瓦器	Pottery
	磁器 見美術遊藝類	Porcelain.　See 6640
.9	其他	Others
2166	石類	STONE OBJECTS
	總錄 依體裁分,用表丁.	General (Subdivide like Table D)
2167.2	造像	Statues
.3	碑銘	Monuments and Tablets
.7	玉器	Jades
2168	金 石類	METAL OBJECTS
	總錄 依體裁分,用表丁.	General (Subdivide like Table D)
2169.1	禮器	Sacrificial Vessels
.2	樂器	Musical Instruments
.3	兵器	Armor and Weapons
.7	鏡鑑	Mirrors
.8	飾物	Personal Ornaments
.9	泉幣	Numismatics
2170	竹木類	BAMBOO AND WOODEN OBJECTS
	總錄 依體裁分,用表丁.	General (Subdivide like Table D)
2171.1	簡牘	Document Straps
.2	符牌	Tallies
.3	造像	Figures

| 2172 | 其他雜質類
依器品種類分. | OBJECTS OF MISCELLANEOUS MATERIALS |
| | | Arrange by kinds of objects |

	地方考古金石志	PARTICULAR SITES AND LOCAL ANTI-QUITIES
2174	全國	Japan as a Whole
2175	關東	Kantō
2176	奧羽	Ou
2177	中部	Chūbu
2178	近畿	Kinki
2179	中國	Chūkoku
2180	四國	Shikoku
2181	九州	Kyushū
2182	琉球	Ryūkyū
2183	北海道	Hokaidō

2185-2188	高麗考古學	KOREA
2185	總錄 依體裁分,用表丁.	GENERAL WORKS (Subdivide like Table D)
2186	專類器	SPECIAL CLASSES OF ARCHAEOLOGICAL REMAINS
.1	甲骨類	SHELLS AND BONES
.2	陶類	TERRA-COTTA
.4	石類	STONE OBJECTS
.6	金類	METAL OBJECTS
.8	竹木類	BAMBOO AND WOODEN OBJECTS
.9	雜質類	OBJECTS OF MISCELLANEOUS MATERIALS

2187	高麗考古學 (續) 地方考古 照朝鮮地誌細分	PARTICULAR SITES AND LOCAL ANTI- QUITIES (Subdivide like 3490-3499)
2188	俄國考古學 亞洲之部	RUSSIA IN ASIA
2190	中印考古學 安南及泰國	INDO-CHINA THAILAND (SIAM)
2189	馬來群島考古學	MALAY ARCHIPELAGO
2191	印度緬甸考古學	INDIA BURMA
2192	伊蘭諸國考古學	IRANIAN COUNTRIES
2193	小亞細亞考古學	ASIA MINOR
2194	阿剌伯考古學	ARABIA
2195	歐洲考古學	EUROPE
2196	非洲考古學	AFRICA
2197	北美洲考古學	NORTH AMERICA
2198	南美洲考古學	SOUTH AMERICA
2199	海洋洲兩極考古學	OCEANIA AND POLAR REGIONS

2200-2249 民族學民族誌 ETHNOLOGY AND ETHNOGRAPHY

2200-2208	民族學總論	COMPARATIVE: GENERAL WORKS ON ALL COUNTRIES
2201.1-.9	總錄	GENERAL (Subdivide by form like Table I)
2202	民族之起源	ORIGINS OF RACES
2203	民族之遷移與 分佈	MIGRATIONS OF RACES
2204-2208	原人風俗制度	CUSTOMS AND INSTITUTIONS OF PRIMITIVE PEOPLES
2204	概論	General Works
2205	物質生活	Material Life
2206	精神生活	Psychic Life
2207	家族生活	Family Life
2208	社會生活	Social Life

各國民族誌與研究　ETHNOLOGY AND ETHNOGRAPHY
OF VARIOUS COUNTRIES

2209-2244	亞洲	ASIA
2209.1-.9	總錄	GENERAL (Subdivide by forms like Table I)
2210-2225	中國	CHINA
2210.1-.9	總錄	General
2211-2212	漢族	The Han (Chinese) Race
2211	由來與遷移	Origin and Migration
2212	與外族之關係	Relation with Other Peoples
2213-2220	中國境內異族	Other Races within China
2213	總錄	General Works
2214	通古斯(東胡)族	The Tungus Tribes
.1	滿洲	Manchu
.3	錫伯	Sibo
.5	索倫	Solon
.7	鄂倫春	Orochon
.9	赫哲	Goldi
2215	蒙古族	The Mongol Tribes
.1	陳巴爾呼	Old Barga or Chipchin
.2	新巴爾呼	New Barga
.3	達呼爾	Daghor
.4	喀爾喀	Khalkha
.5	額魯特	Kalmuch or Olöt
.6	阿爾泰烏梁海	Altai Urianghai
.7	布萊雅	Buriat
.8	韃靼(老朶夷)	Tartar

中國境內異族(續)Other Races within China (Cont.)

2216	突厥(回紇)族	The Turkish Tribes
.1	雅庫特	Yakut
.2	烏梁海	Urianghai or Tuba
.3	撒拉回	Sola
.4	唯吾爾 (纏頭回)	Uigur or <u>Chanton</u>
.5	哈薩克	Kasak
.6	布魯特	Burut
.7	吉爾吉斯	Kirghiz
2217	藏甸(吐番)族	The Tibeto-Burman Tribes
.1	西番	Hsifan
.2	果络	Golok
.3	康巴	Kam-pa
.4	藏巴	Tsang-pa
.5	倮倮	Lolo
.6	摩些	Mosa
.7	怒子	Lutze
.8	傈僳	Lisu
2218	撣(泰)族	The Shan or Tai Tribes
.1	那馬(民家)	Nama
.3	黎	Loi or Li
.8	擺夷	Payi
2219	懵克族	The Mon-Khmer Tribes
.1	苗	Miao
.4	傜	Yao
.8	畲	Hsia

中國境內異族 Other Races within China (Cont.)

2220	其他	Others
.1	費雅喀 (古亞洲族)	Giliak (Palaeo Asiatics)
.2	塔吉克 (伊蘭族)	Tajik (Iranian)

2221-5 地方人種誌 LOCAL ETHNOGRAPHY (Subdivide by Geo-
依地理分. graphical locations)

2221	東三省	Three Eastern Provinces (Manchuria)
.1	遼寧	Liaoning
.4	吉林	Kirin
.7	黑龍江	Heilungkiang
2222	北部諸省	Northern Provinces
.1	河北	Hopei
.2	山東	Shantung
.3	河南	Honan
.4	山西	Shansi
.5	陝西	Shensi
.6	甘肅	Kansu
2223	中部諸省	Central Provinces
.1	西康	Hsikang
.2	四川	Szechuan
.3	湖北	Hupeh
.4	湖南	Hunan
.5	江西	Kiangsi
.6	安徽	Anhwei
.7	江蘇	Kiangsu
.8	浙江	Chekiang

LOCAL ETHNOGRAPHY OF CHINA (cont.)

2224	南部諸省	Southern Provinces
.1	福建	Fukien
.2	廣東	Kwangtung
.3	廣西	Kwangsi
.4	雲南	Yunnan
.5	貴州	Kweichow
2225	邊疆諸省	Outlying Regions
.1	內蒙	Inner Mongolia
.2	熱河	Jehol
.3	綏遠	Suiyuan
.4	察哈爾	Charhar
.5	寧夏	Ninghsia
.6	外蒙	Outer Mongolia
.7	新疆	Sinkiang (Chinese Turkestan)
.8	青海	Chinghai (Kokonor)
.9	西藏	Tibet

2226-2241	日本	JAPAN
2226	總錄	General (Subdivide by form like Table D)
2227	大和族 天孫族	Yamato Race
2228.1	由來	Origin
.4	遷徙	Migration
.7	與外族之關係	Relation with Other Peoples
2229-2234	日本境內異族	Other Tribes and Races within Japan
2229	總錄	General Works
2230	出雲族	
2231	熊襲族	Kumaso
2232	土蜘蛛族	Tsuchigumo
2233	蝦夷族	Aino (Ainu, Ezo)
2233.6	熟蝦夷	Civilized
.7	麤蝦夷	Uncivilized
	中國民族 入中國民族志.	Chinese Race　see 2209-2225
	蕃族 入地方人種志臺灣.	"Ban" Tribe see 2241
2234	其他	Others
2235-2241	地方人種志 依地理區域細分.	Local Ethnography (Subdivide by geo-graphical locations)
2235	本州	Honshū
2236	四國	Shikoku
2236	九州	Kyūshū
2237	琉球	Liuchiu (Ryūkyū)
2239	北海道	Hokkaidō
2240	庫頁島（樺太）	Saghalien (Karafuto)
2241	臺灣	Taiwan (Formosa)

2242-2243	高麗	KOREA
2242.1	總錄	General (Subdivide by form like Table I)
.2	由來	Origin
.3	遷徙	Migration
.4	與外族之關係	Relation with Other Peoples
.5	高勾麗族	Koguryo Race
.6	沃沮族	Wochü Race
.7	挹婁族	Yilou Race
.8	濊族	Hui Race
.9	三韓族	Three Han Races
2243	地方人種志 依地理區域細分.	Local Ethnography (Subdivide like 3491-3499)
2244	其他亞洲諸國	OTHER COUNTRIES OF ASIA
.1	俄國 亞洲之部	Russia in Asia
.2	菲律賓	The Philippines
.3	東印度羣島	Dutch East India Archipelago
.4	馬來半島	The Malay Peninsula
.5	越南 泰國	Indo-China Thailand
.6	印度 緬甸	India Burma
.7	伊蘭諸國 阿富汗,俾路芝 伊蘭.	Iranian Countries (Afghanistan, Baluchistan, Iran)
.8	小亞細亞諸國	Asia Minor
.9	阿剌伯	Arabic
2245	歐洲諸國	EUROPE
2246	非洲諸國	AFRICA
2247	北美洲諸國	NORTH AMERICA

2248　南美洲諸國　SOUTH AMERICA

2249　海洋洲及南北極 OCEANIA AND POLAR REGIONS

2250-2299 譜系 傳記 GENEALOGY AND BIOGRAPHY

2250.1-.9 總錄　　　GENERAL (Form subdivisions like Table I)
依體裁分, 用表一.

.5　譜傳作法　ART OF WRITING GENEALOGY AND BIOGRAPHY

.6　世界人名鑑　WORLD WHO'S WHO

中國譜系紋章 CHINESE GENEALOGY AND HERALDRY

2251　姓譜　　　Surnames, Family Names

2252　氏族譜　　Clan Lineage and History

.1　合譜　　　Collective

.2-.9　專譜　　　Individual (Subdivide chronologically
依時代分, 用表三.　　　　by Table III)

2253　名諱　　　Personal Names

2254　紋章　　　Decorations, Orders, Flags

中國傳記　　CHINESE BIOGRAPHY

2257.1-.9 總錄　　General (Form subdivisions like Table I)
依體裁分, 用表一.

2258　總傳:通代 General Collective Biography - All Periods

2259　總傳:斷代 General Collective Biography - By Periods
(Divide chronologically by dates and
依傳主時代分, 用表三.　names of biographees like Table III)

2260　總傳:地方 General Collective Biography - Local, Table II
用表二.

2261　總傳:專錄 General Collective Biography - Special Types

.1　聖賢　　　Sages

.2　儒林　　　Scholars

.3　忠義　　　Patriots and Martyrs

.4　循吏 縉紳錄 Officials. For civil lists and official
政府職員錄見 4699:9.　registeries, see 4699.9

77

中國傳記(續) CHINESE BIOGRAPHY (Cont.)

2261.5 　列女　　　　　　　Famous Women

.6 　隱逸　　　　　　　Hermits

各學科總傳 Collective subject biography goes with that
如詩人合傳,書畫家　subject, e.g. biography of poets is
合傳等,各從其類.　classified with poetry

2262-2269 別傳　　　　　　Individual Biography.
凡自述,日記,逸話,　Includes autobiography, diaries, personal
言行錄,墓誌,行狀,評　narratives, epitaphs, eulogies, criticism,
論等,皆依傳主時代及　etc. (Divide by period of biographees
姓名照表三細分.　like Table III)

年譜　　　　　　　Nien-pu (Annalistic Biography)

2270 　合刻　　　　　　　Collective

2271-2279 個人　　　　　Individual (Subdivide by period of biographies
依傳主時代及姓　like Table III)
名細分,用表二.

2280-2289 日本譜系紋章 JAPANESE GENEALOGY AND HERALDRY

2280.1 　通錄　　　　　　General

.2 　皇室系譜　　　　　Genealogy of the Imperial House

.3 　姓氏譜　　　　　　Family Names

.4 　族系家傳:合刊　　Clan Lineage and Family History (Collective)

.5 　族系家傳:各家　　Clan Lineage and Family History (Individual)

.6 　名字稱號　　　　　Personal Names

.8 　紋章　　　　　　　Heraldry

2281-2289 日本傳記　　JAPANESE BIOGRAPHY

2281.01-.09 總錄　　　　General (Subdivide by form like Table I)
依體裁分,用表一.

2281.1 　總傳:通代　　　Collective Biography - All Periods
普通人名辭典,　Class general biographical dictionaries
人名表錄入此.　and directories here

2281.2-.9 總傳:斷代　　Collective Biography - By Periods (Subdivide
依時代分,用表三.　chronologically like Table III)

日本傳記　　JAPANESE BIOGRAPHY (Cont.)

2282	總傳：地方 依地理區域分,用表二	Collective Biography - Local (Subdivide by geographical divisions like Table II)
2283	總傳：特種	Collective Biography - Special
.1	肖像	Portraits
.2	生卒表,忌辰錄	Tables of Births and Deaths
.3	人物評論	Critical Biographies
.4		
.5	婦女	Women
.6		
.7	政府職員錄 見4774.8	Civil Lists and Official Registeries see 4774.8
.8	其他專錄	Special Lists or Registery of Special Persons
.9	雜記	Miscellanies
2284-2288	別傳 凡自述,日記,逸話,言行錄,墓誌,行狀,評論等均入此,依傳主時代及姓名細分	Individual Biography. Includes autobiography, diaries, personal narratives, epitaphs, eulogies, criticism, etc. Subdivide by dates and names of biographees
2284.1	上古	Ancient Period (? to 710 A.D.)
.2	奈良時代	Nera Period (710-794)
.3	平安時代	Heian Period (794-1192)
.4	鎌倉時代	Kamakura Period (1192-1333)
2285	室町及安土桃山時代	Muromachi and Azuchi-Momoyama Period (1335-1603)
2286	江戸時代	Yedo Period (1603-1868)
2287	明治時代	Meiji Period (1868-1912)
2288	大正時代	Taishō Period (1912-1926)
2289	現代	Shōwa Period (1926-　　)

2290	朝鮮譜系紋章	KOREAN GENEALOGY AND HERALDRY (Subdivide like 2280)
	仿日本譜系紋章細分	
2291-2294	朝鮮傳記	KOREAN BIOGRAPHY
2291.01-.09	總錄	General (Subdivide by form like Table I)
	依體裁分,用表一.	
2291	總傳:通代	Collective Biography - All periods
2291.1-.9	總傳:斷代	Collective Biography - By periods
	依時代分,參閱朝鮮歷史.	
2292	總傳:地方	Collective Biography - Local (Subdivide by geographical locations like 3490-3499)
	依地理分,參閱 朝鮮地理.	
2293	總傳:特種	Collective Biography - Special
2294.1-.9	別傳	Individual Biography - (Subdivide by periods)
	依時代分,參閱朝鮮歷史.	
2295-2299	他國譜系傳記	GENEALOGY AND BIOGRAPHY OF OTHER COUNTRIES

依地理分,用表二.
例如俄國人合傳,用
2296.4,俄國人別
傳用2296.41至2296.49
細分,其餘依此類推.

Divide by geographical Table II
e.g. Collective biography of Russians is 2296.4 and individual biography of Russians can be subdivided by periods like 2296.41-2296.49

2300-2349 世界歷史 UNIVERSAL HISTORY

	總錄	GENERAL
2305	期刊	Periodicals
2397	會社	Societies
2309	叢集,雜集	Collections
2312	參考書目	Bibliography
2314	字典,辭書	Dictionaries and encyclopedias
2316	年表	Chronology. Charts
2318	教學	Study and Teaching
2320	史學通論	HISTORIOGRAPHY
2322	歷史的哲學	PHILOSOPHY OF HISTORY
2324	世界文化史	HISTORY OF CIVILIZATION AND CULTURE
2328	世界交通史	HISTORY OF WORLD INTERCOURSE

2330	世界通史	GENERAL POLITICAL AND SOCIAL HISTORY
2331	上古	Ancient (Earliest to 500 A. D.)
2333	中古	Medieval (500-1500)
2337	近世 十六世紀	Modern (1500-1599)
2339	十七世紀	Modern (1600-1699)
2341	十八世紀	Modern (1700-1799)
2343	十九世紀	Modern (1800-1899)
2346	二十世紀	Modern (1900-　　)
2348	第一次世界大戰	World War I
2349	第二次世界大戰	World War II

2350-2399　世界地理 WORLD GEOGRAPHY

	總錄	GENERAL
2350	期刊	Periodicals
2352	會社	Societies
2354	叢集, 雜集	Collections
2356	參考書目	Bibliography
2358	教學	Study and Teaching
2360	字典, 辭書	Encyclopedias.　Dictionaries
2361	地名表	Gazetteers
2363	地理學名詞	Geographic Names and Terms
2365	路程表等	Tables.　Distances, geographical positions, etc.
2366	地理學史	HISTORY OF GEOGRAPHY
2368	古地誌	HISTORICAL GEOGRAPHY
2370	今地誌(概論)	GENERAL SYSTEMATIC TREATISES
2375	遊記	VOYAGES AND TRAVELS (General)
2376	雜記	MISCELLANEOUS RECORDS
2380-2399	地圖學 世界地圖	CARTOGRAPHY.　WORLD MAPS AND ATLAS for cartography see

81

2400-2449 亞洲史地 ASIA: HISTORY AND GEOGRAPHY

	總錄	GENERAL
2401	期刊	Periodicals
2402	會社	Societies
2404	叢集	Collections
2406	參考書目	Bibliography
2408	字典,辭書	Dictionaries
2410	年表,大綱	Chronological Tables, Outlines, Atlas
2412	亞洲史學	HISTORIOGRAPHY
2414	亞洲通史	GENERAL HISTORY
2420	亞洲文化史	HISTORY OF CIVILIZATION AND CULTURE
2430	亞洲地名辭典指南	GAZETTEERS, DICTIONARIES, GUIDE BOOKS, ETC.
2432	亞洲地理通論	COMPREHENSIVE WORKS ON GEOGRAPHY
2434	亞洲遊記	DESCRIPTION AND TRAVEL (BY DATE OF BOOK)
2435	依成書年代分	To 1491
2436		1492-1800
2437		1801-1900
2438		1901-1925
2439		1926-Date

2450-2999 中國歷史 CHINA: HISTORY

	總錄	GENERAL
2451	期刊	Periodicals
2452	會社	Societies
2453	史料:檔案等	Historical Sources: Archives, Documents, etc.
2454	史料:官書	Historical Sources: Official Publications
2455	史籍合刻	Collections
2457	字典,辭書	Dictionaries, Encyclopedias
2458	年表	Chronological Tables
2459	圖譜	Charts

2460-2469	中國史學史法	CHINESE HISTORIOGRAPHY
2470-2479	中國文化史	HISTORY OF CHINESE CIVILIZATION (Divide 依時代分,用表三. chronologically like Table III)

中外交通史 及外交史　HISTORY OF INTERCOURSE BETWEEN CHINA AND OTHER COUNTRIES. Diplomatic History

2480-2489	分時代 用表三.	By Periods (Divide like Table III)
2490-2509	分國	By Countries
2491	亞洲古國	Asia: Ancient Countries
2492	亞洲近世諸國 日本高麗除外.	Asia: Modern Countries (except Japan & Korea)
2493	日本及高麗	Japan and Korea
2494	歐洲古國	Ancient European Countries (e.g. Roman Empire)
2495-2504	歐洲近世諸國	Modern Europe
2495	俄國	Russia
2496	英國	Great Britain
2497	法國	France
2498	德國	Germany
2499	奧國,匈牙利	Austria & Hungary
2500	意國	Italy
2501	西班牙,葡萄牙	Spain and Portugal
2502	比利時,荷蘭	Belgium and Holland
2503	斯堪地那威亞	Scandinavia (Denmark, Iceland, Norway, Sweden and Finland)
2504	其他	Other Modern European Countries
2505-2508	美洲諸國	America
2505	加拿大	Canada
2506	美國	United States of America
2507	墨西哥	Mexico
2508	其他	Other Countries
2509	他洲諸國	Other Continents and Countries

of China

2510-2519	中國(全)通史	GENERAL HISTORY (Divide by literary forms)
	依體裁分.	
2511	紀傳	Chi-chuan Style
2512	編年	Annals
2513	紀事本末	Topical Records
2514	史論	Historical Essays
2515	考證及書評	Historical Critiques and Book Reviews
2516	史鈔,課本	Historical Excerpts. Textbooks
2517	雜史	Miscellaneous
2518	書目及索引	Bibliography and Indices

以下各代史皆可依表戊分. If convenient, historical works on each period or dynasty may be subdivided according to Table E.

2520-2999	中國斷代史	HISTORY BY PERIODS
2520	上古史 總錄	ANCIENT HISTORY - GENERAL (Earliest to B. C. 256)
2520.9	傳疑時代 三皇五帝.	Mythical and Legendary Period (The Three Mythical Sovereigns and the Five Legendary Emperors)
2521	三代	The Three Ancient Dynasties (B. C. 2205?-256)
2522	夏	Hsia Dynasty (B. C. 2205?-1766?)
2523	商 (殷)	Shang (Yin) Dynasty (B. C. 1766?-1122?)
2524-2528	周	Chou Dynasty (B. C. 1122?-256)
2524-2525	西周	Western Chou (B. C. 1122?-770)
2526	東周 (春秋)	Eastern Chou or the Ch'un Ch'iu Period (770-479)
2527-2533	晚周 (戰國)	The Last Period of Chou or The Age of the Warring States (B. C. 480-250)
2535	秦漢三國總錄	CH'IN, HAN DYNASTIES AND THE THREE KINGDOMS - GENERAL (B.C. 255-280 A. D.)
2536-2543	秦	CH'IN DYNASTY (B. C. 255-206)
2539	始皇帝以前諸王	Various Kings Previous to the First Emperor (B. C. 255-222)

		Dynastic Title or Temple Name	Length of Reign
2540	始皇帝	Shih Huang-ti	B.C. 221-210
2542	二世皇帝	Erh Shih Huangti	B.C. 209-207
2545	漢	HAN DYNASTY (B. C. 206-220 A. D.)	
2550	前漢 (西漢)	FORMER HAN OR WESTERN HAN (B.C. 206-23 A.D.)	
2551	高帝 (高祖)	Kao Ti or Kao Tsu	B.C. 206-195
2552.1	惠帝	Hui Ti	B.C. 194-188
2552.3	高后 (呂氏)	Kao Hou (Lü Shih)	B.C. 187-180
2552.5	文帝	Wên Ti	B.C. 179-157
2552.7	景帝	Ching Ti	B.C. 156-141)
2553	武帝	Wu Ti	B.C. 140-87
2554.1	昭帝	Chao Ti	B.C. 86-74
2554.2	宣帝	Hsüan Ti	B.C. 73-49
2554.3	元帝	Yüan Ti	B.C. 48-33
2554.4	成帝	Ch'êng Ti	B.C. 32-7
2554.5	哀帝	Ai Ti	B.C. 6-1 A.D.
2554.6	平帝	P'ing Ti	A.D. 1-5
2554.7	孺子嬰	Ju Tzû Ying	6-8
2554.8	新皇帝 (王莽)	Hsin Huang-ti (Wang Mang)	9-23
2554.9	帝玄 (更始帝)	Ti Hsüan or Kêng Shih Ti	23-25
2555	後漢 (東漢)	LATER HAN OR EASTERN HAN (25-220)	
2557	光武帝	Kuang Wu Ti	25-57
2558.1	明帝	Ming Ti	58-75
2558.2	章帝	Chang Ti	76-88
2558.3	和帝	Ho Ti	89-105
2558.4	殤帝	Shang Ti	106
2558.5	安帝	An Ti	107-125

		Dynastic Title or Temple Name	Length of Reign
2558.6	順帝	Shun Ti	126-144
2558.7	沖帝	Ch'ung Ti	145
2558.8	質帝	Chih Ti	146
2559	桓帝	Huan Ti	147-167
2559.7	靈帝	Ling Ti	168-189
2559.8	獻帝	Hsien Ti	189-220
2560	三國	THE THREE KINGDOMS (220-280)	
2563	蜀	The Shu Kingdom	221-263
2565	魏	The Wei Kingdom	220-265
2567	吳	The Wu Kingdom	222-280
2570	兩晉南北朝總彙	CHIN DYNASTY AND THE EPOCH OF SOUTHERN AND NORTHERN DYNASTIES - GENERAL (265-589)	
2571	晉	CHIN DYNASTY (265-420)	
2573	西晉	Western Chin	265-317
2576	東晉	Eastern Chin	317-420
2578	五胡十六國	The Five Barbarian Tribes and the Sixteen Kingdoms	304-439
2580	南北朝	EPOCH OF SOUTHERN AND NORTHERN DYNASTIES (420-589)	
2581	南朝	THE SOUTHERN DYNASTIES (420-589)	
2582	劉宋	(Liu) Sung Dynasty	420-479
2584	南齊	Southern Ch'i Dynasty	479-502
2586	梁	Liang Dynasty	502-557
2588	陳	Ch'ên Dynasty	557-589
2590	北朝	THE NORTHERN DYNASTIES (386-581)	
2591	北魏	Northern Wei	386-534
2593	西魏	Western Wei	535-556
2595	東魏	Eastern Wei	534-550

		Dynastic Title or Temple Name	Length of Reign
2597	北齊	Northern Ch'i	550-577
2599	北周	Northern Chou	557-581
2600	隋唐五代總錄	SUI, T'ANG AND THE FIVE DYNASTIES - GENERAL (589-960)	
2605	隋	SUI DYNASTY (589-618)	
2610	文帝	Wên Ti	589-604
2612	煬帝	Yang Ti	605-618
2617	恭帝侑	Kung Ti Yu	617-618
2618	越王侗	Yüeh Wang T'ung	618
2620	唐	T'ANG DYNASTY	618-
2621	高祖	Kao Tsu	618-626
2622	太宗	T'ai Tsung	627-649
2623	高宗	Kao Tsung	650-683
2624	中宗	Chung Tsung	684, 705-710
2625	武后	Wu Hou, or the Empress Wu	690-710
2626	睿宗	Jui Tsung	684-712
2627	玄宗(明皇帝)	Hsüan Tsung (Ming Wang Ti)	712-756
2628	肅宗	Su Tsung	756-762
2629	代宗	Tai Tsung	763-779
2630	德宗	Tê Tsung	780-805
2631.1	順宗	Shun Tsung	805
2631.5	憲宗	Hsien Tsung	806-820
2632.1	穆宗	Mu Tsung	821-824
2632.5	敬宗	Ching Tsung	825-826
2633	文宗	Wên Tsung	827-840
2634	武宗	Wu Tsung	841-846
2635	宣宗	Hsüan Tsung	847-859
2636	懿宗	I Tsung	860-873

		Dynastic Title or Temple Name	Length of Reign
	唐(續)	T'ANG DYNASTY (Cont.)	
2637	僖宗	Hsi Tsung	874-888
2638	昭宗	Chao Tsung	889-904
2639	昭宣帝	Chao Hsüan Ti	904-906
2640	五代(北)	EPOCH OF THE FIVE DYNASTIES (NORTH) (907-960)	
2642	後梁	Posterior Liang Dynasty	907-923
2644	後唐	Posterior T'ang Dynasty	923-936
2646	後晉	Posterior Chin Dynasty	936-947
2648	後漢	Posterior Han Dynasty	947-951
2649	後周	Posterior Chou Dynasty	951-960
2650	十國(南)	THE TEN KINGDOMS (SOUTH)	
2651	吳	Wu	902-937
2652	閩	Min	909-944
2653	楚	Ch'u	927-951
2654	吳越	Wu Yüeh	907-978
2655	前蜀	Former Shu	907-925
2656	南漢	Southern Han	917-971
2657	南平	Nan P'ing	907-963
2658	後蜀	Posterior Shu	934-965
2659	南唐	Southern T'ang	937-975
2660	北漢	Northern Han	951-979
2662	宋遼金元總錄	SUNG, LIAO, CHIN AND YÜAN DYNASTIES - GENERAL (960-1368)	
2665	宋	SUNG DYNASTY (960-1279)	
2666	北宋	NORTHERN SUNG DYNASTY (960-1127)	
2667	太祖	T'ai Tsu	960-976
2668	太宗	T'ai Tsung	976-997
2669	真宗	Chên Tsung	998-1022

		Dynastic Title or Tem- ple Name	Length of Reign
	北宋 (續)	NORTHERN SUNG DYNASTY (Cont.)	
2670	仁宗	Jên Tsung	1023-1063
2671	英宗	Ying Tsung	1064-1067
2672	神宗	Shên Tsung	1068-1085
2673	哲宗	Chê Tsung	1086-1100
2674	徽宗	Hui Tsung	1101-1125
2675	欽宗	Ch'in Tsung	1126-1127
2676	南宋	SOUTHERN SUNG DYNASTY (1127-1279)	
2678	高宗	Kao Tsung	1127-1162
2679	孝宗	Hsiao Tsung	1163-1189
2680	光宗	Kuang Tsung	1190-1194
2681	寧宗	Ning Tsung	1195-1224
2682	理宗	Li Tsung	1225-1264
2683	度宗	Tu Tsung	1265-1274
2684.3	恭宗	Kung Tsung	1275-1276
2684.5	端宗	Tuan Tsung	1276-1278
2684.7	帝昺	Ti Ping	1278-1279
2685	遼	THE LIAO KINGDOM (916-1201)	
2687	遼 (契丹)	Liao or Ch'i-tan (Kitan)	916-1125
2688	西遼	Western Liao	1125-1201
2690	金	THE CHIN KINGDOM (1115-1234)	
2695	西夏	THE HSI HSIA KINGDOM (982-1227)	
2700	元	YÜAN DYNASTY (1279-1368) 1280	

		Dynastic Title or Temple Name		Length of Reign
		Chinese	Mongolian	
2701	太祖 鐵木真, 成吉思.	T'ai Tsu	(Temuchin or Gengis)	1206-1228
2702	太宗 窩闊台.	T'ai Tsung	(Ogdai or Ogotai)	1229-1245

89

		Dynastic Title or Temple Name		Length of Reign
		Chinese	Mongolian	
2703	定宗 貴由	Ting Tsung	Gayuk or Kuyak	1246-1250
2704	憲宗 蒙哥	Hsien Tsung	Mangu or Mongka	1251-1259
2705	世祖 忽必烈,薩禪	Shih Tsu	Kublai or Sitchen	1260-1294
2706	成宗 鐵木耳	Ch'êng Tsung	Timur or Olcheitu	1295-1307
2707	武宗 海山,曲律	Wu Tsung	Kaisun or Guluk	1308-1311
2708	仁宗 愛育黎拔加八達	Jên Tsung	Ayuli Palpata	1312-1320
2709	英宗 碩德八刺	Ying Tsung	Sotpala	1321-1323
2710	泰定帝 也孫鐵木耳	T'ai Ting Ti	Yesun Timur	1324-1328
2711	明宗 和世瓎	Ming Tsung	Hosila	1328-1329
2712	文宗 圖帖睦爾	Wên Tsung	Tup Timur	1330-1332
2713	順帝 安懽帖睦爾	Shun Ti	Tohan Timur	1333-1368

2718 明清總錄 MING AND CH'ING DYNASTIES - GENERAL (1368-1912)

2720 明 MING DYNASTY (1368-1644)

		Chinese	Title of Reign	Length of Reign
2721	太祖 年號 洪武	T'ai Tsu	Hung-wu	1368-1398
2722	惠帝 建文	Hui Ti	Chien-wên	1399-1402
2723	成祖 永樂	Ch'êng Tsu	Yung-lo	1403-1424
2724	仁宗 洪熙	Jên Tsung	Hung-hsi	1425
2725	宣宗 宣德	Hsüan Tsung	Hsüan-tê	1426-1435
2726	英宗 正統	Ying Tsung	Chêng-tung	1436-1449
2727	景帝(代宗) 景泰	Ching Ti or Tai Tsung	Ching-tai	1450-1457
2728	英宗 復辟 天順	Ying Tsung	T'ien-shun	1457-1464
2729	憲宗 成化	Hsien Tsung	Ch'êng-hua	1465-1487
2730	孝宗 弘治	Hsiao Tsung	Hung-chih	1488-1505
2731	武宗 正德	Wu Tsung	Chêng-tê	1506-1521
2732	世宗 嘉靖	Shih Tsung	Chia-ching	1522-1566

明(續)　MING DYNASTY (Cont.)

			Dynastic Title or Temple Name	Title of Reign	Length of Reign
2733	穆宗	年號 隆慶	Mu Tsung	Lung-ch'ing	1567-1572
2734	神宗	萬歷	Shên Tsung	Wan-li	1573-1620
2735	光宗	泰昌	Kuang Tsung	Tai-ch'ang	1620
2736	熹宗	天啓	Hsi Tsung	T'ien-ch'i	1621-1627
2737	思宗	崇禎	Ssû Tsung	Ch'ung-chên	1628-1644
2738	明季		The Last Four Ming Princes (1644-1662)		
2739.1	福王	弘光	Prince Fu	Hung-kuan	1644-1645
2739.3	唐王	隆武	Prince T'ang	Lung-wu	1645-1646
2739.4	魯王	監國	Prince Lu	Chien-kuo	1646-1651
2739.5	桂王	永歷	Prince Kwei	Yung-li	1647-1662
2740-2959	清		CH'ING DYNASTY (1644-1912)		
2741-2749	通史		GENERAL HISTORY (Subdivided by literary forms		
2741		依體裁分. 紀傳	Chi-chuan		
2742		編年	Annals		
2743		紀事本末	Topical records		
2744		要畧, 課本	Outlines, Textbooks		
2745		表譜, 地圖	Tables, Charts, Atlas, Maps		
2746		雜史 史論	Miscellaneous	*Historical Essays*	
2747		考證 讀引	Critical studies	*and Book Reviews*	
2748		史料, 檔案	Sources, Documents		
2749		書目, 索引	*Bibliographies, Indexes*		
2750-2969	分朝史		HISTORY BY REIGNS AND EVENTS		
2750-2759	未入關時代		The Manchus before their Entry into China		
			Temple Name	Title of Reign	Length of Reign
2760-2779	世祖	順治	Shih Tsu	Shun-chih	1644-1661
2780-2799	聖祖	康熙	Shêng Tsu	K'ang-hsi	1662-1722
2781		內政要畧	Chief Internal Events		
2782					

清(續)　CH'ING DYNASTY (Cont.)

2783	三藩之亂	The Revolt of the Three Viceroys (1674-1681)		
2784	鄭氏據臺灣	Annexation of Formosa (1683)		
2785	準噶爾之役 始末	Expedition against the Jungars (1688-1715)		
2786	西藏之平定	Conquest of Tibet (1706-1720)		
2787	文治政績	Patronage of Arts and Letters		
2788	文字獄	Literary Inquisition		
2789	巡幸	Tours of Inspection		

		Temple Name	Title of Reign	Length of Reign
2800-2809	世宗 雍正	Shih Tsung	Yung-chêng	1723-1735
2801	内政要畧	Chief Internal Events		
2802				
2803	青海之征服	Conquest of Kokonor (1723-1724)		
2804				
2805	準噶爾之役	Expedition against the Jungars (1729-1735)		
2806				
2807	文字獄	Literary Inquisition		
2808				
2809				
2810-2829	高宗 乾隆	Kao Tsung	Ch'ien-lung	1736-1795
2811	内政要畧	Chief Internal Events		
2812	準噶爾之蕩平	Conquest of the Jungars (1754-1755)		
2813	西藏之役	Control over Tibet Established (1751)		
2814	兩金川之役	Pacification of the Rebellions of the Native Tribes of the Tibetan Border (1747-1749, 1755-1779)		
2815	緬甸之役	Expedition against Burma (1765-1769)		
2816	臺灣之變	Revolt in Formosa Suppressed (1768-1769)		
2817	安南之役	Expedition against Annam (1788)		

	Temple Name	Title of Reign	Length of Reign
	清高宗 (續) Kao Tsung (Cont.)		
2818	平回之役	Pacification of the Mohammedan Revolt in Kansu (1781, 1784)	
2819	新疆之蕩平	Conquest of East Turkestan (1792)	
	屯防政策	Border Defense Measures	
2820	尼泊爾之役	Invasion of Nepal (1792)	
2821	朝貢	Tributes by Neighbouring Countries	
2822	朋黨	Party Politics	
2823	文治政績	Patronage of Arts and Letters	
2824	文字獄	Literary Inquisition	
2825			
2826	山東民亂	Rebellion in Shantung (1774)	
2827	貴州苗亂	Suppression of the Revolt of the Miao Tribesmen in Kweichow (1795-1797)	
2828	巡幸	Tours of Inspection	
2829	其他	Other Topics	
2840-2849	仁宗 嘉慶 Jên Tsung	Chia-ch'ing	1796-1820
2841			
2842			
2843	白蓮教	The Pai Lien (White Lotus) Rebellion (1796-1804)	
2844	天理教	The T'ien Li (Heavenly Reason) Rebellion (1813)	
2845	海疆盜寇	Piracies Along the Coast	
2846	其他變亂	Other Rebellions	
2847			
2848			
2849	巡幸	Tours of Inspection	

	清(續)	Temple Name	Title of Reign	Length of Reign
2850-2869	宣宗 道光	Hsüan Tsung	Tao-kuang	1821-1850
2851				
2852	内政要畧	Chief Internal Events		
2853				
2954				
2855	回疆之變	The Mohammedan Revolt in East Turkestan (1820-1831)		
2856				
2857				
2858	黎猺之亂	The Revolt of the Li and Yao Tribes in Hunan, Kwangtung and Kwangsi (1821-1847)		
2859				
2860				
2861	鴉片之戰	"Opium war" with England (1839-1842)		
2862				
2863				
2864				
2865				
2866				
2867				
2868				
2869				
2870-2889	文宗 咸豐	Wên Tsung	Hsien-fêng	1850-1861
2871				
2872	内政要畧	Chief Internal Events		
2873				
2874				
2875	太平天國	The Taiping Rebellion (1850-1864)		

清(續) 文宗(續)	Temple Name Wen Tsung (Cont.)	Title of Reign	Length of Reign
2876			
2877			
2878			
2879			
2880			
2881			
2882			
2883	英法聯軍	War with England and France (1858-1860)	
2884			
2885			
2887	捻匪之勦平	Pacification of the Nien Fei (1853-1868) (Organized bandits in Anhwei, Kiangsu, Shantung and Shansi)	
2888			
2889	雲貴回亂	The Revolt of the Mohammedans in Yunnan and Kweichow (1855-1873)	
2890-2899	穆宗 同治 Mu Tsung	T'ung-chih	1861-1874
2891			
2892	中興政要	Chief Events in Internal Reform under Leadership of Tseng Kuo-fan	
2893			
2894			
2895			
2896			
2897	回亂之勘定	Suppression of the Mohammedan Rebellions in Yunnan, Shensi and Kansu (1863-1873)	
2898			
2899			

	清(續)	Temple Name	Title of Reign	Length of Reign
2900-2919	德宗 光緒	Tê Tsung	Kuang-hsi	1875-1908
2901				
2902				
2903	回部之平定及 新疆省之建立	Pacification of the Revolts in Chinese Tur-kestan, which was organized as a new province entitled "Sinkiang." (1875-1878)		
2904	中法之戰	Sino-Franco War over Indo-China (1882-1885)		
2905	中日之戰	The Sino-Japanese War (1894-1895)		
2906				
2907				
2908				
2910	戊戌政變	The Reform Movement of 1898		
2911				
2912				
2913	義和團之變	The Boxer Uprising in 1900		
2914				
2915				
2916				
2917				
2920	憲政運動	Movement for Constitutional Government		
2940-2959	溥儀帝 宣統	Emperor P'u-i	Hsüan-t'ung	1909-1911
2941				
2942				
2943				
2944				
2945				
2946				
2947				
2948				
2949				
2950				

2960-2969	革命時代	THE REVOLUTION (1911-1912)
2961		
2963		
2965		
2966		
2967		
2968		
2970-2999	中華民國	THE REPUBLIC (1912-)
2971-2974	南京臨時政府	Provisional Government in Nanking (1912)
2975-	袁世凱	President Yüan Shih-k'ai (1912-1916)
2976		
2977		
2978		
2979		
2980	南北分裂時代	Division between North and South (1917-1926)
2981		
2985	國民政府	The Nationalist Government in Nanking (1927-1937)
2987	內政之改進	Internal Progress
2989	國共相爭	The Struggle for Power between the Kuomintang and the Communist Party (1927-1936)
2990	東北事變	Japanese Invasion and the War of National Resistance (1937-)
2991	抗戰建國	Japanese Occupation of the Three Eastern Provinces (Manchuria), 1931

3000-3299 中國地理及方志 CHINA: GEOGRAPHY AND LOCAL HISTORY

3000-3019	總錄	GENERAL (Subdivide like Table I, row 2.)
3020-3031	總志 依體裁分.	GENERAL SYSTEMATIC TREATISES
3020	歷史地理 記歷代者	Historical Geography Of all periods
3021-3028	記一代者 依時代分, 用表三.	Of particular periods (Divide chronologically like Table III)

97

中國地理及方志 (續)
CHINA: GEOGRAPHY AND LOCAL HISTORY (Cont.)

3030	現代地理	Modern Geography (1912 to Date)
3032-3049	專志	SPECIAL WORKS
3033	區域省界	Political Divisions
3034	邊疆防務	Frontiers; Defense Systems
3035	山	Orography

各省之山照表二依省區分著作號碼則取山名之首字左上右下二角及次字左上角號碼，再加修撰時代號碼以點(·)隔開. 如康熙間修廬山志，為 3035.26/012.81, 民國修者為3035.26/012.9.

3037-3040	水	Hydrography (See also 8730
	參見水利工程.	Hydraulic Engineering)
3037	總志	General
3038	海洋	Seas and Oceans
3039	江河	Rivers (Including old works on Irrigation and
	附水利	Flood Control)
3939.1	揚子江	Yangtze River
.2	黃河	Yellow River
.3	黑龍江	Heilung River
.4	運河	Grand Canal
.5	珠江	Pearl River
.6	淮河	Hui River
.7	其他流經數省江河	Other Rivers Crossing Several Provinces
.8	各省水道志	Rivers Within Each Province (Subdivide
	依省區分.	by Provinces)
.9	水利	Irrigation Works
3040	湖泃	Lakes (Arrange by Names of Lakes)
	依湖名排.	
3041-3049	名勝 古蹟	Scenery, Antiquities, etc.
3041	總錄	General
3042	廟宇	Temples
3043	祠堂	Memorial and Ancestral Halls
3044	陵墓	Mausoleums and Tombs
3045	宮殿	Palaces

名勝古蹟(續) Scenery (Cont.)

3046	亭臺樓閣	Pavilions and Galleries
3047		
3048	苑園	Parks and Gardens
3049	其他雜記	Miscellaneous
3050-3079	地方載記及遊記	LOCAL DESCRIPTION AND TRAVEL, GUIDE-BOOKS
3050	總錄	General
3051	北部	Northern Provinces
3052	東三省(滿洲)	The Three Eastern Provinces (Manchuria)
3053	遼寧	Liaoning
3054	吉林	Kirin
3055	黑龍江	Heilungkiang
3056	河北	Hopei
3057	山東	Shantung
3058	河南	Honan
3059	山西	Shansi
3060	陝西	Shensi
3061	甘肅	Kansu
3062	中部	Central Provinces
3063	西康	Hsikang
3064	四川	Szechuan
3065	湖北	Hupei
3066	湖南	Hunan
3067	江西	Kiangsi
3068	安徽	Anhwei
3069	江蘇	Kiangsu
3070	浙江	Chekiang
3071	南部	Southern Provinces
3072	福建	Fukien

	南部	Southern Provinces (Cont.)
3073	廣東	Kwangtung
3074	廣西	Kwangsi
3075	雲南	Yunnan
3076	貴州	Kweichow
3077	藩部	The Outlying Territories
3078.1	内蒙	Inner Mongolia
.2	熱河	Jehol
.3	綏遠	Suiyuan
.4	察哈爾	Charhar
.5	寧夏	Ninghsia
.6	外蒙	Outer Mongolia
3079	西域 總錄	Northwest - General
.1	新疆	Sinkiang (Chinese Turkestan)
.5	青海 西藏	Chinghai (Kokonor) and Tibet
3080-3109	輿圖	MAPS, ATLASES, PLANS OF CITIES, ETC.
3080	全國	National
3081	北部	Northern Provinces
3082	東三省	The Three Eastern Provinces (Manchuria)
3083	遼寧	Liaoning
3084	吉林	Kirin
3085	黑龍江	Heilungkiang
3086	河北	Hopei
3087	山東	Shantung
3088	河南	Honan
3089	山西	Shansi
3090	陝西	Shensi
3091	甘肅	Kansu

	輿圖 (續)	MAPS, ATLASES, PLANS OF CITIES (Cont.)
3092	中部	Central Provinces
3093	西康	Hsikang
3094	四川	Szechuan
3095	湖北	Hupei
3096	湖南	Hunan
3097	江西	Kiangsi
3098	安徽	Anhwei
3099	江蘇	Kiangsu
3100	浙江	Chekiang
3101	南部	Southern Provinces
3102	福建	Fukien
3103	廣東	Kwangtung
3104	廣西	Kwangsi
3105	雲南	Yunnan
3106	貴州	Kweichow
3107.1	蒙古	Mongolia
.2	熱河	Jehol
.3	綏遠	Suiyuan
.4	察哈爾	Charchar
.5	寧夏	Ninghsia
.6	外蒙	Outer Mongolia
3108	新疆	Sinkiang (Chinese Turkestan)
3109	青海,西藏	Chinghai (Kokonor) and Tibet

3110-3299 方志、 GAZETTEERS (OFFICIAL LOCAL HISTORY AND TOPOGRAPHY)

	道與直隸州從府屬,州與廳從縣.	Within each province, Circuits (Tao) and independent Chous or Tings go under number for prefectures (Fu); dependent Chous or Tings go under number for districts (Hsien)
	續志補志須各認為單種書,脂修撰年代分別依表三排列.	Supplementary gazetteers are treated as separate books, independent of their main works. They are distinguished by date of compilation using Table III for period numbers. For arranging individual gazetteers, see note at the end of this section.
3110	北部諸省	Northern Provinces
3114	東三省	The Three Eastern Provinces (Manchuria)
3116-3119	遼寧	Liaoning
3116	全省	Whole Province
3117	府	Prefectures
3118	縣	Districts
3119	市鄉	Towns and Villages
3120-3123	吉林	Kirin
3120	全省	Whole Province
3121	府	Prefectures
3122	縣	Districts
3123	市鄉	Towns and Villages
3124-3127	黑龍江	Heilungkiang
3124	全省	Whole Province
3125	府	Prefectures
3126	縣	Districts
3127	市鄉	Towns and Villages
3128-3135	河北	Hopei (Chihli)
3128	全省	Whole Province
3129	京兆	Chingchao (District of Peking)

方志
北部諸省(續) **Northern Provinces (Cont.)**
河北(續)

3133	府	Prefectures
3134	縣	Districts
3135	市鄉	Towns and Villages
3138-3141	山東	Shantung
3138	全省	Whole Province
3139	府	Prefectures
3140	縣	Districts
3141	市鄉	Towns and Villages
3143-3146	河南	Honan
3143	全省	Whole Province
3144	府	Prefectures
3145	縣	Districts
3146	市鄉	Towns and Villages
3148-3151	山西	Shansi
3148	全省	Whole Province
3149	府	Prefectures
3150	縣	Districts
3151	市鄉	Towns and Villages
3153-3156	陝西	Shensi
3153	全省	Whole Province
3154	府	Prefectures
3155	縣	Districts
3156	市鄉	Towns and Villages
3158-3165	甘肅	Kansu
3158	全省	Whole Province
3159	府	Prefectures
3160	縣	Districts
3161	市鄉	Towns and Villages

方志（續）

3170	中部諸省	Central Provinces
3173-3176	西康	Hsikang
3173	全省	Whole Province
3174	府	Prefectures
3175	縣	Districts
3176	市鄉	Towns and Villages
3178-3181	四川	Szechuan
3178	全省	Whole Province
3179	府	Prefectures
3180	縣	Districts
3181	市鄉	Towns and Villages
3183-3186	湖北	Hupei
3183	全省	Whole Province
3184	府	Prefectures
3185	縣	Districts
3186	市鄉	Towns and Villages
3188-3191	湖南	Hunan
3188	全省	Whole Province
3189	府	Prefectures
3190	縣	Districts
3191	市鄉	Towns and Villages
3193-3196	江西	Kiangsi
3193	全省	Whole Province
3194	府	Prefectures
3195	縣	Districts
3196	市鄉	Towns and Villages

方志
中部諸省（續）　Central Provinces (Cont.)

3198-3201	安徽		Anhwei
3198	全省		Whole Province
3199	府		Prefectures
3200	縣		Districts
3201	市鄉		Towns and Villages
3202-3207	江蘇		Kiangsu
3202	南京		Nanking
3203	全省		Whole Province
3204	府		Prefectures
3205	縣		Districts
3206	市鄉		Towns and Villages
3208-3211	浙江		Chekiang
3208	全省		Whole Province
3209	府		Prefectures
3210	縣		Districts
3211	市鄉		Towns and Villages
3220	南部諸省	Southern Provinces	
3222-3225	福建		Fukien
3222	全省		Whole Province
3223	府		Prefectures
3224	縣		Districts
3225	市鄉		Towns and Villages
3228-3233	廣東		Kwangtung
3228	全省		Whole Province
3229	府		Prefectures
3230	縣		Districts
3231	市鄉		Towns and Villages

南部諸省(續) Southern Provinces (Cont.)

3236-3239	廣西	Kwangsi
3236	全省	Whole Province
3237	府	Prefectures
3238	縣	Districts
3239	市鄉	Towns and Villages
3243-3246	貴州	Kweichow
3243	全省	Whole Province
3244	府	Prefectures
3245	縣	Districts
3246	市鄉	Towns and Villages
3248-3252	雲南	Yunnan
3248	全省	Whole Province
3249	府	Prefectures
3250	縣	Districts
3251	市鄉	Towns and Villages
3255-3299	藩部	The Outlying Territories
3260	西北總錄	Northwest-General
3261	蒙古	Mongolia
3262	內蒙	Inner Mongolia
3263-65	熱河	Jehol
3266-67	綏遠	Suiyuan
3268-70	察哈爾	Charhar
3271-3273	寧夏	Ninghsia
3274	外蒙古	Outer Mongolia
3275-80	新疆	Sinkiang (Chinese Turkestan)
3282-3285	青海	Chinghai (Kokonor)
3290-3299	西藏	Tibet

附註:
各地有府縣志,可照下列三種方法排列.

Note: In arranging individual gazetteers, the following system may be adopted. (1) For provincial gazetteers, use the number for the whole province. The book-number may be found by

(一)省志　用全省號碼著作號或書號,照表三取之,朝代號碼前冠'0.'與分類固號碼以資橫(/)隔開.如雍正山東通志.其排架號為3138/0.82,宣統間修有為3138/0.99.如人關于該有之著述,如丁欽之齊乘,亦用全省號碼惟書名則按著者姓名,依王民四角號碼檢字法綴成之.故其排架號為3138/1488.細則見表四.

(二)合省府縣志　用該省之府或縣號為號,書號則用該府或縣名稱前二字之左上右下角四位號碼,再加表三之朝代號碼.如光緒鎮海(浙江)縣志之排架號為3210/8835.88,民國修者為3210/8835.9.

(三)一縣有古今二名稱者用今名,或某縣又名稱經數次更改者用最近官定名稱如河北有之東安縣志或安次縣志,書名雖異而實指同一地方,應有同樣排架號,故該書號時均用民國改定之名稱其排架號為3134/3438.83及3134/3438.9.如此類推.

以上方法較用任何有固定號碼之地域表排列為便.其優點有三:(1)不用地域表取號碼可省編目時間;(2)辦事員或讀者可於書庫中直接由架上尋書不必再檢目錄以得排架號碼;(3)不受政府屢次修改行政區域表之影響,盍于分類目錄,可隨時將政府所修訂之行政區域表另行排列也.

using Table III for period numbers preceded by zero point (0.)　Thus the <u>Gazetteer of Shantung</u> (Shan tung t'ung chih) compiled during the reign of Emperor Yung-chêng has 3138/0.82, while the edition completed at the time of Emperor Hsüan-t'ung has 3138/0.89 as the call-numbers. Private works on the whole province (as distinguished from official gazetteers) by individuals also use the same class number for the whole province, but the book-number is formed by using Wong's Four-corner Numeral System for the author's name. For applying Wong's Four-corner Numeral System to Book-Numbers or author-numbers, see appendix IV. Thus the <u>Historical Account of Shantung</u> (Ch'i ch'êng) by Yü Ch'in has the call-number 3138/1488

(2)　For prefecture or district gazetteers of a province, use the class number for the <u>Fu</u> or the <u>Hsien</u> in that province. The book-number is formed by abstracting the numbers for the upper left and lower right corners of the first and the second characters of the name of the prefecture or district followed by period numbers from Table III. Thus <u>Chên hai hsien chih</u> (Chekiang) compiled during the reign of Kuang-hsü has the call-no.: 3210/8835.88 while the edition completed in the Republican era bears the call-number 3210/8835.9

(3)　In case a district (hsien) has its name changed, use the present name for abstracting the book-number, or if a place is known by several names, use the latest official name consistently throughout, so that different editions of a gazetteer bearing different titles but referring to the same place may be put together on the shelf by having the same call-number differentiated only by the period numbers following the book-number. Thus the <u>Tung an hsien chih</u> (Hopei) and the <u>An tz'û hsien chih</u> bearing different titles but referring to the same place both have the same call-no. 3134/3438.83 and 3134/3438.9 except for the difference in period numbers, which indicate that the earlier edition was compiled at the time of the Emperor Ch'ien-lung and the latter one finished under the Republic.

The above mechanical arrangement of individual gazetteers has these advantages: (1) it eliminates the necessity of consulting a detailed geographical list of districts and prefectures, which is time-consuming for the cataloger in assigning call-numbers; (2) it enables library assistants and those readers who know Wong's Four-corner System to locate any particular gazetteer quickly in the stack without consulting the catalogue; (3) it offers the possibility of rearranging all gazetteers later without changing the call numbers according to any official list of administrative districts which the Government may issue from time to time. (So far there are at least five such lists: two were of Ch'ing Dynasty, two published by the Peking Government in 1912 and 1918, and one issued by the Nanking Nationalist Government in 1930.)

3300-3399日本歷史 JAPAN : HISTORY

3300-3312	總錄	GENERAL WORKS
3302	期刊	Periodicals
3304	會社	Societies
3305	叢集	Collections
3306	史料	Historical Sources
3308	書目	Bibliographies
3309	教學	Study and Teaching
3310	辭典	Dictionaries
3311	圖譜	Charts
3312	年表	Chronological Tables
3313	史學	HISTORIOGRAPHY
3314-3319	專史	SPECIAL HISTORIES
3314	文化史	History of Civilization
3314.9	交通史	Cultural Relations with Foreign Lands
3315	與中國	With China
3316	與西洋 依地理分,用表二.	With Western Nations (For subdivision, use Table II)
3317	外交史	Diplomatic Relations
3317	分時代者 細分,用表三.	Of different periods (Divide by Table III)
3318	分國者 細分,用表二.	With different countries (Divide by Table II)
3319	單事史	Military History
3320	通史	COMPREHENSIVE GENERAL HISTORY
3321	史論,史話	Historical Essays
3322	史鈔	Historical Excerpts
3324-3399	斷代史	HISTORY BY PERIODS

Period divisions and dates treated by different authors vary greatly. The following scheme is based on two scholarly bibliographies by Kuroita

斷代史　　　　　　HISTORY BY PERIODS (Cont.)

日本歴史時代及其断限,各
家分法出入頗甚.本表根據
黒板勝美之更訂國史の研究,兼
四元次之綜合國史研究兩書目,
並兼參考日本十進分類法(210)
及杜威十進分類法(952).
帝王將軍等統治年代,據大森
金五郎高橋昇造共著之增補最
新日本歴史年表,古代史部分,方
括弧中所註年代取自來希和之英文日
本古代史,圖括弧中所記則為該史
書記事之起訖.

Katsumi and Kurita Mototsugu, with reference
to two existing classification tables, D. C. 952
and N. D. C. 210. The dates of the reigns of
different rulers have been given according to
the revised chronological table of Japanese history compiled by Omori Kingoro in Takahashi
Shozo, 1939. The dates given in brackets are
quoted from Robert Karl Reischauer's Early
Japanese history; those given in parentheses
after book titles show the period treated in
that book.

3324	古代史	Early History	B.C.-1185
3325	古事記	Kojiki, or Furu koto bumi (B.C.-628)　Class the independent Kamiyo no maki in 1947.1	
	神代之部獨立者,入神典.		
3325.8	六國史	Riku kokushi, six national histories	
3326	日本書紀	Nihon shoki (B.C.-696)	
	此為六國史之第一種, 餘五種分入以後各時代. 神代卷獨立者入神典.	This is the first of the six national histories. The others are classified according to their own contents. Class the independent Shindai kan in 1947.2	
3327.2	類聚國史	Ruiju kokushi (B.C.-887) A recompilation of Riku kokushi by subjects	
3327.3	日本紀畧	Nihon kiryaku (B.C.-1017) An abstract of Riku kokushi	
	舊事本紀	Kuji hongi (B.C.-592)　Class in 1947.98	
	入神典.		
	古語拾遺	Kogo shūi (B.C.-c.672)　Class in 1947.3	
	入神典.		
3327.5	水鏡	Mizu kagami (660 B.C.-850)	
3328.2	神皇正統記	Jinnō shōtō ki (B.C.-1339)	
.6	其他	Others	
3328.8	神話時代	Mythologic Age	660 [c.40] B.C.
3328.8	太古史	Primitive History	660 [c.40] B.C.
3329	大和時代	Yamato Period	660 [c.40] B.C.-710 A.D.
3329.1	上古史	Early Ancient History	660 [c.40] B.C.-645 A.D.
3329.1	氏姓時代	Clan-Family (uji-kabane) Age	660 [c.40] B.C.-645 A.D.

古代史(續)Early History (Cont.)

3329.2 　大和開郇騏Founding of Yamato Kingdom　660-98 B.C.
[c.40 B.C.-A.D.230

神武　Jimmu, 660-585 B.C. [c.40-10 B.C.]

綏靖　Suizei, 581-549 B.C. [c.10 B.C.-A.D. 10]

安寧　Annei, 549-511 B.C. [c. A.D. 20-50]

懿德　Itoku, 510-477 B.C. [c.50-80]

孝昭　Kōshō, 475-393 B.C. [c.80-110]

孝安　Kōan, 392-291 B.C. [c.110-140]

孝靈　Kōrei, 290-215 B.C. [c.140-170]

孝元　Kōgen, 214-158 B.C. [c.170-200]

開化　Kaika, 158-98 B.C. [c.200-230]

3329.3 　國土開拓時代Expansion of Yamato Kingdom　97 B.C.-A.D 191
[230-355]

崇神　Sujin, 97-30 B.C. [c.230-258]

垂仁　Suinin, 29 B.C.-70 A.D. [c.259-290]

景行　Keikō, 71-130 [c.291-322]

成務　Seimu, 131-190 [c.323-255]

3329.4 　朝鮮遠攻時代Expedition to Southern Korea　192-507
中國文化輸入 Import of Chinese civilization [c.356-510]

仲哀　Chūai, 192-200 [c.356-362]

神功皇后　Jingō kōgō, 200-269 [c.363-380]

應神　Ōjin, 201-310 [c.380-394]

仁德　Nintoku, 313-399 [c.395-427]

履仲　Richū, 400-405 [c.428-432]

反正　Hanshō, 406-410 [c.433-437]

允恭　Ingyō, 412-453 [c.438-454]

安康　Ankō, 454-456 [c.455-457]

古代史(續)Early History (Cont.)

雄畧	Yūryaku, 457-479 [c.457-489]	
清寧	Seinei, 479-484 [c.490-494]	
顯宗	Kensō, 485-487 [c.495-497]	
仁賢	Ninken, 488-498 [c.498-504]	
武烈	Buretsu, 498-506 [c.504-510]	

3329.5 　　臣連擅權時代 Rise of Soga Family　　508-592 [c.510-592]

繼體	Keitei, 508-531 [c.510-527?]
安閑	Ankan, 531-535 [527?-535?]
宣化	Senka, 535-539 [536?-570?]
蘇我稻目	Soga Iname, 536-570 [536?-570?]
欽明	Kimmei, 539-571 [539?-571]
敏達	Bidatsu, 572-585 [572?-585?]
蘇我馬子	Soga Umako, 572-626 [572?-626]
用明	Yōmei, 585-587 [585?-587]
崇竣	Sushun, 587-592

3329.6 　　飛鳥時代 Asuka Period　　　　　　　　　592-707

　　　　法興肇憲時代 Beginning of Legislations　　592-645

推古(女)	Suiko, 592-628
聖德太子	Shōtoku taishi, 593-621 or 622
蘇我蝦夷	Soga Emishi, 626-645
舒明	Jomei, 628-641
皇極(女)	Kōkyoku, 641-645

3330	公家時代 Court Nobles (Kuge) Age	645-1185
3330	中古史　Late Ancient History　上代史	645-1185
3331	漢化時代　Sinification	645-707
3332	大化改新　Taika Reform	645-661

孝德 大化(壬)白雉(甲)	Kōtoku, 645-654
齊明	Saimei, 654-661

古代史 Early History (Cont.)
(續)

3333	近江時代	Ōmi jidai	661–707
	天智	Tenchi, 661–672	
	弘文	Kōbun, 672	
3334	天武	Temmu, 672–686	
	持統(女) 朱雀	Jitō, 686–697	
	文武 大寶,慶雲	Mommu, 697–797	
3335	奈良時代	Nara Period	710–781
3335	奈良時代	Nara jidai	710–781
3336	元明(女) 慶雲,和銅	Gemmyō, 797–715	
	元正(女) 靈龜,養老	Genshō, 715–724	
3337	聖武 神龜,天平	Shōmu, 724–749	
	孝謙(女) 天平感寶,天平勝寶,天平寶字	Kōken, 749–758	
3338	淳仁 天平寶字	Junnin, 758–764	
	稱德(女) 天平寶字,天平神護,神護景雲	Shōtoku, 764–770	
	光仁 寶龜	Kōnin, 770–781	
3340	平安時代	Heian Period	781–1185
3341	平安初期	Early Heian Period	781–858
3341	平安奠都時代	Building of Heian (Kyōto)	781–833
	桓武 天應,延曆	Kammu, 781–806	
	平城 大同	Heijō, 806–809	
	嵯峨 大同,弘仁	Saga, 809–823	
	淳和 弘仁,天長	Junna, 823–833	
3342	藤原時代	Fujiwara Period	833–1068
3343	攝關新置時代	Appearance of Regents and Imperial Advisers	833–887
	仁明 天長,承和,嘉祥	Nimmyō, 833–850	
	藤原良房	Fujiwara Yoshifusa, udaijin 848–857, dajōdaijin 857–866, sessho 866–872	

古代史 Early History (Cont.)
(续)

文德 嘉祥 仁壽,齊衡,天安　Montoku, 850-858

清和 天安,貞觀　Seiwa, 858-876

藤原基經　Fujiwara Mototsune, sesshō
　　873-880, kampaku 880-891

陽成 貞觀,元慶　Yōzei, 876-884

光孝 元慶,仁和　Kōkō, 884-887

3344　攝關中停時代　Suspension of Regents and Imperial
　　　　　　　Advicers　　　887-967

宇多 仁和,寬平　Uda, 887-897

醍醐 寬平,昌泰,延喜,延長　Daigo, 897-930

朱雀 延長,承平,天慶　Suzaku, 930-946

藤原忠平　Fujiwara Tadahira, sesshō
　　930-941, kampaku 941-949

村上 天慶,天曆,天德,應和,康保　Murakami, 946-967

3345　攝關榮華時代　Prosperity of Regents and Imperial
　　　　　　　Advicers　　　967-1068

冷泉 康保,安和　Reizei, 967-969

藤原實賴　Fujiwara Saneyori, kampaku,
　　967-969, sesshō 969-970

圓融　En'yū, 969-984
安和,天祿,天延,貞元,天元,永觀

藤原伊尹　Fujiwara Koretada, sesshō
　　970-972

藤原兼通　Fujiwara Kanemichi, kampaku
　　973-977

藤原賴忠　Fujiwara Yoritada, kampaku
　　977-986

花山 永觀,寬和　Kazan, 984-986

一條　Ichijō, 986-1011
寬和,永延,永祚,正曆,長德,長保,寬弘

藤原兼家　Fujiwara Kaneie, sesshō
　　986-990

藤原道隆　Fujiwara Michitaka, sesshō
　　990-991, kampaku 991-995

古代史 (續) Early History (Cont.)

藤原道兼	Fujiwara Michikane, kampaku 995	
藤原道長	Fujiwara Michinaga, nairan 995-1016, sesshō 1016-1017	
三條 寬弘, 長和	Sanjō, 1011-1016	
後一條 長和, 寬仁, 治安, 萬壽, 長元	Go-Ichijō, 1016-1036	
藤原賴通	Fujiwara Yorimichi, sesshō 1017-1020, kampaku 1020-1028	
後朱雀 長元, 長曆 長久, 寬德	Go-Suzaku, 1036-1045	
後冷泉 寬德, 永承, 天喜, 康平, 治曆	Go-Reizei, 1045-1068	

3347	上皇實權時代 院政時代	Cloister Government by Retired Sovereigns (in)	1068-1155
	後三條 治曆, 延久	Go-Sanjō, 1068-1073, in 1073	
	白河 延久, 承保, 永曆, 永保, 應德	Shirakawa, 1073-1087, in 1087-1129	
	堀河 應德, 寬治, 嘉保, 永長, 承德, 康和, 長治, 嘉承	Horikawa, 1087-1107	
	鳥羽 嘉承, 天仁, 天永, 天久, 元永, 保安	Toba, 1107-1123, in 1129-1156	
	崇德 保安, 天治, 大治, 天承, 長承, 保延	Sutoku, 1123-1141	
	近衛 永治, 康治, 天養, 久安, 仁平, 久壽	Konoe, 1142-1155	
3347.9	源平時代 前武家時代	Gempei Period Pre-feudal Period	1155-1186
3348	保元平治時代	Emergence of Dominance of Feudal Barons (buke)	1158-1165
	後白河 久壽, 保元	Go-Shirakawa, 1155-1158, in 1158-1179	
	二條 保元, 平治, 永曆 應保, 長寬	Nijō, 1158-1165	
3349	六波羅時代	Rokuhara jidai	1165-1185
3349.2	平家全盛時代	Taira Family Supremacy	1165-1180
	六條 永萬, 仁安	Rokujō, 1165-1168	
	平清盛	Taira no Kiyomori, naidajin, 1166, dajōdaijin 1167-1181	

古代史 Early History (Cont.)
(續)

　　　高倉 仁安,嘉應,承安,安元,治承　Takakura, 1168-1180

　　　平重盛　Tairano Shigemori, naidaijin,
　　　　　　　　1177-1179

3349.7　源氏勃興時代　Rise of Minamoto Clan

　　　安德 治承,養和,壽永　Antoku, 1180-1185

3349.9　武家時代 Feudal Barons (buke) Age　　　　　1156-1863

3349.9　中世及近世史 Medieval and Modern History　　1186 (or 1156)-1868

3350　中世史 Medieval History　　　　　　　　　　1185-1600

3351　近古史鎌倉時代　Kamakura Period　　　　　　　1185-1600
　　　古武家時代
　　　　　　　　Early era of military government

3352　源氏將軍時代 Minamoto shōguns　　　　　　　1185-1221

　　　後鳥羽 壽永,元曆,文治,建久　Go-Toba, 1183-1198, in 1198-1221

　　　源賴朝 鎌倉政所(以文所)創始將軍　Minamoto Yoritomo, shōgunate
　　　　　　　　　　founder 1184, shōgun 1192-1199

　　　大江廣元 公文所別當　Ōe Hiromoto, military civil
　　　　　　　　　secretary 1184-1203

　　　土御門 建久,正治,建仁,元久,建永,承元　Tsuchimikado, 1198-1210

　　　源賴家　Minamoto Yoriie, 1199-1203

　　　源實朝　Minamoto Sanetomo, 1203-1219

　　　北條時政 政所執權　Hōjō Tokimasa, military civil
　　　　　　　　regent (shikken) 1203-1219

　　　北條義時　Hōjō Yoshitoki, 1205-1215,
　　　　　　　　1219-1224

　　　順德 承元,建曆,建保,承久　Juntoku, 1210-1221

3353　藤氏將軍時代 Puppet Fujiwara shōguns under Hōjō
　　　　　　　　Regents　　　　　　　　1221-1246

　　　藤原賴經　Fujiwara Yoritsune, 1219-1244

　　　仲恭 承久　Chōkyō, 1221

　　　後堀河　Go-Horikawa, 1221-1232, in 1232-1234

　　　北條泰時　Hōjō Yasutoki, 1224-1242

115

中世史Medieval History (Cont.)
（續）

四條 貞永,天福,文曆,嘉禎,曆仁,延應,仁治　Shijō, 1232-1242

後嵯峨 仁治,寬元　Go-Saga, 1242-1246, in 1246-1272

北條經時　Hōjō Tsunetoki, 1242-1246

藤原賴嗣　Fujiwara Yoritsugu, 1244-1252

3354　宮將軍時代　Puppet imperial prince shoguns under regents　1246-1321

後深草 寬元,寶治,建長,康元,正嘉　Go-Fukakusa, 1242-1259, in 1287-1290

北條時賴　Hōjō Tokiyori, 1246-1256

宗尊親王　Prince Munetaka, 1251-1266

北條長時　Hōjō Nagatoki, 1256-1264

龜山 正元,文應,弘長,文永　Kameyama, 1259-1274, in 1274-1287

北條政村　Hōjō Masamura, 1264-1268

惟康親王　Prince Koreyasu, 1266-1289

北條時宗　Hōjō Tokimune, 1268-1284

3354.6　文永弘安之役 蒙古襲來　Mongol invasion　1271-1281

後宇多 文永,建治,弘安　Go-Uda, 1274-1287, in 1301-1308, 1318-1321

北條貞時　Hōjō Sadatoki, 1284-1301

伏見 弘安,正應,永仁　Fushimi, 1287-1298, in 1298-1301, 1308-1313

久明親王　Prince Hisaakira, 1289-1308

後伏見 永仁,正安　Go-Fushimi, 1298-1301, in 1313-1318

後二條 正安,乾元,嘉元,德治　Go-Nijō, 1301-1308

北條師時　Hōjō Morotoki, 1301-1311

花園 延慶,慶長,正和,文保　Hanazono, 1308-1318

守邦親王　Prince Morikuni, 1308-1333

北條宗宣　Hōjō Munenobu, 1311-1312

北條熙時　Hōjō Hirotoki, 1312-1315

中世史 Medieval History (Cont.)
(續)

北條基時　　　　　Hōjō Mototoki, 1315-1316

北條高時　　　　　Hōjō Takatoki, 1316-1326

3355　　正中元弘時代　Overthrow of Kamakura shogunate 1318-1333
　　　　後醍醐西明紀入此.
　　　　後醍醐　　　　Go-Daigo, 1318-1339
　　　　　　文保,元應,元亨,正中,嘉曆,元德,元弘,建武,延元.
　　　　赤橋守時　　　Akabashi Moritoki, 1326-1333

3356　　吉野時代　　Yoshino Period　　　　　　　1333-1392
　　　　皇家中興時代,南北朝.
　　　　　　　　　　Era of imperial restoration.

3356　　南朝　　　　　Southern dynasty

　　　　京都親政時代 Government by the emperor　1333-1336

　　　　護良親王　　　Prince Moriyoshi, 1333

　　　　成良親王　　　Prince Nariyoshi, 1335-1336

3358　　南方巡狩時代 Court in Yoshino　　　　　1336-1392

　　　　後村上 延元,興國,正平　Go-Murakami, 1339-1368

　　　　長慶　　　　　Chōkei, 1368-1383
　　　　　　正平,建德,文中,天授,弘和.
　　　　後龜山　　　　Go-Kameyama, 1383-1392

3359　　北朝　　　　　Northern Dynasty

　　　　光嚴 正慶(九二年)　Kōgon, 1331-1333

　　　　足利尊氏　　　Ashikaga Takauji, 1338-1358

　　　　光明 曆應,康永,貞和　Kōmyō, 1338-1348

　　　　崇光 貞和,觀應　Sukō, 1348-1351

　　　　後光嚴　　　　Go-Kōgon, 1352-1371
　　　　　　文和,延文,康安,貞治,應安.
　　　　足利義詮　　　Ashikaga Yoshiakira, 1358-1367

　　　　足利義滿　　　Ashikaga Yoshimizu, 1368-1394

　　　　後圓融　　　　Go-En'yū, 1371-1382

3360　　室町時代　Muramachi Period　　　　　1392-1573
　　　　中武家時代,足利時代.
　　　　　　　　　　Middle era of military government,

　　　　　　　　　　Ashikaga shōguns.

117

中世史 Medieval History (Cont.)
(續)

| 3361 | 幕府專橫時代 Powerful shoguns | 1392-1441 |

後小松 Go-Komatsu, 1382-1412

足利義持 永德,至德,嘉慶,康應明德,應永 Ashikaga Yoshimochi, 1394-1423

稱光 應永 Shōkō, 1412-1428

足利義量 Ashikaga Yoshikazu, 1423-1425

後花園 正長,永享,嘉吉,文安,寶德,享德,康正,長祿,寬正 Go-Hanazono, 1428-1464

足利義教 Ashikaga Yoshinori, 1429-1441

| 3362 | 幕府失威時代 Decline of shōgunate | 1441-1466 |

足利義勝 Ashikaga Yoshikatsu, 1442-1443

足利義政 Ashikaga Yoshimasa, 1449-1473

後土御門 寬正,文正,應仁,文明,長享,延德,明應 Go-Tsuchimikado, 1464-1500

| 3363 | 應仁文明時代 War in and around Kyoto | 1467-1491 |

足利義尚 Ashikaga Yoshihisa, 1473-1489

足利義稙 Ashikaga Yoshimura, 1490-1501

| 3363.9 | 戰國時代 Senkoku jidai | 1491-1590 |

封建制之再編成.

Reconstruction of feudal system

| 3364 | 羣雄爭霸時代 Incessant wars throughout the country | 1491-1578 |

足利義澄 Ashikaga Yoshizumi, 1494-1511

後柏原 明應,大龜,永正,大永 Go-Kashiwabara, 1500-1526

足利義稙 Ashikaga Yoshimura, 1508-1521

足利義晴 Ashikaga Yoshiharu, 1521-1546

後奈良 大永,享祿,天文,弘治 Go-Nara, 1526-1557

足利義輝 Ashikaga Yoshiteru, 1546-1565

正親町 弘治,永祿,元龜,天正. Ōgimachi, 1557-1582

足利義榮 Ashikaga Yoshinaga, 1568

足利義昭 Ashikaga Yoshiaki, 1568-1573

中世史Medieval History (Cont.)

3365	安土桃山時代Azuchi-Momoyama Period	1573-1600

新武家時代, 将軍闕位時代. New era of military government,

Interregnum of shoguns.

3366	織田時代　Unification by Oda	1573-1582

織田信長　　　Oda Nobunaga, 1573-1582

3367	豐臣時代　Unification by Toyotomi	1582-1600

豐臣秀吉　　　Toyotomi Hideyoshi, 1583-1598

後陽成　天正,文禄,慶長　Go-Yōzei, 1586-1611

3368	攻朝鮮　Korean campaigns	1592-1598

文禄慶長之役. 豐臣秀賴　　Toyotomi Hideyori, 1598-1600

3369	關ヶ原之戰　Battle of Sekigahara	1600
3370	近世史Modern History	1600-1867
3370	江戸時代　Edo Period	1600-1867

徳川時代.　　　　Tokugawa shōguns.

3371	幕政創始時代Establishment of shogunate	1600-1651

江戸初世.

3372	徳川家康　　　Tokugawa Ieyasu, 1603-1605	
	徳川秀忠　　　Tokugawa Hidetada, 1605-1623	
	後水尾　　Go-Minoo, 1611-1629	
3373	徳川家光　　Tokugawa Iemitsu, 1623-1651	

島原之亂　　　Shimabara rebellion, 1637-1638

明正(女)寬永　Myōshō, 1629-1643

後光明　寬永,正保(1647)慶安(1649),承應('152-) Go-Kōmyō, 1643-1654

3374	幕政修飾時代Taken on civilization aspects	1651-1716

江戸中世, 元禄時代. Genroku jidai.

徳川家綱　　Tokugawa Ietsuna, 1651-1680

後西院　　　Go-Sai-in, 1654-1663

承應, 明暦(1655), 萬治('58-)寬文('61-)

靈元　　Reigen, 1663-1687

寬文,延寶(1673-),天和('81),貞享('84)

119

近世史 Modern History (Cont.)
(續)

	德川綱吉	Tokugawa Tsunayoshi, 1680-1709
	東山 貞享,元祿(1688-),寶永(1704-)	Higashiyama, 1687-1709
	德川家宣	Tokugawa Ienobu, 1709-1712
	中御門 寶永,正德(1711-),享保('16-)	Nakamikado, 1709-1735

3375　幕政緊張時代 Reemphasis on military aspects　1716-1786
享寶及田沼時代.　　Kyōhō and Tanuma jidai

德川家繼　Tokugawa Ietsugu, 1713-1716
德川吉宗　Tokugawa Yoshimune, 1716-1745
櫻町　Sakuramachi, 1735-1747
享保,元文(1736),寬保('41),延享('44)
德川家重　Tokugawa Ieshige, 1745-1760
桃園　Momozono, 1747-1762
延享,寬延(1748-),寶曆('51)
德川家治　Tokugawa Ieharu, 1760-1786
後櫻町(女)　Go-Sakuramachi, 1762-1770
寶曆,明和(1764-)
後桃園　Go-Momozono, 1770-1779
明和,安永(1779-)
光格　Kōkaku, 1779-1817
安永,天明(1781),寬政('89)享和(1801-),文化(1804-)

3376　幕政彌縫時代 Decline of the shōgunate　1786-1853
江戶季世,文化文政時代.　　Bunka-Bunsei jidai

德川家齊　Tokugawa Ienari, 1787-1837
德川家慶　Tokugawa Ieyoshi, 1837-1853
仁孝　Ninkō, 1817-1846
文化,文政(1818-),天保('30-),弘化('44-)
孝明　Kōmei, 1846-1866
弘化,嘉永(1848-),安政('54),萬延(60)文久('61-),元治('64),慶應(67-)

3377　攘夷開港時代 End of shōgunate and opening of Japan　1853-1867
幕末.

3378　德川家定　Tokugawa Iesada, 1853-1858
日美結約　Visit of Commodore M. C. Perry 1853-1854

3379　德川家茂　Tokugawa Iemochi, 1858-1866
櫻田門之變　Accident of Sakurada　1860

近世史 Modern History (Cont.)
(續)

生麥村之變	Accident of Namamugi, 1862
蛤御門之戰	Battle of Hamagurigamon, 1864
長州征伐	Chōshū extremists subdued, 1864-1886
德川慶喜	Tokugawa Yoshinobu, 1866-1867

3380	憲政時代 Constitutional Age	1867-
3380	現代史 Recent History	1867-
3381	最近世史　維新史　Adoption of Western Civilization	1867-
3381	明治 (睦仁)　Meiji (Mutsuhito), 1867-1912
3382.1	大政奉還 Imperial power reestablishment, 1868
.3	地方動亂 Regional revolts
.4	佐賀之亂 Saga revolt, 1874
.5	秋月之亂 Akizuki revolt, 1876
.6	荻之亂 Ogi revolt, 1876
.7	熊本之亂 Kumamoto revolt, 1876
.8	西南之役 Satsuma extremists rebellion, 1873-1877
3383	擴展史 Political and commercial expansion
.6	攻臺灣 Attack on Chinese Formosa, 1874　見臺灣史地. See 3470.
.8	朝鮮事變 Struggle in Korea with Chinese, 1882-1885　見朝鮮歷史. See 3487.9.
3384	中日戰爭 Sino-Japanese war, 1894-1895　見中國歷史. See 2905.
3385	庚子之變 Siege of Peking, 1900　見中國歷史 See 2913.
3386	日俄戰爭 Russo-Japanese war, 1904-1905
3387	日韓合邦 Annexation of Korea, 1910　見朝鮮歷史 See 3488.

Recent History (Cont.)

3388	大正 (嘉仁)	Taishō (Yoshihito), 1912-1926
3389.3	歐洲戰爭 世界大戰.	World war, 1915-1919
.5	西伯利亞出兵	Siberian Expedition, 1918-1922
3390	昭和 (裕仁)	Shōwa (Hirohito), 1926-
3391	侵畧中國及世界大戰	Invasion of China and World war II, 1931-
.7	滿洲事變 見中國歷史.	Occupation of Northeastern China, 1931- See 2990.
3392	蘆溝橋事變 見中國歷史.	Great campaign in China, 1937- See 2991.
3393	突攻美國及太平洋 其他國家	Attack on the United States of America and other Pacific countries, 1941-
.7	正式向英美宣戰	War with British Empire and the United States

3400-3479　日本：地理 JAPAN: GEOGRAPHY

3401-3406	總錄	GENERAL
3401	期刊	Periodicals
3402	會社	Societies
3403	叢集	Collections
3404	參考書目	Bibliography
3405	教學	Study and Teaching
3406	字典辭書	Dictionaries
3407	地圖	MAPS, ATLASES, PLANS OF CITIES, ETC.

必要細分時參閱地方志 For minute subdivisions see 3410-3479.

.1	關東	Kantō
.2	奧羽	Ou
.3	中部	Chūbu
.4	京畿	Kinki
.5	中國及四國	Chūgoku and Shikoku
.6	九州及琉球	Kyūshū and Ryūkyū
.7	北海道及樺太	Hokkaidō and Karafuto
.8	臺灣	Taiwan
3408	總志	GENERAL SYSTEMATIC TREATISES
3408	歷史地理	Historical Geography (Subdivide like Table III)

依時代分, 用表三.

.2	風土記	Fudo Ki
.8	現代地理	Modern Geography
3409	專志	SPECIAL WORKS
.1	區域界劃	Political Divisions
.2	山志	Orography
.3	水志	Hydrography
.4	名勝古跡	Sceneries, Antiquities, etc.
.5	陵墓	Mausoleums and Tombs

日本地理專志（續）SPECIAL WORKS (Cont.)

3409.6	宮殿	Palaces
.7	亭臺樓閣	Pavilions and Galleries
.8	苑囿	Parks and Gardens
.9	載記及遊記DESCRIPTION AND TRAVEL	
3410-3479	地方史志 LOCAL HISTORY AND GAZETTEERS	
3410	關東地方	Kantō Region
3411	東京府	Tōkyō Metropolitan Prefecture
	武藏國（武）. 參見埼玉縣	Musashi [Bu]; see also Saitama.
3412	東京市	Tōkyō city
3413.1	八王子市	Hachiōji city
.3	西多摩郡	Nishitama district (gun)
.4	南多摩郡	Minamitama district (gun)
.5	北多摩郡	Kitatama district (gun)
.6	大島	Ō shima (islands)
.7	八丈島	Hachijō shima (islands)
.8	小笠原島	Ogasawara jima (islands)
.9	各町村	Towns and Villages
3414	神奈川縣	Kanagawa Prefecture
	相模國（相）. 參見武藏.	Sagami [Sō]; see also Musashi.
.1	橫濱市	Yokohama city
.5	橫須賀市	Yokosuka city
.6	川崎市	Kawasaki city
.7	平塚	Hiratsuka city
.8	各郡	Districts (gun)
.9	各町村	Towns and Villages

日本地方史志(續) LOCAL HISTORY AND GAZETTEERS (Cont.)

3415	千葉縣	Chiba Prefecture
	上總國,下總國,(總) 安房國(房).	Kazusa, Shimōsa [Sō], Awa [Bō].
.1	千葉市	Chiba city
.2	銚子市	Chōshi city
.3	市川市	Ichikawa city
.4	船橋市	Funabashi city
.8	各郡	Districts
.9	各町村	Towns and Villages
3416	茨城縣	Ibaraki Prefecture
	常陸國(常). 參見下總.	Hitachi [Jō]; see also Shimōsa.
.1	水戸市	Mito city
.8	各郡	Districts
.9	各町村	Towns and Villages
3417	埼玉縣	Saitama Prefecture
	武藏國(武).	Musashi [Bu].
.1	川越市	Kawagoe city
.2	川口市	Kawaguchi city
.3	熊谷市	Kumagaya city
.4	浦和市	Urawa city
.8	各郡	Districts
.9	各町村	Towns and Villages
3418	群馬縣	Gumma Prefecture
	上野國(上).	Kōtsuke [Jō].
.1	前橋市	Maebashi city
.2	高崎市	Takasaki city
.3	桐生市	Kiryū city

日本地方史志(續) LOCAL HISTORY AND GAZETTEERS (Cont.)

	群馬縣(續)		
3418.8	各郡	Districts	
.9	各町村	Towns and Villages	
3419	栃木縣	Tochigi Prefecture	
	下野國(野)	Shimotsuke [Ya].	
.1	宇都宮市	Utsunomiya city	
.2	足利市	Ashikaga city	
.3	栃木市	Tochigi city	
.8	各郡	Districts	
.9	各町村	Towns and Villages	
3420	奥羽地方	Ou (Tahoku) Region	
	東北地方.		
3421	福島縣	Fukushima Prefecture	
	岩代國(會津),磐城國.	Iwashiro, Iwaki.	
.1	福島市	Fukushima city	
.2	若松市	Wakamatsu city	
.3	郡山市	Kóriyama city	
.4	平市	Taira city	
.8	各郡	Districts	
.9	各町村	Towns and Villages	
3423	宮城縣	Miyagi Prefecture	
	陸前國. 參見磐城.	Rikuzen; see also Iwaki.	
.1	仙臺市	Sendai city	
.2	石卷市	Ishinomaki city	
.8	各郡	Districts	
.9	各町村	Towns and Villages	
3425	岩手縣	Iwate Prefecture	Mutsu
	陸中國(南部).參見陸奥,陸前.	Rikuchū; see also (Rikuoku) Rikuzen.	
.1	盛岡市	Morioka city	

日本地方史志(續)LOCAL HISTORY AND GAZETTEERS (Cont.)

3425.2	釜石市	Kamaishi city
.8	各郡	Districts
.9	各町村	Towns and Villages
3426	青森縣	Aomori Prefecture
	陸奥國(奥 ,津輕)	Rikuoku [O].
.1	青森市	Aomori city
.2	弘前市	Hirosaki city
.3	八戸市	Hachinohe city
.8	各郡	Districts
.9	各町村	Towns and Villages
3427	秋田縣	Akita Prefecture
	羽後國(羽);參見陸中.	Ugo [U]; see also Rikuchū
.1	秋田市	Akita city
.8	各郡	Districts
.9	各町村	Towns and Villages
3429	山形縣	Yamagata Prefecture
	羽前國(羽);參見羽後.	Uzen [U]; see also Ugo
.1	山形市	Yamagata city
.2	米澤市	Yonezawa city
.3	鶴岡市	Tsuruoka city
.4	酒田市	Sakata city
.8	各郡	Districts
.9	各町村	Towns and Villages
3430	中部地方	Chūbu Region
3431	新潟縣	Niigata Prefecture
	越後國(越);佐渡國(佐).	Echigo [Echi], Sado [Sa].

127

日本地方史志(續)LOCAL HISTORY AND GAZETTEERS (Cont.)

3431.1	新潟市	Niigata city
.2	長岡市	Nagaoka city
.3	高田市	Takaga city
.4	三條市	Sanjō city
.8	各郡	Districts
.9	各町村	Towns and Villages
3432	富山縣 越中國(越).	Toyama Prefecture Etchu [Echi].
.1	富山市	Toyama city
.2	高岡市	Takaoka city
.8	各郡	Districts
.9	各町村	Towns and Villages
3433	石川縣 能登國(能),加賀國(加).	Ishikawa Prefecture Noto [No], Kaga [Ka].
.1	金澤市	Kanazawa city
.8	各郡	Districts
.9	各町村	Towns and Villages
3434	福井縣 越前國(越),若狹國(若).	Fukui Prefecture Echizen [Echi], Wakasa [Jaku].
.1	福井市	Fukui city
.2	敦賀市	Tsuruga city
.8	各郡	Districts
.9	各町村	Towns and Villages
3435	岐阜縣 飛彈國(飛),美濃國(濃).	Gifu Prefecture Hida [Hi], Mino [Nō].
.1	岐阜市	Gifu city

日本地方史志(續)LOCAL HISTORY AND GAZETTEERS (Cont.)

3435.2	大垣市	Ōgaki city
.3	高山市	Takayama city
.8	各郡	Districts
.9	各町村	Towns and Villages
3436	長野縣 信濃國(信).	Nagano Prefecture Shinano [Shin].
.1	長野市	Nagano city
.2	松本市	Matsumoto city
.3	上田市	Ueda city
.4	岡谷市	Okatani city
.5	飯田市	Iida city
.8	各郡	Districts
.9	各町村	Towns and Villages
3437	山梨縣 甲斐國(甲).	Yamanashi Prefecture Kai [kō].
.1	甲府市	Kōfu city
.8	各郡	Districts
.9	各町村	Towns and Villages
3438	靜岡縣 伊豆國(豆),駿河國(駿),遠江國(遠).	Shizuoku Prefecture Izu [Zu], Suruga [Sun], Totomi [Yen].
.1	靜岡市	Shizuoku city
.2	濱松市	Hamamatsu city
.3	沼津市	Numazu city
.4	清水市	Shimizu city
.5	熱海市	Atami city
.8	各郡	Districts
.9	各町村	Towns and Villages

日本地方史志(續)LOCAL HISTORY AND GAZETTEERS (Cont.)

3439	愛知縣	Aichi Prefecture
	三河國(參),尾張國(尾).	Mikawa [San], Owari [Bi].
.1	名古屋市	Nagoya city
.2	豐橋市	Toyohashi city
.3	岡崎市	Okazaki city
.4	一宮市	Ichinomiya city
.5	瀨戶市	Seto city
.6	半田市	Handa city
.8	各郡	Districts
.9	各町村	Towns and Villages
3440	近畿地方	Kinki Region
3441	京都府	Kyōto Metropolitan Prefecture
	山城國(城),丹波國(丹),丹後國(丹).	Yamashiro [Jō], Tamba [Tan], Tango [Tan].
.1	京都市	Kyōto city
3442.1	福知山市	Fukuchiyama city
.8	各郡	Districts
.9	各町村	Towns and Villages
3443	大阪府	Osaka Metropolitan Prefecture
	攝津國(攝),河內國(河),和泉國(泉).	Settsu [setsu], Kawachi [Ka], Izumi [sen].
.1	大阪市	Osaka city
3444.1	堺市	Sakai city
.2	岸和田市	Kishiwada city
.3	布施市	Fuse city
.4	豐中市	Toyonaka city
.8	各郡	Districts
.9	各町村	Towns and Villages

日本地方史志(續)LOCAL HISTORY AND GAZETTEERS (Cont.)

3445	兵庫縣	Hyōgo Prefecture
	但馬國(丹),播磨國(播),淡路國(淡);參見丹波,攝津.	Tajima [Tan], Harima [Ban], Awaji [Tan]; see also Tamba, Settsu.
.1	神户市	Kōbe city
.2	姬路市	Himeri city
.3	尼崎市	Amagasaki city
.4	明石市	Akashi city
.5	西宫市	Nishinomiya city
.8	各郡	Districts
.9	各町村	Towns and Villages
3446	和歌山市	Wakayama Prefecture
	紀伊國 (紀).	Kii [Ki].
.1	和歌山市	Wakayama city
.2	新宫市	Shingū city
.3	海南市	Kainan city
.8	各郡	Districts
.9	各町村	Towns and Villages
3447	奈良縣	Nara Prefecture
	大和國 (和)	Yamato [Wa].
.1	奈良市	Nara city
.8	各郡	Districts
.9	各町村	Towns and Villages
3448	三重縣	Mie Prefecture
	伊賀國(伊),志摩國(志),伊勢國(勢);參見紀伊.	Iga [I], Shima [Shi[, Ise [Sei]; see also Kii.
.1	津市	Tsu city
.2	四日市	Yokkaichi city

日本地方史志 (續)LOCAL HISTORY AND GAZETTEERS (Cont.)

3448.3	宇治山田市	Ujiyamada city
.4	松阪市	Matsuzaka city
.5	桑名市	Kuwana city
.8	各郡	Districts
.9	各町村	Towns and Villages
3449	滋賀縣	Shiga Prefecture
	近江國 (江).	Ōmi [Gō].
.1	大津市	Ōtsu city
.2	彥根市	Hikone city
.8	各郡	Districts
.9	各町村	Towns and Villages
3450	中國四國地方	Chūgoku, Shikoku Region
	中國:	
3451	鳥取縣	Tottori Prefecture
	因幡國 (田),伯耆國 (伯).	Inaba [In], Hōki [Haku].
.1	鳥取市	Tottori city
.2	米子市	Yonago city
.8	各郡	Districts
.9	各町村	Towns and Villages
3452	島根縣	Shimane Prefecture
	出雲國 (雲),石見國 (石), 隱岐國 (隱)	Izumo [Un], Iwami [Seki], Oki [In]
.1	松江市	Matsue city
.8	各郡	Districts
.9	各町村	Towns and Villages
3453	山口縣	Yamaguchi Prefecture
	周防國 (防),長門國 (長).	Suō [Bō], Nagato [Chō].
.1	山口市	Yamaguchi city

日本地方史志(續)LOCAL HISTORY AND GAZETTEERS (Cont.)

3453.2	下關市	Shimonosiki city
.3	宇部市	Ube city
.4	萩市	Hagi city
.5	德山市	Tokuyama city
.6	防府市	Hōfu city
.8	各郡	Districts
.9	各町村	Towns and Villages
3454	廣島縣	Hiroshima Prefecture
	備後國(備),安藝國(藝).	Bingo [Bi], Aki [Gei].
.1	廣島市	Hiroshima city
.2	吳市	Kure city
.3	尾道市	Onomichi city
.4	福山市	Fukuyama city
.5	三原市	Mihara city
.8	各郡	Districts
.9	各町村	Towns and Villages
3455	岡山縣	Okayama Prefecture
	美作國(作),備前國(備),備中國(備).	Mimasaka [Saku], Bizen [Bi], Bitchū [Bi].
.1	岡山市	Okayama city
.2	倉敷市	Kurashiki city
.3	津山市	Tsuyama city
.8	各郡	Districts
.9	各町村	Towns and Villages
	四國地方:	
3456	香川縣	Kagawa Prefecture
	讚岐國(讚).	Sanuki [San].

日本地方史志(續) LOCAL HISTORY AND GAZETTEERS (Cont.)

3456.1	高松市	Takamatsu city
.2	丸龜市	Marugame city
.8	各郡	Districts
.9	各町村	Towns and Villages
3457	德島縣	Tokushima Prefecture
	阿波國(阿).	Awa [A].
.1	德島市	Tokushima city
.8	各郡	Districts
.9	各町村	Towns and Villages
3458	愛媛縣	Ehime Prefecture
	伊豫國(豫).	Iyo [Yo].
.1	松山市	Matsuyama city
.2	今治市	Imabari city
.3	宇和島市	Uwajima city
.4	八幡濱市	Yawatahama city
.5	新居濱市	Niihama city
.8	各郡	Districts
.9	各町村	Towns and Villages
3459	高知縣	Kōchi Prefecture
	土佐國(土).	Tosa [To].
.1	高知市	Kōchi city
.8	各郡	Districts
.9	各町村	Towns and Villages
3460	九州地方	Kyūshū (Seinan) Region
	西南地方,西海道.	
3461	福岡縣	Fukuoka Prefecture
	筑前國,筑後國(筑); 筑紫.	Chikuzen [Chiku], Chikugo [Chiku].

日本地方史志(續)LOCAL HISTORY AND GAZETTEERS (Cont.)

3461.1	福岡市	Fukuoka city
.2	久留米市	Kurume city
.3	門司市	Moji city
.4	小倉市	Kokura city
.5	若松市	Wakamatsu city
.6	大牟田市	Ōmuta city
.7	八幡市	Yawata city
.71	戶畑市	Tobata city
.72	直方市	Nōgata city
.73	飯塚市	Iizuka city
.8	各郡	Districts
.9	各町村	Towns and Villages
3462	佐賀縣	Saga Prefecture
	肥前國 (肥).	Hizen [Hi].
.1	佐賀市	Saga city
.2	唐津市	Karatsu city
.8	各郡	Districts
.9	各町村	Towns and Villages
3463	長崎縣	Nagasaki Prefecture
	壹岐國(壹),對馬國(對).	Iki [I], Tsushima [Tai]
.1	長崎市	Nagasaki city
.2	佐世保市	Sasebo city
.8	各郡	Districts
.9	各町村	Towns and Villages
3464	熊本縣	Kumamoto Prefecture
	肥後國 (肥).	

日本地方史志(續)LOCAL HISTORY AND GAZETTEERS (Cont.)

3464		Higo [Hi].
.1	熊本市	Kumamoto city
.8	各郡	Districts
.9	各町村	Towns and Villages
3465	大分縣	Ōita Prefecture
	豐前國,豐後國(豐).	Buzen [Hō], Bungo [Hō].
.1	大分市	Ōita city
.2	別府市	Beppu city
.3	中津市	Nakatsu city
.8	各郡	Districts
.9	各町村	Towns and Villages
3466	宮崎縣	Miyazaki Prefecture
	日向國(日).	Hyūga [Nichi].
.1	宮崎市	Miyazaki city
.2	都城市	Miyakonojō city
.3	延岡市	Nobeoka city
.8	各郡	Districts
.9	各町村	Towns and Villages
3467	鹿兒島縣	Kagoshima Prefecture
	薩摩國(薩),大隅國(隅).	Satsuma [Satsu], Ōsumi [Gū].
.1	鹿兒島市	Kagoshima city
.8	各郡	Districts
.9	各町村	Towns and Villages
3468	琉球	Liuchiu (Ryūkyū)
3468	沖繩縣	Okinama Prefecture
.1	那霸市	Naha city

日本地方史志(續)LOCAL HISTORY AND GAZETTEERS (Cont.)

3468.2	首里市	Shuri city
.8	各郡	Districts
.9	各町村	Towns and Villages
3469	北海道 蝦夷	Hokkaido (Ezo)
.1	石狩國	Ishikari Kuni
.11	札幌市	Sapporo city
.12	旭川市	Asahikawa city
.13	石狩支廳	Ishikari Shitei
.14	空知支廳	Sorachi Shitei
.15	上川支廳	Kamikawa Shitei
.19	各町村	Towns and Villages
.2	後志國	Shiribeshi Kuni
.21	小樽市	Otaru city
.22	後志支廳	Shiribesi Shitei
.24	各町村	Towns and Villages
.25	渡島國	Oshima Kuni
.26	函館市	Hakodate city
.27	檜山支廳	Hiyama Shitei
.28	渡島支廳	Oshima Shitei
.29	各町村	Towns and Villages
.3	膽振國	Iburi Kuni
.31	室蘭市	Muroran city
.32	膽振支廳	Iburi Shitei
.34	各町村	Towns and Villages
.35	日高國	Hidaka Kuni
.35	日高支廳	Hidaka Shitei
.39	各町村	Towns and Villages

日本地方史志(續)LOCAL HISTORY AND GAZETTEERS (Cont.)

3469.4	十勝國	Tokachi Kuni
.41	帶廣市	Obihiro city
.4	十勝支廳	Tokachi shitei SUB PREFECTURE
.49	各町村	Towns and Villages
.5	釧路國	Kushiro Kuni
.51	釧路市	Kushiro city
.5	釧路支廳	Kushiro shitei SUB PREFECTURE
.59	各町村	Towns and Villages
.6	根室國及千島國	Nemuro and Chishima Kuni
.6	根室支廳	Nemuro shitei SUB PREFECTURE
.69	各町村	Towns and Villages
.7	北見國	Kitami Kuni
.73	網走支廳	Abashiri shitei SUB PREFECTURE
.76	宗谷支廳	Sōya shitei SUB PREFECTURE
.79	各町村	Towns and Villages
.8	天鹽國	Teshio Kuni
.8	留萌支廳	Rumoe shitei SUB PREFECTURE
.89	各町村	Towns and Villages
.9	樺太(庫頁島)	Karafuto (Kuyehtao; Saghalien)
.93	各支廳	Shitei SUB PREFECTURE
.98	各郡	Districts
.99	各町村	Towns and Villages
3470	臺灣	TAIWAN (FORMOSA)
3471	臺北州	Taihoku (Taipei)
.1	臺北市	Taihoku (Taipei) city
.2	基隆市	Kirun (Chilung) city

日本地方史志(續) LOCAL HISTORY AND GAZETTEERS (Cont.)

臺北州(續)

3471.7	各郡	Districts
.8	各街庄	Towns and Villages
3472	新竹州	Sinchiku (Shinchu)
.1	新竹市	Sinchiku (Shinchu)
.7	各郡	Districts
.8	各街庄	Towns and Villages
3473	臺中州	Taichū (Taichung)
.1	臺中市	Taichū (Taichung) city
.2	彰化市	Shōka (Changhua) city
.7	各郡	Districts
.8	各街庄	Towns and Villages
3474	臺南州	Tainan
.1	臺南市	Tainan city
.2	嘉義市	Kagi (Chia yi) city
.7	各郡	Districts
.8	各街庄	Towns and Villages
3475	高雄州	Takao (Kaohsiung)
.1	高雄市	Takao (Kaohsiung) city
.2	屏東市	Heitō (Pingtung) city
.7	各郡	Districts
.8	各街庄	Towns and Villages
3476	臺東廳	Taitō (Taitung)
.7	各郡	Districts
.8	各街庄	Towns and Villages
3477	花蓮港廳	Karenkō (Hualienkang)
.7	各郡各支廳	Districts & SUB PREFECTURES
.8	各街庄各區	Towns and Villages

139

日本地方史志(續)LOCAL HISTORY AND GAZETTEERS (Cont.)

3478	澎湖廳	Bōko (P'êng hu; Pescadores)	
.8	各街庄	Towns and Villages	
3479	蕃地	Aboriginal districts	

3480-3489 朝鮮歷史 KOREA: HISTORY

3480	總錄 細分用表一.	GENERAL WORKS (Subdivide by Table I)	
3481	文化史	CULTURAL HISTORY	
3482	通史	GENERAL HISTORY	
	時代史	HISTORY BY PERIODS	
3483	古朝鮮時代	Ancient Period	-108 B.C.
	傳説時代	Legendary Period	2317-1122 B.C.
	箕子時代	Chitze (Kija) Dynasty	1122-194 B.C.
	衛滿時代	Wei-Man (Wiman) Dynasty	194-108 B.C.
3484	樂浪郡時代	Lo Lang Chun (Nang nang gun) Period	108 B.C.-313 A.D.
	滄海郡,樂浪郡,瑞屯郡,玄菟郡真蕃郡,辰韓,馬韓,弁韓.		
3485	三國時代	Three Kingdoms Period	313 A.D.-935 A.D.
.2	新羅 辰韓	Silla (Hsin lo, Shiragi), 57 B.C.-935 A.D.	
.5	高句麗	Koguryō (Kaokouli; Kōkuri), 37 B.C.-668 A.D.	
.8	百濟 馬韓	Paekche (Pochi; Kudara), 18 B.C.-663 A.D.	
3486	高麗時代	Koryo (Kaoli; Kōrai) Period	918-1392
3487	朝鮮時代	Choson (Chaohsien; Chōsen) Period	1392-1895
.9	韓國時代	Han'guk (Kankoku; Hankuo) Period	1896-1910
3488	日韓合併	Annexed by Japan	1910-

3490-3499 朝鮮地理 KOREA: GEOGRAPHY

3490	總錄	GENERAL WORKS

朝鮮地理 (續) KOREA: GEOGRAPHY (Cont.)

3491	京畿道	Kyŏngki to (Keiki tō, prefecture)
.1	京城府	Kyŏngsŏng pu (Keijō fu, Soeul, city)
.2	仁川府	Inch'ŏn pu (Jinsen fu, city)
.3	開城府	Kaesŏng pu (Kaijō fu, city)
.7	各郡	Districts (kun)
.8	各邑面	Towns and Villages (ŭp myŏn)
3492	忠清北道	Ch'ung-ch'ŏng puk to (Chūsei hoku tō)
.3	各郡	Districts (kun)
.4	各邑面	Towns and Villages (ŭp myŏn)
3492.5	忠清南道	Ch'ung-ch'ong nam to (Chūsei nan tō)
.7	各郡	Districts
.8	各邑面	Towns and Villages
3493	全羅北道	Chŏnra puk to (Zenrahoku tō)
.1	群山府	Kunsan pu (Kunsan fu)
.2	全州府	Chŏnchu pu (Zenshu fu)
.7	各郡	Districts
.8	各邑面	Towns and Villages
3494	全羅南道	Chŏnra nam to (Zenra nan tō)
.1	木浦府	Mokp'o pu (Moppo fu)
.2	光州府	Kwangchu pu (Kōshū fu)
.7	各郡	Districts
.8	各邑面	Towns and Villages
.9	濟州島	Chechu to (Saishū tō, Quelpart island)
3495	慶尚北道	Kyŏngsang puk to (Keishōhoku tō)
.1	大邱府	Taeku pu (Taikyū fu)
.3	各郡	Districts
.4	各邑面	Towns and Villages

朝鮮地理 (續) KOREA: GEOGRAPHY (Cont,)

3495.5	慶尚南道	Kyǒngsang nam to (Keishōnan tō)
.6	釜山府	Pusan pu (Husan fu)
.7	馬山府	Masan pu (Masan fu)
.8	各郡	Districts
.9	各邑面	Towns and Villages
3496	黄海道	Hwanghae to (Kōkai tō)
.7	各郡	Districts
.8	各邑面	Towns and Villages
3497	平安南道	P'yǒngan nam to (Heian nan tō)
.1	平壤府	P'yǒngyang pu (Heijō fu)
.2	鎮南浦府	Chinnamp'o pu (Chinnampo fu)
.3	各郡	Districts
.4	各邑面	Towns and Villages
.5	平安北道	P'yǒngan puk to (Heianhoku tō)
.6	新義州府	Sinnichu pu (Singishū fu)
.7	各郡	Districts
.8	各邑面	Towns and Villages
3498	江原道	Kang wǒn to (Kōgen tō)
.7	各郡	Districts
.8	各邑面	Towns and Villages
3499	咸鏡南道	Hamkyǒng nam to (Kankyō nan tō)
.1	元山府	Wǒnsan pu (Genzan fu)
.2	咸興府	Hamhǔng pu (Kankō fu)
.3	各郡	Districts
.4	各邑面	Towns and Villages

朝鮮地理(續)KOREA: GEOGRAPHY (Cont.)

3499.5	咸鏡北道	Hamkyŏng puk to (Kankyō-hoku tō)
.6	清津府	Ch'ŏngchin pu (Seisin fu)
.7	羅津府	Rachin pu (Rasin fu)
.8	各郡	Districts
.9	各邑面	Towns and Villages

3500-3599 亞洲其他各國 OTHER COUNTRIES IN ASIA

3500-3509	俄國(亞洲之部)	Russia in Asia (Siberia, Central Asia, Turkestan)
3500	西伯利亞,中央細亞,土國其斯坦. 歷史	History
3501-3509	地理	Geography
3510-3519	菲律賓	Philippine Islands
3510	歷史	History
3511-3519	地理	Geography
3520-3529	東印度羣島	East Indies Islands
3520	歷史	History
3521-3529	地理	Geography
3530-3539	馬來半島	Malay Peninsula
3530	歷史	History
3531-3539	地理	Geography
3540-3543	泰國 暹羅	Thailand (Siam)
3540	歷史	History
3542-3543	地理	Geography
3544-3546	越南	Indo-China
3544	歷史	History
3545-3546	地理	Geography

3547-3549	緬甸	Burma
3547	歷史	History
3548-3549	地理	Geography
3550-3559	印度	India
3550	歷史	History
3551-3559	地理	Geography
3560-3564	阿富汗	Afghanistan
3560	歷史	History
3561-3564	地理	Geography
3565-3566	俾路芝	Baluchistan
3565	歷史	History
3566	地理	Geography
3567-3568	尼泊爾	Nepal
3567	歷史	History
3568	地理	Geography
3570-3576	伊蘭 波斯	Iran (Persia)
3570	歷史	History
3571-3576	地理	Geography
3577-3578	伊拉克	Iraq (Mesopotamia)
3580-3589	阿剌伯	Arabia
3580	歷史	History
3581-3589	地理	Geography
3590	土耳其 (亞洲之部) 小亞細亞	Turkey in Asia.　Asia Minor
3590	歷史	History
3591-3599	地理	Geography

3600-3799 歐洲史地 EUROPE: HISTORY AND GEOGRAPHY

3601-3609	總志	General
3610-3619	土耳其 (歐洲之部)	Turkey in Europe
3620-3621	巴爾幹半島	Balkan Peninsula
3622-3626	保加利亞	Bulgaria
3627-3628	亞爾巴尼亞	Albania
3630-3634	希臘	Greece
3635-3639	羅馬尼亞	Rumania
3640-3649	俄國	Russia
3650-3659	波蘭	Poland
3660-3669	波羅的海各國 立陶宛, 拉脫維亞, 愛沙尼亞.	Baltic States: Lithuania, Latvia, Esthonia
3670-3679	斯堪地那維亞 芬蘭, 瑞典, 那威, 丹麥及冰島.	Scandinavian Countries: Finland, Sweden, Norway, Denmark (including Iceland)
3680-3685	捷克斯拉夫	Czechoslovakia
3686-3689	巨哥斯拉夫	Jugoslavia
3690-3695	匈牙利	Hungary
3696-3699	奧地利	Austria
3700-3719	德國	Germany
3720-3729	瑞士, 盧森堡	Switzerland. Luxembourg
3730-3735	荷蘭	Holland
3736-3739	比利時	Belgium
3740-3749	法國	France
3750-3759	意大利	Italy
3760-3769	西班牙	Spain
3770-3779	葡萄牙	Portugal
3780-3799	英國	Great Britain
3780-3789	歷史 分時代	History by periods

英國 (續)　　　GREAT BRITAIN (Cont.)

3790-3799	地理	Geography and Local History
3791-3794	英格蘭	England
3795	威爾斯	Wales
3796-3797	蘇格蘭	Scotland
3798-3799	愛爾蘭	Ireland

3800-3899　美洲史地　THE AMERICAS: HISTORY AND GEOGRAPH

3805	北美	NORTH AMERICA
3810-3829	坎拿大	CANADA
3810-3819	歷史	HISTORY BY PERIODS
3811	發現時代	Discovery
3812	法屬時代	French Regime, 1524-1763
3815	英屬時代	British Occupation, 1763-1867
3817-3819	自治時代	Dominion of Canada, 1867-
3820	地理	GEOGRAPHY AND LOCAL HISTORY
3821	英屬哥侖比亞	British Columbia
3822	西北諸省	Northwest Provinces
3823	東北諸省	Northeast Provinces
3824	安大略	Ontario
3825	魁卜克	Quebec
3826	新布隆瑞克	New Brunswick
3827	愛德華島	Prince Edward Island
3828	新蘇格的亞	Nova Scotia
3829	紐芬蘭 拉布剌達	Newfoundland. Labrador

3830-3849	美國	UNITED STATES OF AMERICA
3830	歷史	HISTORY BY PERIODS
3831	發現時代	Discovery (to 1607)
3832	殖民時代	Colonial (1607-1775)
3833	革命時代	Revolution (1775-1789)
3834	憲政時代	Constitutional (1789-1809)
3835	英美二次戰爭	War of 1812 (1809-1845)
3836	美墨戰爭	War with Mexico (1845-1861)
3837	内戰時代	Civil War (1861-1865)
3838	十九世紀末	Later 19th Century (1865-1901)
3839	二十世紀	20th Century (1901-　　)
3840	地理	GEOGRAPHY AND LOCAL HISTORY
3841	北大西洋諸州	North Atlantic States
3842	中大西洋諸州	Middle Atlantic States
3843	南大西洋諸州	South Atlantic States
3844	南密河諸州	South Mississippi States
3845	中密河諸州	Middle Mississippi States
3846	北密河諸州	North Mississippi States
3847	西部諸州	Western States
3848	北太平洋諸州	Pacific States (North)
3849	南太平洋諸州	Pacific States (South)
3850-3859	墨西哥	MEXICO
3860-3869	中美	CENTRAL AMERICA
3862	危地馬拉	Guatemala (State and city)
3863	英領洪都拉斯	British Honduras
3864	洪都拉斯	Honduras

3865	薩爾瓦多	Salvador
3866	尼加拉瓜	Nicaragua
3867	哥斯達黎加	Costa Rica
3868-3869	巴拿馬	Panama, Isthmus and Canal Zone
3870-3879	西印度羣島	WEST INDIES
3871	古巴	Cuba
3872	海地,多米尼加	Haiti, Dominican Republic
3874	波特黎各	Puerto Rico
3875	牙買加	Jamaica
3876	巴哈馬	Bahama Islands
3877	百慕大羣島	Bermuda Islands
3880-3889	南美	SOUTH AMERICA
3881	可倫比亞	Colombia
3882	委內瑞辣	Venezuela
3883	基阿那	The Guianas (British, Dutch and French)
3884	巴西	Brazil
3885	玻利維亞	Bolivia
3886	巴拉圭,烏拉圭	Paraguay, Uruguay
3887	阿根廷	Argentina
3888	智利	Chile
3889	秘魯,厄瓜多爾	Peru, Ecuador
3900-3999	非洲大洋洲及兩極史地	AFRICA, OCEANIA AND POLAR REGIONS
3910	北非	North Africa
3911	埃及	Egypt
3920	法屬及赤道非洲	French West and Equatorial Africa

3930	中非	Central Africa
3940	南非	South Africa
3950	澳大利亞	Australia
3960	新西蘭	New Zealand
3970	大洋洲, 夏威夷	Oceania. Hawaii
3980	南極	Antarctic Regions
3990	北極	Arctic Regions

4000-4999 社會科學類 SOCIAL SCIENCES

4000-4019	社會科學總論	SOCIAL SCIENCE IN GENERAL (Subdivide by Table I) 依體裁分,用表一.
4020-4099	統計學	STATISTICS (General only; special with subject) 一般統計入此,專科入各該科.
4020-4029	統計理論	GENERAL THEORY
4030-4099	各國統計	GENERAL STATISTICS OF SPECIAL COUNTRIES
4030-4039	中國	CHINA
4030.1-4030.9	全國	National
4031-4039	各省 用表二細分	Provincial (By Table II)
4040-4049	日本	JAPAN
4040.1-4040.9	全國	National
4041-4049	各地 用表二細分	Regional (By Table II)
4050-4059	亞洲其他各國	OTHER COUNTRIES IN ASIA
4050	俄國 亞洲部分	Russia in Asia
4051	菲律賓	Philippine Islands
4052	東印度羣島	East Indies Islands
4053	馬來半島	Malay Peninsula
4054	泰國 越南	Thailand (Siam) Indo-China
4055	印度 緬甸	India Burma
4056	阿富汗 俾路芝	Afghanistan Baluchistan
4057	伊蘭 伊拉克	Iran Iraq
4058	阿剌伯	Arabia
4059	小亞細亞	Asia Minor
4060-4079	歐洲各國 用表二.	EUROPE Table II
4080-4089	美洲各國 用表二.	AMERICAS ,, ,,
4090-4099	非洲 大洋洲 用表二.	AFRICA OCEANIA ,, ,,

4100-4299	社會學	SOCIOLOGY
4101-4109	總錄	GENERAL (Subdivide by Table I)
4110-4128	各論	SPECIAL TREATISES ON GENERAL SOCIOLOGY
4110	社會學學說	Sociological Theories
4120	社會心理學	Social Psychology
4125	公意	Public Opinion
4127	群眾及其他	Crowds, mobs, etc.
4129-4149	社會歷史及狀況	SOCIAL HISTORY, CONDITIONS AND INVESTIGATIONS
4129	總志	General
4130-4139	中國	China
4130	分時代	Subdivide by periods　Table III
4131-4139	分地方	Subdivide by Regions　Table II
4140-4148	日本	Japan
4140	分時代	Subdivide by Periods　Table III
4141-4148	分地方	Subdivide by Regions　Table II
4149	其他各國	Other Countries.　Divide like Table II
4150-4169	習俗	CUSTOMS AND MANNERS
4150	概論	General Treatises
4151	服制	Dresses.　Costume
4152	飲食吸煙及癖好	Eating, Drinking and Other Habits
4153	居住	Houses.　Dwellings
4155	生壽	Birth
4156	嫁娶	Marriage Customs
4157	喪葬	Treatment of the Dead
4158	祭祀	Offering Ceremonies
4159	賓讌	Banquets.　Parties
4160	節令	Festivals.　Holidays
4161	射御	Archery and Chariotry
4162	其他	Other Customs and Manners

151

4164	各業習俗	Customs Relating to Special Occupations
4165	士	Scholars
4166	農	Farmers
4167	工	Artisans
4168	商	Merchants
4169	其他	Other Classes
4170-4179	家庭與婦女	FAMILY AND WOMEN
4170	總錄	General
4172	兩性關係	Sex Relations
4174	婚姻	Marriage
4176	婦女	Women. Feminism
4180-4209	會社組織	SOCIAL ORGANIZATION
4181	祕密會社	Secret Societies
4182	各省市會館	Provincial Clubs
4184	宗教團體	Religious Societies
4185	種族團體	Racial Societies
4186	職業團體	Occupational Societies
4187	政治團體	Political and Patriotic Societies
4188	俱樂部	Special Clubs
4190	各種社會	Communities
4192	城市社會	Urban groups: The City
4196	鄉村社會 參見鄉村社會學(8075).	Rural groups: The Country (See also 8075)
4200	階級 附奴婢制度.	Classes and Slavery
4208	種族	Races as Social Groups
4210-4279	社會病象 救濟及改良	SOCIAL PATHOLOGY: PHILANTHROPY, CHARITIES AND CORRECTIONS
4210	慈善事業	Philanthropy (General)
4212	國家與慈善事業	State and Charities

社會病象 SOCIAL PATHOLOGY (Cont.)

救濟及改良（續）

4214	慈善事業組織	Charity Organization
4216	社會改良運動	Social Welfare
4220	保護及救濟	Protection, Assistance and Relief, etc.
4222	童孺	Children
4223	老弱	Aged
4224	青年	Young Men and Women
4225	殘廢	Defectives
4227	同業救濟	Persons of Special Occupations
4229	乞丐	Pauperism
4230	各種墮落	Degeneration, Intemperance, Drug Habits, etc.
4231	鴉片	Opium
4232	煙草	Tobacco
4233	娼妓 依地理細分 用表二.	Prostitution (Subdivide by Table II)
4240	犯罪學	Criminology
4260	刑罰學	Penology
4266	警察, 偵探	Police. Detectives
4270	監獄	Prisons. Punishment
4275	感化所	Reformatories
4280-4299	社會改造	SOCIAL RECONSTRUCTION: SOCIALISM, COMMUNISM, UTOPIAS AND ANARCHISM
4280	社會主義	Socialism
4290	共產主義	Communism
4295	烏托邦	Utopias
4296	無政府主義	Anarchism

4300-4599	經濟學	ECONOMICS
4301-4309	總錄 依體裁分;用表一.	GENERAL (Subdivide by Table I)
4310-4329	經濟理論及 思想史	ECONOMIC THEORY AND THOUGHT: ''SYSTEMS'', COMPENDS, HISTORIES, ETC.
4310-4319	通論 創作以著者年代分排; 思想史以討論時代分排.	General Treatises (Arrange original works by authors' dates and historical works by the periods discussed therein)
4311-4313	中國著述	Chinese Works
4311	上古	Ancient
4312	中古	Medieval
4313	近世	Modern
4313-4315	日本著述	Japanese Works
4314	明治以前	Pre-Meiji (　　-1868)
4315	明治以後	Post-Meiji (1868-Date)
4316-4319	西洋著述	Western Works
4316	不分時代	General
4317	亞當斯密以前	Before Adam Smith (to 1766)
4318	經典時代	Classical Period (1766-1876)
4319	現代	Modern Period (1876-Date)
4320-4339	專論	Special Topics
4321	價值論,物價論	Value and Price
4322	地租論	Land and Rent
4323	工資論	Labor and Wages
4324	資本論,利息論	Capital and Interest
4325	利潤論,收益論	Profit and Income
4326	財富論,資產論	Wealth and Property
4327	分配論	Distribution
4328	消費論	Consumption
4329	生產論	Production

經濟理論
專論(續)　Special Topics (Cont.)

4330-4339　人口論　Population Theory. Demography
人口研究入此.　(Monographs and Studies only. Statistics
人口統計入各國　of population go in 4020-4099)
統計.

4337　中國人口研究　Studies of Chinese Population

4338　日本人口研究　Studies of Japanese Population

4340-4379　經濟史地 ECONOMIC HISTORY, GEOGRAPHY AND CONDITIONS
及狀況
通論　General and Comparative

4341-4347　總錄　General (Form subdivisions. See Table I)
依體裁分. 用表一.

4348　經濟史　Economic History: General Treatises

4349　經濟地理　Economic Geography: General Treatises

4350-4379　分國　By Countries

4351-　中國　China

4351　經濟史地叢集　Collections: Economic History and Geography

4352　經濟史概論　Economic History: General Treatises

4353　上古至明　Earliest to Ming Dynasty (1644)

4354　清　Ch'ing Dynasty (1644-1912)

4355　民國　The Republic (1912-date)

4356　經濟地理概論 Economic Geography: General Treatises

4357　各省經濟地理 Economic Geography by Provinces (Divide
依表二細分.　by Table II)

4358　實業通志　Economic Surveys: General
凡論農工商,劳與運輸,金融及財政狀況者入此,專論殺法者入二實.

4359　各省實業志　Economic Surveys by Provinces (Divide by
依表二細分.　Table II)

4360-4369　日本　Japan

4361　經濟史地叢集　Collections: Economic History and Geography

4362　經濟史概論　Economic History: General Treatises

4363　上古至德川時代　Earliest to the end of Tokugawa
Period (　-1868)

4364　明治時代　Meiji Period (1868-1912)

4365　大正以後　Taishō to the Present (1912-date)

經濟史地及狀況
日本(續) Japan (Cont.)

4366	經濟地理概論	Economic Geography: General Treatises
4367	各地經濟地理	Economic Geography: Regional (Divide by Table II)
	依表二細分,但臺灣及朝鮮經濟地理入產業志後.	
4368	產業通志	Economic Surveys: General
4369	各地產業志	Economic Surveys: Regional (Divide by Table II)
	依表二細分.臺灣經濟地理及產業志,4369.8; 朝鮮,4369.9.	

4380-4419　土地與農業 LAND AND AGRICULTURE
農業經濟書歸在普　(See also 8020-8099. In a general library works
通圖書館宜入此;在　on agricultural economics are classified here.
農業圖書館宜入農業.　In an agricultural library it is better to place
them in 8020-8099)

4380-4389	通論	General and Comparative
4383	土地及農業經濟概論	General Treatises on Land and Agricultural Economics
4385	農業及土地制度通史	General History of Agriculture and Land Systems
4386	地產經營	Real Estate Business
4387	農業階級	Agricultural Classes
4388	租佃制度及政策	Land Tenure and Policy
4389	土地利用及耕種	Utilization and Culture of Special Classes of Land
4390-4419	分國	By Countries
4390-4399	中國	China
4392	法令	Law and Documents
4394	歷史及現狀	History and Description
4396	政策	Policy
4398	各地狀況	Local Conditions (Divide by Table II)
	依表二細分.	
4400-4409	日本	Japan
4402	法令	Law and Documents
4404	歷史及現狀	History and Description
4406	政策	Policy
4408	各地狀況	Local Conditions (Divide by Table II)
	依表二細分.	

4410-4419	其他各國 依表二細分.	Other Countries (See Table II)
4420-4449	工業	INDUSTRY
4420.1-.9	總錄 依體裁分,用表一.	GENERAL (Form subdivisions, see Table D
4422	工業制度	Industrial Systems: house industry, handicrafts, trades, factory system, etc.
4424	工業組織	Industrial organization: corporations, trusts, etc.
4426	政府與工業 工業政策.	State and Industry: industrial policy
4427	國有與市有工業	State and Municipal Industries
4431	中央工業報告	National Industrial Reports
4432	各地工業報告 依地理分,用表二.	Industrial Reports of Various Provinces (Subdivide by geographical Table II)
4434-4449	各種工業	SPECIAL INDUSTRIES

關於歷史及經濟方面著述 入此, 技術方面著述 入農業工藝類.
(Historical and economic treatises only. Technical go in 8280-8899)

4435	農產品工業	Agricultural Products
4438	礦業	Mineral Industries
4441	工程	Engineering
4443	製造品:化學類	Manufactures: Chemical
4444	五金類	Metal
4445	木材類	Lumber
4446	皮革類	Leather
4447	紙類	Paper
4448	紡織類	Textiles
4449	雜類	Miscellaneous
4450-4476	勞工	LABOR
4451-4459	總錄 依體裁分,用表一.	General (Form subdivisions, see Table D
4460-4476	專論	Special Topics
4460	歷史及現狀 依地理分,用表二.	History and Conditions (Subdivide by geographical Table II)

勞工(續) LABOR (Cont.)

4461	勞工制度	Labor Systems
4462	工資	Wages
4463	工作時間	Hours
4464	罷工	Strikes
4465	失業	Unemployment
4466	職業介紹	Employment Agencies and Ways of Employment
4467	女工童工	Woman and Child Labor
4468	勞工生活問題	Social Condition of Labor
4469	工人保險等	Workingmen's Insurance; Mutual Aid, etc.
4470	工人衛生	Labor Hygiene; Welfare Institutions
4471	勞工法令	Labor and the State: Law and Legislation
4474	行會工團	Guilds, Trade Unions, etc.
4475	糾紛及仲裁	Disputes and Arbitration

4477-4479	合作	COOPERATION
4477.1-.9	總錄 依體裁分, 用表一.	General (Subdivide by Table I)
4478	歷史及現狀	History and Conditions (Subdivide by Geographical Table II)
4479	各種合作社 關于各業之合作 分入其類例如農 業合作入農業.	Kinds of Cooperative Associations (Cooperation relating to other subjects are classified with those subjects, e.g. 8093 Cooperation in Agriculture)
.1	信用合作 參見金融.	Credit Cooperatives　　See also 4565-4576
.4	購買合作 參見家政.	Purchasing Cooperatives　　'' '' 8251
.5	消費合作 參見家政.	Consumer's Cooperatives　　'' '' 8251
.6	銷售合作 參見營業技術.	Marketing Cooperatives　　'' '' 4557
.7	生產合作 參見農家工藝.	Producers' Cooperatives　　'' '' 8093

4480-4529	運輸交通	TRANSPORTATION AND COMMUNICATION
4481-4486	總錄 依體裁分, 用表一.	General form subdivisions. See Table I.

運輸及交通(續) TRANSPORTATION (Cont.)

4487	指南, 年鑑	Shippers' Guides. Directories. Tables
4488	通史	History in General
4489	政策	Public Policy — General Treatises
4490	公路	Roads and Highways
4495	汽車運輸	Motor Transportation
4500	鐵路	Railways
4510	水運 海運, 運河, 等.	Water Transportation. Shipping
4515	空運	Air Transportation
4518	他種運輸	Other Means of Transportation
4520	郵政	Postal Service
4525	電報, 電話	Telegraph and Telephone
4529	他種交通	Other Means of Communication
4530-4549	商業貿易	COMMERCE TRADE
4530	期刊	Periodicals
	商會報告	Reports of Chambers of Commerce, etc.
4531	中國	China
4532	日本	Japan
4533	其他各國 照地理分, 用表二.	Other Countries. See Table II
4534	叢集	Collections: Pamphlets. Tracts, etc.
4535	書目	Bibliography
4536	字典指南	Dictionaries. Directories. Guides
4537	年鑑	Yearbooks and Almanacs
4539	概論	General Treatises and Compends
4540	商業政策	Commercial Policy
4541	商業史	Commercial History Better classified with 4340-4379
4542	商業地理 商業史地以併入經濟史地為宜.	Commercial Geography

商業貿易(續) COMMERCE (Cont.)

4543-4545	國內商業	Internal Trade (Domestic Commerce)
4543	中國	China
4544	日本	Japan
4545	其他各國 依地理分,用表二.	Other Countries (Subdivide by Table II)
4546-4549	國際貿易	International Trade
4546	統計及公牘	Statistics and Documents
4547	理論, 概說	Theory Treatises
4548	關稅政策及歷史	Tariff - Policy and History. See also 4594
4549	其他問題 例如津貼及補助.	Other Topics e.g. Subsidies and Bounties
4550-4559	營業技術	BUSINESS METHODS
4551.1-.9	總錄 依體裁分,用表一.	General (Subdivide by Table I)
4552	營業組織及管理	Business Organization and Administration
4553	公事房管理法	Office Economy
4554	商業算術	Business Arithmetic
4555	簿記會計	Bookkeeping. Accounting
4556	廣告	Advertising
4557	販賣銷售	Marketing. Salesmanship
4558	堆棧倉庫	Warehousing and Storage
4559	各項商業管理法	Special Lines of Business; Management, Method, etc.
4560-4579	金融	FINANCE
4560.1-.19	總錄 依體裁分,用表一.	General (Form subdivisions. See Table I)
4561	貨幣	Money
4562	物價	Prices and Price Indexes
4565	銀行	Banking
4569	信用	Credit
4570	國外匯兌	Foreign Exchange

金融(續)　　FINANCE (Cont.)

4572	公司財務	Corporation Finance. Stock Companies, etc.
4574	投資	Investments. Speculation, Stock Exchange, etc.
4576	保險	Insurance
4577	人壽保險	Life Insurance
4578	火災保險	Fire Insurance
4579	傷損保險	Casualty Insurance
4580-4599	財政	PUBLIC FINANCE
4580.1-.9	總錄 依體裁分, 用表一.	General (Subdivide by Table I)
4581-4589	各國財政	Finances of Different Countries
4581-4582	中國	China
4581	中央	National
4582	地方	Local (Subdivide by Geographical Table II)
4583-4584	日本 依地理分, 用表二.	Japan
4583	中央	National
4584	地方	Local (Subdivide by Geographical Table II)
4585	亞洲其他諸國 依地理分, 用表二.	Other Countries in Asia
4586-4589	其他各國 依地理分, 用表二.	Other Countries
4590-4599	財政專論	Special Topics
4590	財務行政及預算制度	Financial Administration and the Budget System
4591-4596	賦稅	Taxation
4591	丁役　田賦	Poll Tax　Land Tax
4592	鹽稅	Salt Tax
4593	酒榷　烟稅	Wine and Tobacco Taxes
4594	關稅	Customs
4595	釐金	Likin
4596	其他各稅	Other Taxes

財政 (續) PUBLIC FINANCE (Cont.)

4597	公債	Public Debt (Loans and Public Securities)
4598	官産官業及其收益	State Property, State Enterprises and Their Income
4599		

4600-4899	政法學	POLITICS AND LAW
4601-4607	總錄 依體裁分,用表一	GENERAL (Subdivide by Table I)
4608-4612	政法思想史	HISTORY OF POLITICAL AND LEGAL THOUGHT
4608	中國	China
4609	日本	Japan
4610	其他東方諸國	Other Oriental Countries (Subdivide by Table II)
4611	西洋 依地理分,用表二.	Western (Subdivide by Table II)
4612	世界	Universal and Comparative

4614-4629	政法哲學	POLITICAL AND LEGAL PHILOSOPHY
4614-4618	中國人專著	Treatises by Chinese Authors
4614	古代	Ancient Period (Earliest to 206 B.C.)
4615	漢至隋	Han Dynasty to Sui Dynasty (B.C. 206-618 A.D
4616	唐至明	T'ang Dynasty to Ming Dynasty (618-1644)
4617	清	Ch'ing Dynasty (1644-1912)
4618	民國	The Republic (1912-Date)
4622-4625	日本人專著	Treatises by Japanese Authors
4622	上古至室町時代	Ancient to the End of Muromachi Period (Earliest to 1603)
4623	德川時代	Tokugawa Period (1603-1868)
4624	明治時代	Meiji Period (1868-1912)
4625	現代	Contemporary (1912-Date)
4626-4628	西洋人專著	Treatises by Western Authors
4626	上古	Ancient
4627	中古	Medieval

政法學(續) POLITICS AND LAW (Cont.)

4628	近代	Modern
4629	現代	Contemporary
4630-4649	比較政府:中央	COMPARATIVE GOVERNMENT - CENTRAL
4630-4637	總錄 依體裁分, 用表一.	General (Subdivide by Table D
4638	政制史	History
4639	概論	General Treatises
4641-4643	各部制度	Special Branches of Government
4641	立法	Legislative
4642	行政	Executive
4643	司法	Judicial
4644-4648	其他制度	Special Topics
4644	公民	Citizenship
4645	選舉權	Suffrage
4646	選舉制度	Electoral System
4647	代議制度	Representation
4648	政黨	Political Parties
4650-4659	比較政府:地方	COMPARATIVE GOVERNMENT - STATE AND LOCAL
4650	總錄 依體裁分, 用表一.	General
4651	省政府	State or Provincial Government
4652-4659	地方及市政府	Local Government. Municipal Government
4653	法令	Charters. Laws
4654	組織及行政	Organization and Administration
4656	公共事業	Public Works, etc.
4660-4799	各國政府	GOVERNMENTS OF VARIOUS COUNTRIES
4660-4769	中國政府	THE CHINESE GOVERNMENT
4660.1-.9	總錄 依體裁分用表一.	General (By form division Table D

中國政府(續) THE CHINESE GOVERNMENT (Cont.)

4661.1-.9	詔令 依時代分	Edicts, Decrees, etc. (Subdivide chronologically
4662.1-.9	奏議公牘專集 依著者時代分.	Memorials and Official Papers of Individual Authors (Subdivide chronologically)
4664.1-.9	奏議公牘彙刊 依時代分.	Memorials and Official Papers: Collections (Subdivide chronologically)
4665-4669	貢舉考試	Selection and Examination Systems
4665	古代至五代	Earliest to the Five Dynasties (to 960)
4666	宋元	Sung and Yüan Dynasties (960-1368)
4667	明	Ming Dynasty (1368-1644)
4668	清	Ch'ing Dynasty (1644-1912)
4669	民國	The Republic (1912-)
4670-4674	吏治要覽	Manuals for Officials
4670	官規,政績,從政錄,等. 古代至五代	Earliest to the Five Dynasties (to 960)
4671	宋元	Sung and Yüan Dynasties (960-1368)
4672	明	Ming Dynasty (1368-1644)
4673	清	Ch'ing Dynasty (1644-1912)
4674	民國	The Republic (1912-)
4676-4680	儀注典禮	Rites and Ceremonies
4676	古代至五代	Earliest to the Five Dynasties (to 960)
4677	宋元	Sung and Yüan Dynasties (960-1368)
4678	明	Ming Dynasty (1368-1644)
4679	清	Ch'ing Dynasty (1644-1912)
4680	民國	The Republic (1912-)
4681-4688	政制通考	General Works on Political Institutions
4681	古部總論, 通代	On All Periods
4682	古代至隋	Earliest to Sui Dynasty (to 618)
4683	唐五代	T'ang and the Five Dynasties (618-960)

中國政府(續) THE CHINESE GOVERNMENT (Cont.)

4684	宋	Sung Dynasty (960-1279)
4685	元	Yüan Dynasty (1280-1368)
4686	明	Ming Dynasty (1368-1644)
4687	清	Ch'ing Dynasty (1644-1912)
4688	民國	The Republic (1912-)
4690-4735	中央各部制度	The Departments of the Central Government (Includes works on the history, organization, 凡論各部之沿革組 regulations and rules, decrees and proclama- 織章則法令政實者 tions, and anecdotes of each department under 入此. 各部下依朝代 which the arrangement is chronological. Works 排列. 總論歷代政府 on the Government of Each Dynasty should go with 者入政制通考. 4681-9, General Works on Political Institutions.)
4690-4693	元首	CHIEF OF THE STATE
4690	通論	General
4691	皇帝, 內務府, 宗人府	The Emperor, Imperial Household, Imperial Clan Court
4692	總統府	Office of the President
4693	國民政府	State Council of the National Government
.2	委員會 文官處	Civil Affairs Dept.
.3	參軍處	Military Affairs Dept.
.4	主計處	The Comptroller-General's Office
4694-4698	行政中樞	CENTRAL EXECUTIVE ORGANS
4695	內閣	Neiko (Grand Secretariat on Imperial Chancery)
4696	軍機處	Chün Chi Ch'u (Council of State or Grand Council)
4697	國務院	Kuo Wu Yüan (The Cabinet)
4698	行政院	Executive Yüan
4699.1-.9	各委員會	Different Special Commissions under the Execu- tive Yüan
4701-4702	禮教	RITES AND EDUCATION
4701	禮部	Board of Rites
4701.9	學部	Board of Learning
4702	教育部	Ministry of Education

中國政府(續)　　THE CHINESE GOVERNMENT (Cont.)

4703-4706	財政	FINANCE
4703	户部	Board of Revenue
.9	度支部	Board of Finance
4704	財政部	Ministry of Finance
4705	鹽務署	Salt Revenue Administration
4706	關務署	Customs Administration

4707-4710	工商農鑛	PUBLIC WORKS, AGRICULTURE, MINES, INDUSTRY AND COMMERCE
4707	工部	Board of Public Works
4707	商部	Board of Trade
4707	農工商部	Board of Agriculture, Industry and Commerce
4708	農商部	Ministry of Agriculture and Commerce
4709	農鑛部	Ministry of Agriculture and Mines
4709	工商部	Ministry of Industry and Commerce
4710	實業部經濟部	Ministry of Industries and of Economic Affairs

4711-4712	交通	COMMUNICATION AND TRANSPORT
4711	郵傳部	Board of Posts and Communications
	交通部	Ministry of Communications
4712	鐵道部	Ministry of Railways

4713-4714	内政	INTERNAL AFFAIRS
4713	民政部	Board of Civil Affairs
4713	内務部	Ministry of Interior
.8	中央防疫處	National Epidemic Prevention Bureau
4714	内政部	Ministry of Internal Affairs
.8	衛生署	Public Health Administration

4715	外交	FOREIGN AFFAIRS
	總理衙門	Tsung-li Yamen
	外務部	Board of Foreign Affairs
	外交部	Ministry of Foreign Affairs

中國政府(續)　THE CHINESE GOVERNMENT (Cont.)

4716	藩政僑務	DEPENDENCIES, OVERSEAS AFFAIRS
.1	理藩院	Board of Dependencies
.3	蒙藏院	Dep't. of Mongolian and Tibetan Affairs
.5	蒙藏委員會	Commission on Mongolia and Tibet
.9	僑務委員會	Commission on Overseas Chinese Affairs
4718-4721	國防	NATIONAL DEFENSE
4718	兵部	Board of War
4719	陸軍部	Ministry of Army
.6	海軍部	Ministry of Navy
4720	軍政部	Ministry of Military Affairs
.8	航空署	Department of Aviation
4721	參謀部	General Staff
	將軍府	Council of Generals
	軍事委員會	National Military Council
4722-4723	立法	LEGISLATIVE PROCESS
4722	資政院	National Assembly
	國會	The Parliament
4723	立法院	Legislative Yüan
4724-4725	司法	ADMINISTRATION OF JUSTICE
	法院判例及解釋見法典法規	(For Decisions and Interpretations of the Supreme and other Courts, see 4885-4886)
4724.8	刑部	Board of Punishments
	法部	Board of Justice
.9	司法部	Ministry of Justice
4725	司法院	Judicial Yüan
.2	司法行政部	Ministry of Judicial Administration
.4	最高法院	Supreme Court
.6	行政法院	Administrative Court

中國政府(續)　THE CHINESE GOVERNMENT (Cont.)

4726-4727	考試	CIVIL SERVICE EXAMINATION (For history of the examination system, see 4665-4668)
4726	吏部	Board of Civil Appointments
4727	考試院	Examination Yüan
.6	銓敘部	Ministry of Personnel
4728-4729	監察	CONTROL SYSTEM
4728	都察院	The Censorate
4729	監察院	Control Yüan
.8	審計部	Ministry of Audits
4730-4735	其他各部	OTHER DEPARTMENTS
4730		
4731	翰林院	The Hanlin Academy
4732	中央研究院	Academia Sinica
4733		
4734		
4735		
4737	政黨	POLITICAL PARTIES
4738.10-.99	國民黨	Kuomintang
.10-27	黨義	Principles
	孫文主義	Sun-Yat-senism
.10	全集	Complete Works
.11	選集	Selections
.12	解說	Secondary Works of Interpretations
	三民主義	Three-people Principles
.13	全書	Complete Works
.14	節選	Selections
.15	解說	Secondary Works of Interpretations

國民黨(續)KUOMINTANG　　　(Cont.)

4738.16	民族主義 Principle of Nationalism
.17	民權主義 Principle of Democracy
.18	民生主義 Principle of People's Livelihood
.19	建國方署 Plans for National Reconstruction
.20	建國大綱 Outline of National Reconstruction
.21	五權憲法 Five-power Constitution
.22	革命方署 Plans for Revolution
.23	其他政策及宣言 Other Policies and Declarations Announced by Dr. Sun
.24	講演集　Collection of Dr. Sun's Lectures
.25	函牘雜文 Dr. Sun's Letters and Miscellaneous Essays
.26	黨章　　Party Regulations
.27	政論　Party Platforms

4738.28-.32	史傳　HISTORY AND BIOGRAPHY
.28	全史　　General
.29	民元以前 Earliest to 1911
.30	民元以後 1912-present
.31	傳記　Biography (Divide by biographees) 依傳主姓名分
.32	史屑　Miscellaneous Historical Works
4738.33-.96	組織　ORGANIZATION
	全國　National - General
.33	黨內編著 Official Publications
.34	黨外編著 Unofficial Publications
	全國代表會議 National Convention
.35	黨內編著 Official Publications
.36	黨外編著 Unofficial Publications

國民黨(續)KUOMINTANG (Cont.)

中央執行委員會Central Executive Committee

4738.37	黨內編著	Official Publications
.38	黨外編著	Unofficial Publications

常務委員會Standing Committee of C.E.C.

.39	黨內編著	Official Publications
.40	黨外編著	Unofficial Publications

政治委員會Political Council

.41	黨內編著	Official Publications
.42	黨外編著	Unofficial Publications
.43	其他委員會Other Councils (Divide by names of councils) 依名稱排列.	

組織部 Organization Department

.44	黨內編著	Official Publications
.45	黨外編著	Unofficial Publications

宣傳部 Propaganda Department

.46	黨內編著	Official Publications
.47	黨外編著	Unofficial Publications

訓練部 Training Department

.48	黨內編著	Official Publications
.49	黨外編著	Unofficial Publications

青年部 Young People's Department

.50	黨內編著	Official Publications
.51	黨外編著	Unofficial Publications

婦女部Women's Department

.52	黨內編著	Official Publications
.53	黨外編著	Unofficial Publications

國民黨(續)KUOMINTANG (Cont.)

海外部　Overseas Department

4738.54	黨內編著	Official Publications
.55	黨外編著	Unofficial Publications
.56	其他各部	Other Departments
.57-.86	省黨部	Provincial Organizations (Divide by names of provinces)
	依省名分 省下再依 區名分	(Under each province, divide by the names of the districts)
.87-.99	特別黨部	Special Areas' Organizations (Divide by names of the areas)
.87	南京	Nanking
.88	上海	Shanghai
.89	廣州	Canton
.90	武漢	Wuhan
.91	北平天津	Peiping and Tientsin
.92	東三省	The Three Eastern Provinces
.93	香港	Hongkong
.94	其他國內地方	Others
.95	美洲	America
.96	歐洲	Europe
.97	日本	Japan
.98		
.99	其他	Others
4739	其他政治問題	OTHER PROBLEMS OF CHINESE GOVERNMENT
4740-4769	省市地方政府	CHINESE PROVINCIAL, LOCAL AND MUNICIPAL GOVERNMENTS
4740	省市地方政府總論	General treatises on provincial, local and municipal governments of more than one province

中國省市地方政府 CHINESE PROVINCIAL, LOCAL AND MUNICIPAL
(續) GOVERNMENTS (Cont.)

4741	省政府總論	General treatises on provincial governments of more than one province
4742	市政地方政府總論	General treatises on local and municipal governments of several provinces.
4743-4769	各省市或地方政府	Provincial, local and municipal governments of one province

各省之縣市政府
用該省號碼添小
數點再依王氏四角
號碼法加該縣市
名稱首二字之第一角
號碼. 例如河北
省為4745 天津
市則4745.13.

(For county (hsien) and municipal (shih) governments of each province, the province number should be followed by a decimal point and a number for the county or city. Such a number may be formed by taking the first corner each [using Wong's Four-corner System] of the two characters forming the name of the county or ci

4743	遼寧	Liaoning
4744	吉林	Kirin
4745	黑龍江	Heilungkiang
4746	河北	Hopei
4747	山東	Shantung
4748	河南	Honan
4749	山西	Shansi
4750	陝西	Shensi
4751	甘肅	Kansu
4752	四川	Szechuan
4753	西康	Hsikang
4754	湖北	Hupeh
4755	湖南	Hunan
4756	江西	Kiangsi
4757	安徽	Anhwei
4758	江蘇	Kiangsu

中國省市地方政府 CHINESE PROVINCIAL LOCAL AND MUNICIPAL
(續) GOVERNMENTS (Cont.)

4759	南京	Nanking
4760	浙江	Chekiang
4761	福建	Fukien
4762	廣東	Kwangtung
4763	廣西	Kwangsi
4764	雲南	Yunnan
4765	貴州	Kweichow
4766.1	熱河	Jehol
..2	綏遠	Suiyuan
.3	寧夏	Ninghsia
.4	察哈爾	Charhar
4767	外蒙古	Outer Mongolia
4768	新疆	Sinkiang (Chinese Turkestan)
.6	青海	Chinghai (Kokonor)
4769	西藏	Tibet

4770-4787	日本政府	THE JAPANESE GOVERNMENT
4771	總論	GENERAL TREATISES
4772	政治制度史	POLITICAL AND LEGAL INSTITUTIONS
.2	公家制度	Kuge (Court nobles) Institutions
.3	武家制度	Buke (Feudal barons) Institutions
.4	藩政	Administration of Clans
.5	憲政制度	Constitutional Institutions. See also 3380, 4890
	參見日本現代史及憲法.	
4773	儀制典例	CEREMONIES AND RITES
	有職故實入此.	
.1	讓位, 踐祚, 即位	Abdication, accession and coronation
	大嘗祭入神道.	For the great thanksgiving, see 1948.2

173

日本政府 THE JAPANESE GOVERNMENT (Cont.)
(續)

4773.2	行幸啟,御成	Imperial Visits
.3	元服,年賀	Majority Ceremonies
.4	立太子,立坊,立后,女御入内,御産	Selection of Crown Prince, Empress, etc.
.5	改元	Renaming of Era
.6	歲事,節會,拜賀	Rituals of the Year
.7	親王及將軍宣下,任大臣,除目,宣旨	Imperial Appointments
.8	供御,膳部,裝束,服色,調度,輿車	Imperial Wardrobe and Household Fixtures
.9	大喪,服忌,觸穢機	Imperial Funerals
4774-4785	中央政府	THE CENTRAL GOVERNMENT

各部之歷史,規程及官書之須集中一處者入此。其餘之書,即係政府機關出版,亦依内容,各歸其類。
Class here works on the history, regulation etc. of each department, and the official do ments of the various departments which sh be kept together as a group. However, wor relative to special subjects though issued b the departments, should go with those subje

4774.1	總錄	GENERAL
.2	官書叢集	Collection of Official Documents
.3	通論	General Treatises (Subdivide by dynasties like Table III)
	依時代細分,用表三.	
.8	職員錄	Civil Lists. Official Registers
4775	皇帝(天皇)	EMPEROR
.1	皇室	Imperial Family
.2	宮内省	Department of Imperial Household
.9	内大臣府	Office of the Privy Seal
4776.1	樞密顧問	PRIVY COUNSELLORS
.3	元老	Genro
.5	樞密院	Privy Council

日本政府 THE JAPANESE GOVERNMENT (Cont.)

4777	内閣	CABINET
4777.1	内務省	Department of Home Affairs
.2	文部省	Department of Education
.3	厚生省	Department of Welfare
.4	大藏省	Department of Finance
.5	農林省	Department of Agriculture and Forestry
.6	商工省	Department of Commerce and Industry
.7	遞信省	Department of Communications
.8	鐵道省	Department of Railways
.9	司法省	Department of Justice
4778.1	外務省	Department of Foreign Affairs
.2	拓務省	Department of Colonial Affairs
.5	大本營	IMPERIAL HEADQUARTERS
.52	侍從武官府	Office of Aide-de-camp
.54	元帥府	Board of Marshals and Fleet Admirals
.55	軍事參議院	Supreme War Council
.56	國防總部	Central Defense Headquarters
.58	參謀本部	General Staff Headquarters
.59	教育總監部	Military Education Department
.6	陸軍省	Department of War
.79	海軍軍令部	Naval General Staff Board
.8	海軍省	Department of Navy
4779	考試監察機關	EXAMINATION AND CONTROL ORGANS
.2	文官試驗委員會	Commission on Civil Service Examination
.5	行政裁判所	Court of Administrative Litigation
.8	會計檢查院	Board of Audit

日本政府 THE JAPANESE GOVERNMENT (Cont.)
(續)

4780	議會	IMPERIAL DIET
4781	貴族院	House of Peers
4782	眾議院	House of Representatives
4783	選舉制	Electoral System
4784	政黨	POLITICAL PARTIES
4785	地方政府	LOCAL GOVERNMENTS (GENERAL TREATISES)
.1	府縣郡制及其行政	Prefectural System
.2	府縣會	Prefectural Assemblies
.3	町村制及其行政	Town and Village System
.4	町村會	Town and Village Assemblies
.5	都市制及其行政	Municipal Governments
.6	都市會	Municipal Councils
4786	各地方政府 依地方分,用表二.	GOVERNMENTS OF PARTICULAR PREFECTS, CITIES AND TOWNS (Subdivide by geographical Table)
4787	屬地行政	ADMINISTRATION OF DEPENDENCIES
.1	朝鮮總督府	Chosen Government General
.2	臺灣總督府	Taiwan Government General
.3	樺太廳	Karafuto Administration
.4	南洋廳	South Sea Mandated Islands Administration
.5	關東廳	Kwantung Administration
4788-4789	其他亞洲各國政府 參見殖民地行政組織.	GOVERNMENTS OF OTHER ASIATIC COUNTRIES (See also 4804 Colonial Administration and Governments of Controlling European Countries)
4788.1	韓國	KOREA (Before 1910 only, After 1910, see 4787.1)
.2		
.3		
.4	泰國	THAILAND

其他亞洲各 GOVERNMENTS OF OTHER ASIATIC COUNTRIES (Cont.)
國政府(續)

4788.5		
.6		
.7		
.8	印度	INDIA (only independent native states)
.9		
4789.1	阿富汗	AFGANISTAN
.2	俾路芝	BALUCHISTAN
.3	伊蘭	IRAN
.4	伊拉克	IRAQ
.5	阿剌伯	ARABIA
.6		
.7		
.8		
.9		

4790-4799	西洋各國政府	THE GOVERNMENTS OF OTHER WESTERN COUNTRIES
4790	歐美政府	EUROPE AND AMERICA (GENERAL)
4791	英國及屬領	Great Britain and British Empire
4792	法國	France
4793	德國	Germany
4794	瑞士	Switzerland
4795	意大利	Italy
4796	俄國	Russia
4797	其他歐洲各國	Other European Countries
4798	美國	United States of America
4798.9	南美各國	Latin American Countries
4799	非洲及海洋洲各國 參見殖民地行政組織.	Other Countries in Africa and Oceania (See also 4804 Colonial Administration and governments of controlling countries)

4800-4859	國際政治及公法	INTERNATIONAL POLITICS AND LAW
4800.1-.19	總集 依體裁分，用表一.	GENERAL (Subdivide by forms like Table I)
4801-4809	殖民及移民	COLONIZATION AND IMMIGRATION
4801	移民論	Immigration
4802	殖民論	Colonization and Emigration
.1	中國僑務政策	Chinese Emigration Policies
.2	日本殖民政策	Japanese Colonization Policies
4803	殖民地種類	Forms and Classes of Colonies
.1	外人在華租界及特區	Foreign Concessions and Special Territories in China
.2		
.3		
.7	國聯委託管理區域	Mandated Territories
4804	殖民地行政組織	Colonial Organization and Administration
4805-4809	各國殖民移民狀況及管理	Conditions and Government of Colonists and Immigrants in Special Countries (Subdivide by country of settlement like Table II. A capital letter indicating the country of origin is to be added to the class number. e.g. 4808.4C, 4808.4J and 4808.4G are the numbers for the Chinese, Japanese and German immigrants in the U. S. A.)

依移入國，照表二分．華僑及日僑在各國者，于分類號碼後加C或J來表之，他國僑民類推．例如在美國之華僑，日僑，德僑，其號碼為4808.4C，4808.4J，4808.4G.

4805	亞洲	Asia
4806-4807	歐洲	Europe
4808	美洲	America
4809	非洲及大洋洲	Africa and Oceania
4811-4819	條約及公牘	TREATIES AND DOCUMENTS
4811	概論	General
4812-4813	中國	China
4812	彙集 依時代分，用表三.	Collections. By periods according to Table III

國際政治及 INTERNATIONAL POLITICS AND LAW (Cont.)
公法

4813	彙集 分國	By Countries
.1	俄國	Russia
.2	英國	England
.3	美國	United States
.4	法國	France
.5	日本	Japan
.6	德國	Germany
.7	意國	Italy
.8	其他	Minor Countries
4814-4815	日本	Japan
4814	彙集 依時代分用表三.	Collections. By periods according to Table III
4815	彙集 分國	By Countries
.1	俄國	Russia
.2	英國	England
.3	美國	United States
.4	法國	France
.5	中國	China
.6	德國	Germany
.7	意國	Italy
.8	其他	Minor Countries
.9	其他亞洲各國	Other Countries in Asia
4816-4819	歐美諸國 依地理分, 用表二.	Other Countries. See Table II
4820-4829	國際關係, 邦交	INTERNATIONAL RELATIONS. DIPLOMACY

凡汎論國際關係, 外
交政策, 外交問題者入
此; 叙述純粹事實者
入各國外交史.

(Only works on general international relations, diplomatic systems and policies are classed here. For factual accounts of relations between countries, see diplomatic history of the countries involved.)

國際關係 邦交 INTERNATIONAL RELATIONS. (Cont.)

4820.1-.9	總錄 依體裁分, 用表一.	General (Subdivide by forms like Table I)
4821	外交行政	Organization and Administration
4822	使節	The Diplomatic Service
4823	領事制度	Consuls, Consular Systems
4824	治外法權	Extraterritoriality
.1	在中國者	In China
4825-4829	各國外交政策及問題 依地理分, 用表二.	Diplomacy of Special Countries (Subdivide by geographical Table II)
4825	亞洲	Asia
.1	中國	China
.2	日本	Japan
4826-4827	歐洲	Europe
4828	美洲	America
4829	非洲及大洋洲	Africa and Oceania
4830-4839	國際政府	INTERNATIONAL GOVERNMENT
4830	國際仲裁	International Arbitration
4833	世界法庭	World Court
4835	國際會議	International Congresses
4836		
4837	國際聯盟	League of Nations
4839		
4840-4859	國際法	INTERNATIONAL LAW
4841-4842	通論 歷史, 原理, 及例案.	General Treatises (History, Theory and Cases)
4841	上古及中古	Ancient and Medieval
4842	近世	Modern (1500-date)

國際法 (續) INTERNATIONAL LAW (Cont.)

4843-4859	專論	Special Topics
4843	平時法	Law of Peace
4844	法人、國權	Persons. Rights
4845	訂約	Treaty Making
4846	陸海空領權	Jurisdiction, General: land, sea, air
4847	其他	Other Topics
4848	戰時法	Law of War
4849	交戰	Belligerency
4850	海上法	Maritime War: Prize law, right of search
4851	戰時物權	Property in War
4852	中立	Neutrality
4853	制裁方法	Measures Short of War
4854	其他	Other Special Topics
4855	國際私法	Private International Law
4856	國際民法	Civil Law (International)
4857	國際商法	Commercial Law (International)
4858	國際刑法	Criminal Law (International). Extradition
4859	國際訴訟法	Procedure in International Private Law

4860-4899	法律法學 LAW JURISPRUDENCE
4861-4869	總錄 依體裁分,用表一. GENERAL (Subdivide by form like Table D
4870-4880	法制史 法理學史 HISTORY OF LEGAL SYSTEMS AND OF JURISPRUDENCE

4870-4877	中國	China
4870	概論	General
4871	先秦	Earliest to Han Dynasty (206 B.C.)

法律法學(續)LAW JURISPRUDENCE (Cont.)

4872	漢至隋	Han Dynasty to Sui Dynasty (B.C. 206-618 A.D.)
4873	唐,五代	T'ang Dynasty and the Five Dynasties (618-960)
4874	宋元	Sung and Yüan Dynasties (960-1368)
4875	明	Ming Dynasty (1368-1644)
4876	清	Ch'ing Dynasty (1644-1912)
4877	民國	The Republic (1912-date)
4878	日本 依時代分,用表三.	Japan (Subdivide chronologically by Table III)
4879	亞洲其他諸國 依地理分,用表二.	Other Countries in Asia (Subdivide geographically by Table II)
4880	西洋諸國 依地理分,用表二.	Western Countries (Subdivide geographically by Table II)
4881-4889	法彙法典律例判釋	COLLECTIONS OF LAW, CODES, STATUTES AND CASES, DECISIONS AND INTERPRETATIONS
4881-4886	中國	China
4881	上古至隋	Earliest to Sui Dynasty (618 A.D.)
4882	唐及五代	T'ang Dynasty and the Five Dynasties (618-960)
4883	宋元	Sung and Yüan Dynasties (960-1368)
4884	明	Ming Dynasty (1368-1644)
4885	清	Ch'ing Dynasty (1644-1912)
4886	民國	The Republic (1912-date)
4886.01-.09	此處專列六法及判釋彙編,各部官規應入中央行政及地方政府. 立法院及最高法院 依時代分,用表三.	Central Legislative Yüan and the Supreme Court (Subdivide by periods like Table III)
4886.11-.39	各省法院 依省區分,用表二.	Provincial Courts (Subdivide geographically by Table II)
4887	日本	Japan
.1	上古至室町時代	Ancient to End of Muramachi Period (-1603)
.2	德川時代	Tokugawa Period (1603-1868)

法律法學(續) LAW. JURISPRUDENCE (Cont.)

4887.3	明治時代	Meiji Period (1868-1912)
.4	現代	Contemporary Period (1912-date)
.4	中央	Central
.41	地方	Local
4888	亞洲其他各國 依地理分, 用表二.	Other Countries in Asia (Subdivide geographi cally by Table II)
4889	西洋諸國 依地理分, 用表二.	Western Countries (Subdivide geographically by Table II)

4890-4899	法律各論	**LAW OF SPECIAL TOPICS**
4890	憲法	Constitutional Law
.1-.2	中國	China
.3-.4	日本	Japan
.5	亞洲其他各國 依地理分, 用表二.	Other Countries in Asia (Subdivide geo- graphically by Table II)
.6-.7	西洋諸國 依地理分, 用表二.	Western Countries (Subdivide geographi- cally by Table II)
4891	民法 中國及日本	Civil Law (Chinese and Japanese)
.1	總則	General principles
.2	債權	Obligation (Contracts, Agency, Damages, Sales, Bailments, Partnership, Suretyship)
.3	物權	Property Rights over things
.4	親屬	Consanguinity Family
.5	承繼	Inheritance and Succession
.8	其他	Others
.9	其他各國民法 依地理分, 用表二.	Civil Laws of Other Countries (Subdivide geographically by Table II)
4892	商法 中國及日本	Commercial Law (Chinese and Japanese)
.1	商人通例	General Regulation of Traders
.2	公司法 會社法.	Corporation Company

法律法學(續) LAW JURISPRUDENCE (Cont.)

4892.3	商行為法	Business Transaction
.4	票據法 手形法	Bills and Notes
.5	海商法	Maritime Commerce
.6	保險法	Insurance
.7	出版法	Copyright and Publication
.8	破產法	Bankruptcy
.9	銀行法	Banks and Banking
4893.1	商標法	Trade Mark
.2	商會法	Chambers of Commerce
.3	工廠法	Factory
.4	工會法	Trade Union
.8	其他	Others
.9	其他各國商法 依地理分,用表二.	Commercial Laws of Other Countries (Subdivide geographically by Table II)
4894	刑法 中國及日本	Criminal Law (Chinese and Japanese)
.1	犯罪學 或入社會學.	Criminology or class in 4240
.2	總則	General
.3	分則 罪.	Crimes and Offenses
.4	刑名	Punishments
.5	案例	Cases and Precedents
.6	刑罪學 或入社會學.	Penology or class in 4260
.7	特別犯人	Special Classes of Criminal Offenders
	少年	Juvenile
	婦女	Women
	精神病者	Mentally Defective
.9	其他各國刑律 依地理分,用表二.	Penal Codes of Other Countries (Subdivide geographically by Table II)

法律法學 (續) LAW JURISPRUDENCE (Cont.)

4896	法院組織法 裁判所構成法	Court Organization and Rules
4897	訴訟法 中國及日本	Trials and Procedure (Chinese and Japanese)
.1	通論	General
.2	陪審制度	Jury System
.3	律師 辯訴	Lawyers Pleading
.4	證據、證人	Evidence Witness
.5	民事訴訟法	Code of Civil Procedure
.6	刑事訴訟法	Code of Criminal Procedure
.7	和議	Arbitration
.8	其他	Others
.9	其他各國訴訟法 依地理分, 用表二.	Procedure Codes of Other Countries (Subdivide geographically by Table II)
4898	行政法 行政法通論入此; 各國 行政制度法規入各國政府.	Administrative Law (General treatises only; for administration laws of special countries, see governments of those countries 4660-4799)
4899	法醫學	Medical Jurisprudence

教育 EDUCATION

4900-4999	教育	EDUCATION
4900-4907	總錄 依體裁分, 用表一.	GENERAL (Subdivide by form like Table I)
4909-4916	歷史與現狀	HISTORY AND CONDITIONS
4909	概論 世界教育史.	General, Universal
4911-4912	中國	China
4911	全國 依時代分, 用表三.	National (Subdivide by periods like Table III)
4912	地方 依省區分, 用表二.	Local (Subdivide geographically by Table II)
4913 4914	日本	Japan
4913	全國 依時代分, 用表三.	National (Subdivide by periods like Table III)
4914	地方 依地理分, 用表二.	Local (Subdivide geographically by Table II)
4915	其他諸國	

185

教育 (續)　　EDUCATION (Cont.)

4916-4930	組織及行政	ORGANIZATION AND ADMINISTRATION
4916	概論	General Treatises
4917-4922	公報及統計	Official Publications and Statistics (Laws, Regulations, etc.)
4917-4918	中國	China
4917	中央	Central
4918	地方 依地理分,用表二.	Local (Subdivide geographically by Table II)
4919-4920	日本	Japan
4919	中央	Central
4920	地方 依地理分,用表二.	Local (Subdivide geographically by Table II)
4921	亞洲其他諸國 依地理分,用表二.	Other Countries in Asia (Subdivide geographically by Table II)
4922	西洋諸國 依地理分,用表二.	Western Countries (Subdivide geographically by Table II)
4923-4929	學制及行政機關	Educational Systems and Organs
4923	概論	Comparative and General
4924-4925	中國	China
4924	全國	National
4925	地方 依地理分,用表二.	Local (Subdivide geographically by Table II)
4926-4927	日本	Japan
4926	全國	National
4927	地方 依地理分,用表二.	Local (Subdivide geographically by Table II)
4928	亞洲其他諸國 依地理分,用表二.	Other Countries in Asia (Subdivide geographically by Table II)
4929	西洋其他諸國 依地理分,用表二.	Western Countries (Subdivide geographically by Table II)

教育(續)　　EDUCATION (Cont.)

4930	教育行政問題	Other Educational Administrative Problems
4930.1-.4	經費 參見財政.	Educational Finance. See also 4580 Public Finance
.1	概論	General
.2	中國	China
.3	日本	Japan
.4	其他各國 依地理分, 用表二.	Other Countries (Subdivide geographically by Table II)
4930.5-.8	視察	Inspection and Supervision
.5	概論	General
.6	中國	China
.7	日本	Japan
.8	其他各國 依地理分, 用表二.	Other Countries (Subdivide geographically by Table II)
.9	其他	Others
4931-4934	教育學說	EDUCATIONAL THEORIES
4931	概論	General
4932	中國教育學說	Chinese Educational Theories
4933	日本教育學說	Japanese Educational Theories
4934	西洋教育學說	Western Educational Theories
4935	各派教育學說	Different Types of Educational Philosophy
4936-4938	教育心理及統計	EDUCATIONAL PSYCHOLOGY AND STATISTICS
4936	教育心理	Educational Psychology
4937	教授法	Methods of Teaching
4938	教育統計及測驗	Educational Statistics and Measurement
4940-4954	管理與訓育	MANAGEMENT AND SUPERVISION
4940	通論學校管理與訓育者入此; 關於各級學校之管理與訓育者, 宜入各級學校. 概論	General

教育(續)　　EDUCATION (Cont.)

4941	組織及檔案	School Organization and Records
4942	財務	School Finance
4943	庶務	Business Management
4946	建築	Architecture
.1	校址	School Sites
.2	校舍	Buildings
.4	試驗室	Laboratories
.6	圖書館及博物館	Library and Museums
4945	設備	Equipment
4946	衛生	School Hygiene
4947	教員	Faculty
4948	入學手續	Admission
4949	課室管理	Classroom Management
4950	課程	Curriculum
4951	考試	Examinations
4952	記分	Marking
4953	訓導	Discipline
4954	學生生活	School Life
4955~4960	初等教育	ELEMENTARY EDUCATION
4955	總錄 依體裁分,用表一	General (Form subdivisions, see Table I)
4956	歷史及現狀	History and Conditions
4957	原理	Theory
4958	兒童研究	Child Study
4959	幼稚園及其管理	Kindergartens and Their Management
4960	小學及其管理	Elementary Schools and Their Management

教育(續)　　EDUCATION (Cont.)

4962-4965	中等教育	SECONDARY EDUCATION
4962	總錄 依體裁分, 用表一.	General (Form subdivisions, see Table I)
4963	歷史及現狀	History and Conditions
4964	管理及訓育	Management and Supervision
4965	其他	Other Topics
4966-4974	師範教育 師資訓練.	NORMAL SCHOOLS. TRAINING FOR TEACHERS
4966	總錄 依體裁分, 用表一.	General (Form subdivisions, see Table I)
4967	訓練	Training
4968	檢定	Qualifications. Examinations. Certificates
4969	聘任及委派	Appointment. Organization of Teaching Force
4970	地位及待遇	Professional Status and Compensation
4971	管理及訓育	Management and Supervision
4972-4974	各級師範學校	Kinds of Normal Schools
4975-4978	高等教育	HIGHER EDUCATION
4975	總錄 依體裁分, 用表一.	General (Form subdivisions like Table I)
4976	歷史及現狀	History and Conditions
4977	原理	Theory
4978	管理	Management
4980-4989	職業教育	VOCATIONAL AND PROFESSIONAL EDUCATION
4981	職業教與士大夫教育	Vocational vs Liberal
4982	職業指導	Vocational Guidance
4983	實業教育	Industrial Education
4984	商業教育	Commercial Education
4985	農業教育	Agricultural Education
4986	工程教育	Engineering Education

教育(續)　　　EDUCATION (Cont.)

4987	法政教育	Law and Politics
4988	醫學教育	Medical Education
4989	其他	Others
4991	特殊教育	SPECIAL FORMS OF EDUCATION
.1	德育	Moral Education
.2	宗教教育	Religious Education
.3	家庭教育	Home Education
.4	自修	Self Education
.5	教育推廣	Extension
	成人教育	Adult education
	夜校	Evening schools
	暑期學校	Vocational schools
	函授學校	Correspondence schools
.6	私家學校	Private Schools
	私塾家塾等	
.7	公民教育	Education for Citizenship
.8	民眾教育	Mass Education
4992	特種人教育	EDUCATION FOR SPECIAL CLASSES
.1	婦女	Women
.2	華僑	Overseas Chinese
.3	特別種族	Special Races
.4	特別階級	Special Social Classes
.5	孤兒教育	Orphans and Neglected
.6	殘廢教育	Defectives
.7	低能教育	Mentally Deficient
4993-4999	各院校刊物	INDIVIDUAL INSTITUTIONS AND THEIR PUBLICATIONS
4993-4997	中國	CHINA
4993-4996	舊時國學及書院志	Imperial Academies and Shu-yüan in former times

教育(續)　　　EDUCATION (Cont.)

各院校刊物(續)INDIVIDUAL INSTITUTIONS AND THEIR PUBLI-
CATIONS (Cont.)

4993	五代及以前	Earliest to the End of the Five Dynasties (-960)
4994	宋元	Sung and Yüan Dynasties (960-1368)
4995	明	Ming Dynasty (1368-1644)
4996	清	Ch'ing Dynasty (1644-1912)
4997	近代學校	Modern Colleges and Schools (1912-date) (Subdivide first by provinces like Table II and then arrange material by names of institutions)

校章及學生刊物等.
清末新式學校之刊物亦入此.
先照省區分,用表二,次按校名排.

4998	日本	JAPAN
.01-.09	分時代	By Periods use Table III
	用表三.	
.1-.9	分地	By Areas use Table II)
	用表二.	

各地學校刊物依校名排. (In each area arrange material by names of institutions)

4999	其他各國	OTHER COUNTRIES (Subdivide geographically by Table II)

依地理分,用表二.

5000-5999 語言文學類 LANGUAGE AND LITERATURE

5000-5039 語言學總論 LINGUISTICS IN GENERAL

語文學,言語學, 比較語言學. COMPARATIVE PHILOLOGY

5001-5009	總錄 依體裁分,用表一.	GENERAL (Form subdivisions like Table I)
5010	語言學概論	SCIENCE OF LANGUAGE: GENERAL WORKS
5012	語言生理學	PHYSIOLOGY OF SPEECH
5013	比較文法	COMPARATIVE GRAMMAR
5014	音韻學 . 聲韻學.	Phonólogy. Phonetics
5015	國際音標	International Phonetic Script
5017	文字形體學	Morphology. Orthography. Word-formation
5018	詞類之區分	Parts of Speech (Morphology and Syntax)
5025	造句法	Syntax. Arrangement of Words. Sentence
5027	語原學 字源學.	Etymology
5029	語義學 字義學.	Semantics
5030	字典辭書學	COMPARATIVE LEXICOGRAPHY
5032	繙譯法	ART OF TRANSLATION
5033	述記法	STENOGRAPHY. SHORTHAND
5034	方言學	DIALECTOLOGY
5035	人造語 國際語,世界語.	ARTIFICIAL LANGUAGE. ESPERANTO
5036-5039	世界各語系	LINGUISTIC GROUPS OF THE WORLD
5036	印度支那語系	Indo-Chinese Sino-Tibetan
5037	烏拉阿爾泰語系	Ural-Altaic Altaic
5038	印歐語系	Indo-European
5039	其他	Others
5040-5059	文學總論 比較文學.	LITERATURE IN GENERAL. COMPARATIVE LIT.
5041	期刊雜誌	Periodicals
5042	會社	Societies

	文學總論(續)	LITERATURE IN GENERAL (Cont.)
5043	叢書彙刊	Collections
5044	書目	Bibliography
5045	教學法	Teaching and Study
5046	字典,辭書	Dictionaries. Encyclopedias
5047	文學摘錦	Books of Quotations
5048	世界文學史	History of World Literature
5049	文學理論	Theories of Literature
5050	文學批評	Literary criticism
5051	修辭學	Rhetoric
5052	詩歌作法,詩韻	Poetic Art. Prosody
5053	戲曲作法	Technique of Dramatic Composition
5054	小説作法	Technique of Writing Fiction
5055	演説學	Oratory
5056	傳記作法	Technique of Writing Biography
5057		
5058		
5059		
5060-5199	中國語文字學	CHINESE PHILOLOGY. CHINESE LANGUAGE
5061-5069	總錄 作體裁分,用表	GENERAL (Subdivide by forms like Table I)
5070-5089	訓詁	SEMANTIC STUDIES
5071-5080	爾雅	Êrh-ya
5071-5079	白文注疏傳説圖解補修等 依作者時代分,用表三.	Texts, Commentaries, Treatises, Illustrations, Amendations, etc. (Subdivide chronologically by authors like Table III)
5080	專字解釋	Studies of Individual Characters
5081-5089	羣雅	Other Works similar to Êrh-ya
5081	小爾雅	Hsiao-êrh-ya

中國語設字學(續) CHINESE PHILOLOGY (Cont.)

5082	釋名	Shih-ming
5083	廣雅	Kuang-ya
5084-5089	其他	Others
5084	六朝至五代	Six Dynasties to Five Dynasties (265-960)
5085	宋	Sung Dynasty (960-1279)
5086	元	Yüan Dynasty (1280-1368)
5087	明	Ming Dynasty (1368-1644)
5088	清	Ch'ing Dynasty (1644-1912)
5089	民國	The Republic (1912-date)

專書傳注及專類書音義雖
係訓詁著作,但宜隨原書分入
各類,如經典釋文入經類,班
馬字類入史部,餘類推.

Vocabularies for particular books or special classes of books are better classified with those books or classes.

方言派之訓詁著述,入
方言類.

Yang Hsiung's Fang-yen and other similar works are to be classified in 5150-5159 Dialects

5090-5119	文字	GRAPHIC AND ETYMOLOGICAL STUDIES

參見中國考古學(古文
字學)及中國書法.

See also 2050-2125 Paleography (Chinese Archaeology)
6070-6189 Chinese Calligraphy

5090	說文以前字書	Works Prior to Shuo-wên

如史籀倉頡急就篇.

5091-5109	說文	Shuo-wên
5091	書目	Bibliography
5092	叢集	Collections
5093	大徐(鉉)本	Elder Hsü's Text and Commentary
5094	小徐(鍇)本	Younger Hsü's Text and Commentary
5095-5099	其他注釋	Other Commentaries (with text)
5095	唐五代	T'ang Dynasty and the Five Dynasties (618-960)
5096	宋元	Sung and Yüan Dynasties (960-1368)
5097	明	Ming Dynasty (1368-1644)
5098	清	Ch'ing Dynasty (1644-1912)

文字(續)　　GRAPHIC AND ETYMOLOGICAL STUDIES (Cont.)

5099	民國	The Republic (1912-date)
5100-5109	專題研究	Special Topics in Shuo-wên
5101	六書	The Six Groups of Scripts
5102	聲韻	Pronunciation of Characters
5103	引經	Characters used in the Classics
5104	古語	Ancient Words and Phrases
5105	古籀	Ancient Forms of Characters
5106	重文	Duplicate Characters in Variant Forms
5107	新補,新附,逸字	Added Characters that were Originally Missing
5108	部首	Radicals (Classifiers)
5109	其他 如索引等.	Others (e.g. Indexes)
5110-5119	説文後各書	Other Works Similar to Shuo-wên
5111	字林	Tzû-lin
5112	玉篇	Yü-p'ien
	其他	Others
5113	六朝至五代	Six Dynasties to Five Dynasties (265-960)
5114	宋 類篇.	Sung Dynasty (960-1279)
5115	元	Yüan Dynasty (1280-1368)
5116	明	Ming Dynasty (1369-1644)
5117	清	Ch'ing Dynasty (1644-1912)
5118	民國	The Republic (1912-date)
5120-5139	音韻	PHONOLOGICAL STUDIES
5120	通論	General Treatises
5121	古音 上古至漢末.	Archaic Pronunciation (Earliest to cir. 265)
5123-5125	今音	Ancient Pronunciation (265-1279)

音韻(續)　　　PHONOLOGICAL STUDIES (Cont.)

5123	晉至隋 聲類切韻.	Chin Dynasty to Sui Dynasty (265-618)
5124	唐五代 唐韻.	T'ang Dynasty and the Five Dynasties (618-960)
5125	宋 廣韻.	Sung Dynasty (960-1279)
5126-5129	國音 現代音.	Modern Pronunciation
5126	元 中原音韻.	Yüan Dynasty (1280-1368)
5127	明	Ming Dynasty (1368-1644)
5128	清	Ch'ing Dynasty (1644-1912)
5129	民國	The Republic (1912-date)
5130-5139	音韻專著	Special Topics in Phonology
5131		
5132	聲調	The System of Tones
5133	反切	Method of Indicating Pronunciation of a Character by two other Characters giving the Initial and Final of the Desired Character
5134		
5135		
5136	注音符號	National Phonetic Script
5137	羅馬字拼音法	Romanization Systems
5140-5149	文法	GRAMMAR
5140	通論	General Treatises
5143	虛字	Particles
5146	章句	Sentence Construction
5147	標點符號	Punctuation
5150-5159	方言	DIALECTS
5151	揚雄方言	Yang Hsiung's Study of Ancient Dialects
5152		
5153		

方言(續)　　DIALECTS (Cont.)

5154	國語宣話.	National Language; Mandarin
5155	吳語	Wu Dialects
5156	閩語	Min Dialects
5157	粵語	Yüeh Dialects
5158	其他	Other Dialects

5160-5162　蒙求教本 INSTRUCTION BOOKS

| 5161 | 前代學語教本 | Early Works |
| 5162 | 現代學語教本 | Modern Works |

5163-5169　其他文字問題 OTHER PROBLEMS OF CHINESE LANGUAGE

5163

5164	基本字彙	Basic Chinese
5165	簡字,俗字	Simplified and Colloquial Forms of Characters
5167	檢字法	Methods of Arranging Characters
5169	速記法	Chinese Short-hand Systems

5170-5179　字典辭書 LEXICOGRAPHY DICTIONARIES

就廣義言訓詁古類之爾雅,文字類之說文,及音韻類之廣韻等,皆係字典,此處所列者,乃現代體式之辭書耳. In a wide sense all the works in the previous three groups, namely, Semantic Studies, Graphic Studies, and Phonological Studies, are dictionaries. Here are classed works that are the immediate fore-runners of modern dictionaries.

5172-5174　依部首編排者 Those Arranged According to Radical System

5172	明代編撰字彙,正字通.	Works Compiled in Ming Dynasty
5173	康熙字典	K'ang-hsi Dictionary
5174	康熙以後編撰	Works after K'ang-hsi Dictionary
5175	依音韻編排者	Those Arranged According to Rhyme or Phonetic System
5176	依號碼編排者	Those Arranged According to Numeral System
5178	依字義編排者分類者.	Those Arranged According to Classified Categories
5179	特殊字典	Other Special Dictionaries

5185-5199	對譯字典	CHINESE-FOREIGN LANGUAGES DICTIONARIES
5187	中日字典	Chinese-Japanese Dictionaries
5188	漢滿字典	Chinese-Manchu ,,
5189	漢蒙字典	Chinese-Mongolian ,,
5190	漢暹字典	Chinese-Siamese ,,
5191	漢藏字典	Chinese-Tibetan ,,
5192	漢梵字典	Chinese-Sanskrit ,,
5193	中文希臘文字典	Chinese-Greek ,,
5194	中文拉丁文字典	Chinese-Latin ,,
5195	中法字典	Chinese-French ,,
5196	中英字典	Chinese-English ,,
5197	中德字典	Chinese-German ,,
5198	中俄字典	Chinese-Russian ,,
5199	其他	Others
5200-5799	中國文學	CHINESE LITERATURE
5201-5211	總錄	GENERAL
5202	期刊	Periodicals
5204	會社	Societies
5206	年刊	Year-Books
5208	書目	Bibliographies
5209	辭書,事彙	Dictionaries and Encyclopaedias
5210-5211	教學法 附修詞學.	Teaching and Studying (Includes works on Rhetoric)
5212-5217	詩文評	LITERARY CRITICISM
5212	通評	General Treatises
5213	詩話 (通代) 附詩律.	Critique on Poetry -- of all Periods (Includes works on Prosody)

中國文學(續)CHINESE LITERATURE (Cont.)

5214	詩話（斷代）依時代排,用表三.	Critique on Poetry -- of particular Periods (Subdivide by periods like Table III)
5215	賦話	Critique on Fu
5216	散文評	Critique on General Prose
5217	騈文評	Critique on Prose of Paired Sentences
5218-5229	文學史傳	HISTORY AND BIOGRAPHY
5218	文學家合傳(通代)	General Collective Biography of All Periods
5219	文學家合傳(斷代)依時代細分,用表三.	General Collective Biography of Particular Periods (Subdivide by Periods like Table III
5220	文學史（通代）	General History of Chinese Literature
5221-5229	文學史（斷代）依時代分,用表三.	History of Special Periods (Subdivide by Periods like Table III
5235.1-.9	專集彙刊 彙刊諸家別集者入此. 依時代分,用表三.	COLLECTIONS OF INDIVIDUAL COMPLETE WORKS (TS'UNG-SHU)
5236-5241	總集 如所選者為某一代文作品,先加該時代號碼,再加選輯者時代號碼,不限時代之總集,則先須加°O,,再加選輯者時代號碼. 用表三.	GENERAL ANTHOLOGY
5236	諸體總集	Anthology of Literary Selections of All Forms
5237	詩總集	Anthology of Poetry (Subdivide by periods like Table III)
5238	文總集	Anthology of Prose (Subdivide by periods like Table III)
5239	騈文總集	Anthology of Prose of Paired Sentences
5240	賦總集 楚辭,古賦,律賦.	Anthology of Fu or Descriptive Prose-Poems (Includes Elegies of Ch'u, ancient odes)
5241	地方總集 依地域分,用表二. 不分體裁	LOCAL LITERARY COLLECTIONS (Divide by geographical Table II)
5242-5569	別集 專刊個人詩文彙刊 及諸體合集不能折 散者.每人下依表庚 排列.	COLLECTED LITERARY WORKS OF INDIVIDUAL AUTHORS (Mainly Poetry and Prose, but collections that cannot be broken should be classed here. The works for each author may be arranged according to Table G)
5242-5243	周秦	Chou and Ch'in Dynasties (1122-206 B.C.)
5242	屈平	Ch'ü P'ing (B.C. 343-290 ?)
5243	宋玉	Sung Yü (B.C. 290-222 ?)

別集(續) COLLECTED LITERARY WORKS, etc. (Cont.)

5244-5256	漢三國	Han Dynasty and the Three Kingdoms B.C. 206-265 A.D.
5244	枚乘	Mei Ch'êng (B.C. ? -140 ?)
5245	其他同時作者	Other Contemporary Writers
5246	賈誼	Chia I (B.C. 200-168)
5247	司馬相如	Ssu-ma Hsiang-ju (? - B.C. 118)
5248	其他同時作者	Other Contemporary Writers (B.C. 140-24 A.D.)
5249	揚雄	Yang Hsiung (B.C. 53-18 A.D.)
5250	其他同時作者	Other Contemporary Writers (25-75 A.D.)
5251		Other Contemporary Writers (76-146 A.D.)
5252	蔡邕	Ts'ai Yung (133-192 A.D.)
5253	其他同時作者	Other Contemporary Writers (147-189 A.D.)
5254	曹植	Ts'ao Chih (192-232)
5255	稽康	Chi K'ang (223-262)
5256	其他三國時作者	Other Writers of the Three Kingdoms (189-265 A.D.)
5257-5264	晉	Chin Dynasty (265-420)
5257	太康期間作者	Writers floruit during the period of 265-290
5258	陸機	Lu Chi (261-303)
5259	陸雲	Lu Yün (262-303)
5260	潘岳	P'an Yo (? -300)
5261	左思	Tso Ssu (? -306)
5262	其他西晉作者	Other Contemporary Writers
5263	陶潛	T'ao Ch'ien (365-427)
5264	其他東晉作者	Other Contemporary Writers

	別集 (續)	COLLECTED LITERARY WORKS, etc. (Cont.)
5265-5279	南北朝	Northern and Southern Dynasties (420-589)
5266	謝靈運	Hsieh Ling-yün (385-433)
5267	顏延之	Yen Yen-chih (384-456)
5268	鮑照	Pao Chao (421?-465?)
5269	其他宋代作者	Other Sung Dynasty Writers (420-479)
5270	謝朓	Hsieh T'iao (464?-499?)
5271	其他齊代作者	Other Chi Dynasty Writers (479-502)
5272	江淹	Chiang Yen (444-505)
5273	沈約	Shên Yo (441-513)
5274	蕭統	Hsiao T'ung (501-531)
5275	其他梁代作者	Other Liang Dynasty Writers (502-557)
5276	徐陵	Hsü Ling (507-583)
5277	其他陳代作者	Other Ch'ên Dynasty Writers (557-589)
5278	北朝作者	Northern Dynasty Writers (386-581)
5279	庾信	Yü Hsin (513-581)
5280-5283	隋	Sui Dynasty (589-618)
5281	楊廣	Yang Kuang (Emperor, Yang Ti, 569-618)
5283	其他隋代作者	Other Sui Dynasty Writers
5284-5326	唐	T'ang Dynasty (618-907)
5285	魏徵	Wei Ch'êng (580-463)
5286	王勃	Wang Po (648-675)
5287	楊烱	Yang Ch'iung (? - 692)
5288	盧照鄰	Lu Chao-lin (641?-680?)
5289	駱賓王	Lo Pin-wang (? -684)
5290	陳子昂	Ch'ên Tzû-ang (656?-698?)
5291	沈佺期	Shen Ch'üan-ch'i (675 chin-shih)

別集(續)　　　　COLLECTED LITERARY WORKS, etc. (Cont.)

5291.9	宋之間	Sung Chi-wên (? - 713?)
5292	其他初唐作者	Other Writers floruit in the period of (618-712)
5293	張說	Chang Yüeh (667-730)
5294	蘇頲	Su T'ing (669-727)
5295	張九齡	Chang Chiu-ling (673-740)
5296	孟浩然	Mêng Hao-jan (689-740)
5297	王維	Wang Wei (699-759)
5298	李白	Li Po (701-762)
5299	杜甫	Tu Fu (712-770)
5300	高適	Kao Shih (? - 765)
5301	王昌齡	Wang Ch'ang-ling (? - 756?)
5302	岑參	Ts'ên Ts'an (744 chin-shih)
5303	其他盛唐作者	Other writers floruit in the period of (713-766)
5304	韋應物	Wei Ying-wu (737?-829?)
5305	劉長卿	Liu Ch'ang-Ch'ing (733 chin-shih)
5306	顏真卿	Yen Chên-ch'ing (709-784)
5306.9	錢起及其他 大歷十才子	Ch'ien Ch'i (751 chin-shih) and his nine literary friends
5307	陸贄	Lu Chih (754-805)
5308	韓愈	Han Yü (768-824)
5309	柳宗元	Liu Tsung-yüan (773-819)
5310	張籍	Chang Chi (765? - 830?)
5311	孟郊	Mêng Chiao (751-814)
5312	李賀	Li Ho (790-816)
5312.9	賈島	Chia Tao (788-843)
5313	劉禹錫	Liu Yü-hsi (772-842)

	別集(續)	COLLECTED LITERARY WORKS, etc. (Cont.)
5314	白居易	Po Chü-i (772-846)
5315	元稹	Yüan Chên (779-831)
5316	其他中唐作者	Other Writers floruit in the period of (766-835)
5317	杜牧	Tu Mu (803-852)
5318	李商隱	Li Shang-yin (813-858)
5319	温庭筠	Wên T'ing-chün (? - 880?)
5320	陸龜蒙	Lu Kuei-mêng (? - 881?)
5321	皮日休	Pi Jih-hsiu (867 chin-shih)
5322	韓偓	Han Wu (889 chin-shih)
5323	其他同時作者	Other Contemporary Writers
5324	羅隱	Lo Yin (833-909)
5325	司空圖	Ssŭ-k'ung T'u (837-908)
5326	杜荀鶴	Tu Hsün-hao (846-904)
5327	其他晚唐作者	Other Writers floruit in the period of (836-907)
5328-5330	五代	Five Short Dynasties (907-960)
5328	韋莊	Wei Chuang (cir. 855-920)
5329	杜光庭	Tu Kuang-t'ing (850-933)
5330	其他五代作者	Other Contemporary Writers
5331-5369	宋	Sung Dynasty (960-1279)
5331	徐鉉	Hsü Hsüan (916-991)
5332	楊億	Yang I (947-1020)
5333	柳開	Liu K'ai (948-1001)
5334	王禹偁	Wang Yü-ch'êng (954-1001)
5335	穆修	Mu Hsiu (979-1032)
5336	寇準	K'ou Chun (961-1045)
5336.9	石介	Shih Chieh (1005-1045)

別集 (續)   COLLECTED LITERARY WORKS, etc. (Cont.)

5337	梅堯臣	Mei Yao-ch'ên (1002-1060)
5338	歐陽修	Ou-Yang Hsiu (1007-1072)
5338.9	蘇舜欽	Su Shun-ch'in (1008-1048)
5339	蘇洵	Su Hsün (1009-1066)
5340	邵雍	Shao Yung (1011-1077)
5341	司馬光	Ssû-ma Kuang (1019-1086)
5342	曾鞏	Tsêng Kung (1019-1083)
5343	王安石	Wang An-shih (1021-1086)
5344	其他同時作者	Other Contemporary Writers
5345	蘇軾	Su Shih (1036-1101)
5346	蘇轍	Su Ch'ê (1039-1112)
5347	黃庭堅	Huang T'ing-chien (1045-1110)
5348	秦觀	Ch'in Kuan (1049-1101)
5349	陳師道	Ch'ên Shih-tao (1053-1101)
5350	其他北宋作者	Other Writers of the Northern Sung Dynasty (960-1127)
5350.9	葉夢得	Yeh Mêng-tê (1077-1148)
5351	陳與義	Ch'ên Yü-i (1090-1138)
5352	王十朋	Wang Shih-p'êng (1112-1171)
5353	楊萬里	Yang Wan-li (1124-1206)
5354	陸游	Lu Yu (1125-1210)
5355	范成大	Fan Ch'êng-ta (1126-1193)
5356	朱熹	Chu Hsi (1130-1200)
5356.9	呂祖謙	Lü Tsu-ch'ien (1137-1181)
5357	陸九淵	Lu Chiu-yüan (1139-1192)
5358	其他同時作者	Other Contemporary Writers
5358.9	陳亮	Ch'ên Liang (1143-1190)

	別集 (續)	COLLECTED LITERARY WORKS, etc. (Cont.)
5359	葉適	Yeh Shih (1150-1223)
5359.9	徐照及永嘉四靈	Hsü Chao (? -1211) and his three literary friends
5360	真德秀	Chên Tê-hsiu (1178-1235)
5361	魏了翁	Wei Liao-wêng (1178-1237)
5362	其他同時作者	Other Contemporary Writers
5363	劉克莊	Liu K'o-chuang (1178-1269)
5364	其他同時作者	Other Contemporary Writers
5365	文天祥	Wên T'ien-hsiang (1236-1282)
5367	其他同時作者	Other Contemporary Writers
5368	謝枋得	Hsieh Fang-tê (1226-1289)
5370-5379	遼金	Liao (916-1201) and Chin (1115-1234) Kingdoms
5371	王若虛	Wang Jo-hsü (1174-1243)
5372	元好問	Yüan Hao-wên (1190-1257)
5376	其他同時作者	Other Contemporary Writers
5380-5399	元	Yüan Dynasty (1280-1368)
5381	元初作者	Writers at the beginning of Yüan Dynasty
5382	許衡	Hsü Hêng (1209-1281)
5383	戴表元	Tai Piao-yüan (1244-1310)
5384	吳澄	Wu Ch'êng (1249-1331)
5385	其他同時作者	Other Contemporary Writers
5386	趙孟頫	Chao Mêng-fu (1254-1322)
5387	袁桷	Yüan Chüeh (1267-1327)
5388	柳貫	Liu Kuan (1270-1342)
5389	楊載	Yang Tsai (1271-1323)
5390	虞集	Yü Chi (1272-1348)

		別集(續)	COLLECTED LITERARY WORKS, etc. (Cont.)
5391		范梈	Fan P'êng (1272-1330)
5392		揭奚斯	Chieh-hsi-ssû (1274-1344)
5393		其他同時作者	Other Contemporary Writers
5394		黃溍	Huang Chin (1277-1357)
5395		其他同時作者	Other Contemporary Writers
5396		吳萊	Wu Lai (1292-1340)
5397		楊維楨	Yang Wei-chên (1296-1370)
5398		戴良	Tai Liang (1317-1383)
5399		其他同時作者	Other Contemporary Writers
5400-5429	明		Ming Dynasty (1368-1644)
5401		明初作者	Writers between Yüan and Ming Dynast
5402		宋濂	Sung Lien (1310-1381)
5403		劉基	Liu Chi (1311-1375)
5404		高啟	Kao Ch'i (1336-1374)
5405		其他同時作者	Other Contemporary Writers
5406		方孝孺	Fang Hsiao-ju (1357-1402)
5407		楊士奇	Yang Shih-ch'i (1365-1444)
5409		其他同時作者	Other Contemporary Writers
5410		李東陽	Li Tung-yang (1447-1516)
5411		王守仁	Wang Shou-jen (1472-1529)
5412		李夢陽	Li Mêng-yang (1472-1529)
5413		其他同時作者	Other Contemporary Writers
5414		何景明	Ho Chin-ming (1483-1521)
5415		歸有光	Kuei Yu-kuang (1506-1567)
5416		唐順之	T'ang Shun-chih (1507-1560)
5417		其他同時作者	Other Contemporary Writers

別集 (續)　　　　COLLECTED LITERARY WORKS, etc. (Cont.)

5418	李攀龍	Li P'an lung (1514-1570)
5419	其他同時作者	Other Contemporary Writers
5420	王世貞	Wang Shih-chên (1526-1590)
5422	其他同時作者	Other Contemporary Writers
5423	高攀龍	Kao P'an-lung (1562-1626)
5424	其他同時作者	Other Contemporary Writers
5425	袁宏道	Yüan Hung-tao (1578?-1610?)
5426	鍾惺	Chung Hsing (1574-1625)
5427	其他同時作者	Other Contemporary Writers
5428	黃道周	Huang Tao-chou (1585-1646)
5429	其他明末作者	Other Writers at End of Ming Dynasty
5431-5532	清	Ch'ing Dynasty (1644-1912)
5431	清初作者	Other Writers between Ming and Ch'ing Dynasties
5432	錢謙益	Ch'ien Ch'ien-i (1582-1664)
5433	其他同時作者	Other Contemporary Writers
5434	吳偉業	Wu Wei-yeh (1609-1671)
5436	其他同時作者	Other Contemporary Writers
5437	黃宗羲	Huang Tsung-hsi (1610-1695)
5438	宋琬	Sung Wan (1614-1673)
5439	其他同時作者	Other Contemporary Writers
5440	顧炎武	Ku Yen-wu (1613-1682)
5441	其他同時作者	Other Contemporary Writers
5442	侯方域	Hou Fang-yü (1618-1654)
5443	其他同時作者	Other Contemporary Writers
5444	施潤章	Shih Jun-chang (1618-1683)
5445	尤侗	Yu T'ung (1618-1704)

別集(續)　　COLLECTED LITERARY WORKS, etc. (Cont.)

5446	其他同時作者	Other Contemporary Writers
5447	王夫之	Wang Fu-chih (1619-1692)
5449	其他同時作者	Other Contemporary Writers
5450	毛奇齡	Mao Chi-ling (1623-1716)
5451	魏禧	Wei Hsi (1624-1680)
5452	彭孫遹	P'êng Sun-yü (1631-1700)
5453	其他同時作者	Other Contemporary Writers
5454	王琬	Wang Wan (1624-1690)
5455	其他同時作者	Other Contemporary Writers
5456	陳維崧	Ch'ên Wei-sung (1625-1682)
5457	其他同時作者	Other Contemporary Writers
5458	姜宸英	Chiang Ch'ên-ying (1628-1699)
5459	朱彝尊	Chu I-tsun (1629-1709)
5460	其他同時作者	Other Contemporary Writers
5461	王士禎	Wang Shih-chên (1634-1711)
5462	邵長蘅	Shao Ch'ang-hêng (1637-1704)
5463	其他同時作者	Other Contemporary Writers
5464	查慎行	Ch'a Shên-hsing (1650-1727)
5465	趙執信	Chao Chih-hsin (1662-1744)
5466	其他同時作者	Other Contemporary Writers
5467	方苞	Fang Pao (1668-1749)
5468	沈德潛	Shên Tê-ch'ien (1673-1769)
5470	其他同時作者	Other Contemporary Writers
5470.9	藍鼎元	Lan Ting-yüan (1680-1733)
5471	厲鶚	Li Ê (1692-1750)
5472	其他同時作者	Other Contemporary Writers

	別集 (續)	COLLECTED LITERARY WORKS, etc. (Cont.)
5472.9	胡天游	Hu T'ien-yu (1696-1758)
5473	劉大櫆	Liu Ta-k'uei (1698-1780)
5473.9	杭世駿	Hang Shih-chün (1696-1773)
5474	全祖望	Ch'üan Tsu-wang (1705-1755)
5475	其他同時作者	Other Contemporary Writers
5475.9	鄭燮	Chêng Hsieh (1693-1765)
5476	清高宗	Ching Kao Tsung (1711-1799)
5477	袁枚	Yüan Mei (1715-1797)
5477.9	邵齋燾	Shao Ch'i-tao (1718-1769)
5478	盧文弨	Lu Wên-ch'ao (1717-1795)
5479	戴震	Tai Chên (1723-1777)
5480	蔣士銓	Chiang Shih-ch'üan (1725-1784)
5480.9	王鳴盛	Wang Ming-shêng (1722-1797)
5481	其他同時作者	Other Contemporary Writers
5481.9	趙翼	Chao I (1727-1814)
5482	紀昀	Chi Yün (1724-1805)
5483	錢大昕	Ch'ien Ta-hsin (1728-1805)
5484	其他同時作者	Other Contemporary Writers
5485	姚鼐	Yao Nai (1731-1815)
5486	翁方綱	Wêng Fang-kang (1733-1818)
5487	其他同時作者	Other Contemporary Writers
5488	汪中	Wang Chung (1744-1794)
5489	吳錫麒	Wu Hsi-ch'i (1746-1818)
5490	其他同時作者	Other Contemporary Writers
5491	洪亮吉	Hung Liang-chi (1746-1809)
5491.9	黃景仁	Huang Ching-jen (1749-1783)

別集（續）　　COLLECTED LITERARY WORKS, etc. (Cont.)

5492	孔廣森	K'ung Kuang-sên (1752-1786)
5493	其他同時作者	Other Contemporary Writers
5494	孫星衍	Sun Hsing-yen (1753-1818)
5495	惲敬	Yün Ching (1757-1817)
5495.9	張問陶	Chang Wên-t'ao (1764-1814)
5496	其他同時作者	Other Contemporary Writers
5496.9	舒位	Shu Wei (1765-1815)
5497	張惠言	Chang Hui-yen (1761-1802)
5498	曾燠	Tsêng Yü (1760-1831)
5498.9	焦循	Chiao Hsün (1763-1820)
5499	阮元	Juan Yüan (1764-1849)
5499.9	郭麐	Kuo Lin (1767-1831)
5500	其他同時作者	Other Contemporary Writers
5501	陳壽祺	Ch'ên Shou-ch'i (1771-1834)
5502	張維屏	Chang Wei-p'ing (1780-1859)
5503	其他同時作者	Other Contemporary Writers
5503.9	李兆洛	Li Chao-lo (1769-1841)
5504	梅曾亮	Mei Tsêng-liang (1786-1856)
5506	其他同時作者	Other Contemporary Writers
5506.9	劉開	Liu K'ai (1781-1821)
5507	龔自珍	Kung Tzû-chên (1792-1841)
5508	其他同時作者	Other Contemporary Writers
5509	鄭珍	Chêng Chên (1806-1864)
5510	其他同時作者	Other Contemporary Writers
5510.9	姚燮	Yao Hsieh (1805-1864)
5511	曾國藩	Tsêng Kuo-fan (1811-1872)
5513	其他同時作者	Other Contemporary Writers

	別集(續)	COLLECTED LITERARY WORKS, etc. (Cont.)
5514	何紹基	Ho Shao-chi (1799-1873)
5515	金和	Chin Ho (1818-1885)
5516	俞樾	Yü Yüeh (1821-1906)
5517	其他同時作者	Other Contemporary Writers
5519	張裕釗	Chang Yü-chao (1823-1894)
5521	其他同時作者	Other Contemporary Writers
5523	翁同龢	Wêng T'ung-ho (1830-1904)
5524	譚獻	T'an Hsien (1832-1901)
5525	李慈銘	Li T'zû-ming (1829-1894)
5526	其他同時作者	Other Contemporary Writers
5527	吳汝綸	Wu Ju-lun (1840-1903)
5528	其他同時作者	Other Contemporary Writers
5529	譚嗣同	T'an Ssû-t'ung (1865-1898)
5530	黃遵憲	Huang Tsun-hsien (1848-1905)
5531	其他同時作者	Other Contemporary Writers
5532-5569	民國	The Republic (1912-date)
5532	王闓運	Wang K'ai-yün (1832-1916)
5533	樊增祥	Fan Tsêng-hsiang (1846-1931)
5534	林紓	Lin Shu (1852-1924)
5535	嚴復	Yen Fu (1853-1921)
5536	沈曾植	Shên Tsêng-chih (1853-1922)
5537	馬其昶	Ma Ch'i-ch'ang (1855-1930)
5538	康有為	K'ang Yu-wei (1855-1927)
5539	梁鼎芬	Liang Ting-fên (1859-1919)
5540	李詳	Li Hsiang (1859-1931)
5541	陳三立	Ch'ên San-li (1859-1937)

	別集 (續)	COLLECTED LITERARY WORKS, etc. (Cont.)
5542	易順鼎	I Shun-ting (1858-1920)
5543	鄭孝胥	Chêng Hsiao-hsü (1860-1938)
5544	姚永概	Yao Yung-k'ai (1866-1923)
5545	章炳麟	Chang Ping-Lin (1868-1936)
5546	陳衍	Ch'ên Yen (1868-1937)
5547	孫德謙	Sun Tê-ch'ien (1869-1935)
5548	梁啟超	Liang Ch'i-ch'ao (1873-1929)
5549		
5550	其他同時作者	Other Contemporary Writers
5551	吳闓生	Wu K'ai-shêng (1878-)
5552	王國維	Wang Kuo-wei (1877-1927)
5553	周樹人	Chou Shu-jên (1881-1936)
5554	章士釗	Chang Shih-chao (1881?-)
5555	劉師培	Liu Ssû-pei (1884-1919)
5556	胡適	Hu Shih (1891-)
5557	徐志摩	Hsü Chih-mo (1897-1931)
5558	其他同時作者	Other Contemporary Writers
5560	日本作者	Japanese Writers
5570-5649	詞	TZ'Û (POEMS OF UNEVEN SYLLABLES)
5571-5579	通錄	GENERAL
5571	期刊	Periodicals
5572	會社	Societies
5573	叢刊	Miscellanies
5574	書目	Bibliographies
5575	詞譜	Rules for Composition

詞 (續)　TZ'Û (Cont.)

5576	詞韻	Rhyming books and dictionaries
5577	詞話	Critiques and Comments
5578	詞史	History of the Development of Tz'û
5579	詞人合傳	Collective Biography of Tz'û Writers
5580	總集	COLLECTIONS (Series of complete works of individual writers issued in sets; may be divided chronologically by Table III)

凡刊歷代詞家專集者入此,
得依内容時代排,用表三.

| 5582 | 選集 | ANTHOLOGIES OF CHOICE SELECTIONS (Subdivide chronologically by Table III) |

依内容時代細分,用表三.

5583-5649	專集	COLLECTED WORKS OF INDIVIDUAL AUTHORS
5583-5588	唐五代	T'ang and the Five Dynasties (618-960)
5583.1	張志和	Chang Chih-ho (730?-810?)
.3	劉禹錫	Liu Yü-hsi (772-842)
.4	白居易	Po Chü-i (772-846)
.9	其他中唐作者	Other Writers in the period of (766-835)
5584.1	溫庭筠	Wên T'ing-Yün (? -880?)
.7	韓偓	Han Wu (889 Chin-shih)
.8	皇甫松	Huang-fu Sung (810?-880?)
.9	其他晚唐作者	Other Writers in the period of (836-907)
5585.1	李存勗	Li-Ts'un-hsü (? -926)
.2	韋莊	Wei Chuang (cir. 855-920)
.5	牛嶠	Niu Chiao (878 Chin-shih)
5586	馮延己	Fêng Yen-chi (? -960)
5587	李璟	Li Ching (916-961)
	李煜	Li Yü (937-978)

以上南唐二主

| 5588 | 其他五代作者 | Other Writers in the period of (907-960) |

詞 (續)　　TZ'Û (Cont.)

5589-5620	宋	Sung Dynasty (960-1279)
5589	晏殊	Yen Shu (? -1055)
5590.1	范仲淹	Fan Chung-yen (989-1052)
.5	宋祁	Sung Chi (998-1062)
5591	歐陽修	Ou-yang Hsiu (1007-1072)
5592	張先	Chang Hsien (990-1078)
5593	柳永	Liu Yung (1034 Chin-shih)
5594	晏幾道	Yen Chi-tao (? -1080?)
.9	王安石	Wang An-shih (1021-1086)
5595	蘇軾	Su Shih (1036-1101)
5596	秦觀	Ch'in Kuan (1049-1101)
5597	黃庭堅	Huang T'ing-chien (1045-1105)
5598	晁補之	Chao Pu-chih (1053-1110)
5599	周邦彥	Chou Pang-yen (1057-1121)
5600	賀鑄	Ho Chu (1063-1120)
5601	朱淑真	Chu Shu-chen (cir. 1130)
5602	李清照	Li Ch'ing-chao (1081-1140?)
5603	向鎬	Hsiang Hao (cir. 1110- ?)
5604	其他北宋作者	Other Writers in the Northern Dynasty (960-1127)
5605	葉夢得	Yeh Mêng-tê (1077-1148)
5606	朱敦儒	Chu Tun-ju (1080?-1155)
5607	陸游	Lu Yu (1125-1210)
5608	辛棄疾	Hsin Ch'i-chi (1140-1207)
5609	范成大	Fan Ch'êng-ta (1126-1193)
5610	劉過	Liu Kuo (1150-1220)
5611	姜夔	Chiang Kúei (1155-1235)

詞 (續)　TZ'Û (Cont.)

5612	史達祖	Shih Ta-tsu (1155?-1220?)
5613	吳文英	Wu Wên-ying (?-1260?)
5614	劉克莊	Liu K'o-chuang (1178-1269)
5615	王沂孫	Wang I-sun (? -1290?)
5616	周密	Chou Mi (1232-1308)
5617	張炎	Chang Yen (1248-1320?)
5618	蔣捷	Chiang Chieh (1235?-1320?)
5619	其他宋末作者	Other Contemporary Writers
5620-5624	金元	Chin Kingdom (1115-1234) and Yüan Dynasty (1279-1368)
5620	元好問	Yüan Hao-wên (1190-1257)
5621	仇遠	Ch'iu Yüan (1247- ?)
5622	張雨	Chang Yü (1277-1348)
5623	張翥	Chang Chu (1287-1368)
.9	倪瓚	Ni Tsan (1301-1374)
5624	其他作者	Other Contemporary Writers
5625-5630	明	Ming Dynasty (1368-1644)
5625	劉基	Liu Chi (1311-1375)
.9	其他同時作者	Other Contemporary Writers
5626	楊慎	Yang Shên (1488-1559)
.9	其他同時作者	Other Contemporary Writers
5627	王世貞	Wang Shih-chên (1526-1590)
.9	其他同時作者	Other Contemporary Writers
5628	施紹莘	Shih Shao-hsin (cir. 1630)
5629	陳子龍	Ch'ên Tzû-lung (1608-1647)
5630	其他同時作者	Other Contemporary Writers

詞 (續)　　　TZ'Û (Cont.)

5631-5642	清	Ch'ing Dynasty (1644-1912)
5631	吳偉業	Wu Wei-yeh (1609-1671)
.9	其他清初作者	Other Contemporary Writers
5632	陳維崧	Ch'ên Wei-sung (1625-1682)
5633	納蘭性德	Na-lan-hsin-tê (1655-1685)
5634	朱彝尊	Chu I-tsun (1629-1709)
5635.1	顧貞觀	Ku Chên-kuan (1637- ?)
.5	彭孫遹	P'êng Sun-yü (1631-1700)
5636	厲鶚	Li Ê (1692-1750)
.9	其他康雍間作者	Other Contemporary Writers
5637	張惠言	Chang Hui-yen (1761-1802)
5638	張琦	Chang Ch'i (1764-1833)
5639	郭麐	Kuo Lin (1767-1831)
.9	其他乾嘉間作者	Other Contemporary Writers
5640.1	周濟	Chou Chi (1781-1839)
.3	董士錫	Tung Shih-hsi (1782- ?)
.5	項鴻祚	Hsiang Hung-tsu (1798-1835)
.7	龔自珍	Kung Tzû-chên (1792-1841)
.9	其他道光間作者	Other Contemporary Writers
5641.1	蔣敦復	Chiang Tun-fu (1808-1867)
.3	蔣春霖	Chiang Ch'un-lin (1818-1868)
.9	其他咸同間作者	Other Contemporary Writers
5642.1	譚獻	T'an Hsien (1832-1901)
.5	王鵬運	Wang P'êng-yün (1849-1904)
.9	其他光宣間作者	Other Contemporary Writers

詞 (續)　TZ'Û (Cont.)

5643-5649	民國	The Republic (1912-____)
5643	鄭文焯	Chêng Wên-ch'ao (1856-1918)
5644	況周頤 (儀)	Huang Chou-i (1859-1926)
5645	朱祖謀	Chu Tsu-mou (1857-1932)
5646	王國維	Wang Kuo-wei (1877-1927)
5647	其他	Other Contemporary Writers
5650-5730	曲及戲劇	SONGS AND DRAMA
5651-5658	總錄	GENERAL
5651	會社, 期刊	Societies, Periodicals
5652	叢刊	Collections
5653	書目	Bibliographies
5654	事彙, 類書	Encyclopedias
5655	概說, 通論	General Treatises
5656	史傳	History and Collective Biography
5657	曲話, 劇評	Critiques and Comments
5658	曲律, 曲韻	Rules for Composition and Rhyming Handbooks
5659-5660	散曲 小令套數	SAN CH'Û (SONGS WITHOUT DIALOGUES)
5659	總集, 選集	Collections and Selections
5660	專集	Works of Individual Writers
.6	元	Yüan Dynasty (1280-1368)
.7	明	Ming Dynasty (1368-1644)
.8	清	Ch'ing Dynasty (1644-1912)
.9	民國	The Republic (1912-____)

5661-5699	雅部劇本 雜劇與傳奇	CLASSICAL DRAMA: Northern Short Plays and Southern Long Plays
5661-5664	總集 凡院本,戲文,南戲,雜劇及全本 傳奇而成叢書者入此,僅依內容時代排,不再分體裁.	Collections; Ts'ung-shu (Subdivide chronologically by periods)
5661	宋金元	Sung, Chin & Yüan Dynasties (960-1368)
5662	明	Ming Dynasty (1368-1644)
5663	清	Ching Dynasty (1644-1912)
5664	民國	The Republic (1912-)
5665	選集 凡選刊散折雜劇及散曲 傳奇而成集者入此	Selections (Anthologies of choice portions of Northern and Southern Plays)
5666-5699	專集 一人所作之劇本依下列次序: (一)全集(二)選刊(三)雜劇(四)雜劇殘散 折排折所出之雜劇殘總(五)傳奇(六)傳奇殘散 曲(總本與角本)(七)樣折所出(傳奇樣折)(八)他人 對于該作者之評論與研究.	Collected Works of Individual Dramatists (Single plays or parts of a play by the same author are to be arranged after his complete collected works.)
5666-5676	南宋金元	Southern Sung, Chin and Yüan Dynasties (1127-1368)
5666	董解元	Tung Chieh-yüan (cir. 1160-1210)
.9	其他宋金作者	Other Sung and Chin Writers
5667	關漢卿	Kuan Han-ch'ing (cir. 1200-1270)
5668	王實甫	Wang Shih-p'u (cir. 1210-1280)
5669	馬致遠	Ma Chih-yüan (cir. 1210-1280)
5670	白樸	Po P'u (1226-1285)
5671	其他元初作者	Other Writers in the Period of (1240-1280)
5672	鄭光祖	Chêng Kuang-tsu (cir. 1250-1310)
.9	宮天挺	Kung T'ien-t'ing (cir. 1260-1330)
5673	喬吉	Ch-iao Chi (? - 1345)
5674	其他元一統時代作者	Other Writers in the Period of (1280-1340)
5675	其他元末作者	Writers in the last period of Yüan Dynasty (1341-1368)

雅部劇本 (續)   WORKS OF INDIVIDUAL DRAMATISTS (Cont.)

| 5676-5690 | 明 | Ming Dynasty (1368-1644) |

5676　　高明 琵琶記　　　Kao Ming (1345 chin-shih)

.9　　其他元末明初南戲作者 Other Writers of Southern Plays at
荊釵記,白兔記,拜月亭,殺狗記,等入此. the beginning of the Ming Dynast

5677　　賈仲名　　　Chia Chung-ming (fl. 1383)

.9　　其他明初雜劇作者 Other Writers of Northern Plays at
the Beginning of the Mind Dynasty

5678　　朱有燉　　　Chu Yu-tun (1377-1439)

.9　　其他正統正德間雜劇作者 Other Writers of Northern Plays in th
period of (1436-1521)

5679　　鄭若庸　　　Chêng Jo-yung (fl. 1535)

5680　　徐渭　　　Hsü Wei (1521-1593)

5681　　汪道昆　　　Wang Tao-k'un (1547 chin-shih)

5682　　張鳳翼　　　Chang Fêng-i (1527-1613)

5683　　梁辰魚　　　Liang Ch'ên-yü (fl. 1551)

5684　　其他同時作者　　　Other Contemporary Writers

5685　　沈璟　　　Shên Ching (1574 chin-shih)

5686　　湯顯祖　　　T'ang Hsien-tsu (1550-1617)

5687　　其他同時作者　　　Other Contemporary Writers

5688　　馮夢龍　　　Fêng Mêng-lung (? -1646)

5689　　阮大鋮　　　Juan Ta-ch'êng (? -1646)

5690　　其他明末作者　　　Other Contemporary Writers

| 5691-5711 | 清 | Ch'ing Dynasty (1644-1912) |

5691　　李玉　　　Li Yü (fl. 1644)

5692　　徐石麒　　　Hsü Shih-ch'i (fl. 1644)

5693　　吳偉業　　　Wu Wei-yeh (1609-1671)

5694　　李漁　　　Li Yü (1611- ?)

5695　　尤侗　　　Yu T'ung (1618-1704)

雅部劇本 (續) WORKS OF INDIVIDUAL DRAMATISTS (Cont.)

5696	洪昇	Hung Shêng (1659-1704)
5697	孔尚任	Kung Shang-jên (1648-1715)
5698	萬樹	Wan Shu (fl. 1692)
5699	其他順康間作者	Other Writers in the Period of (1644-1723)
5700	張堅	Chang Chien (1681-1771)
5701	唐英	T'ang Ying (fl. 1736)
5702	董榕	Tung Yung (fl. 1736)
5703	夏綸	Hsia Lun (1680-1753?)
5704	蔣士銓	Chiang Shih-ch'üan (1725-1784)
5705	楊潮觀	Yang Chao-kuan (fl. 1745)
5706	舒位	Shu Wei (1765-1815)
5707	其他雍乾嘉作者	Other Writers in the Period of (1723-1821)
5708	黃燮清	Huang Hsieh-ch'ing (1835 chu-jên)
5709	楊恩壽	Yang Ên-shou (fl. 1862)
5710	其他道咸間作者	Other Writers in the Period of (1821-1862)
5711	同光宣間作者	Writers floruit in the Period of (1862-1912)
5712-5713	民國	The Republic (1912-)
5712	吳梅	Wu Mei (1880-)
5713	其他	Others
5714-5717	花部劇本	POPULAR DRAMA
	亂彈俗劇	(The popular drama, except the I-yang and Kao-yang plays, is different from the classical drama not only in singing but also in the composition of the songs and the dialogues which are more colloquial and "coarse" than the classical ones. The themes and stories

花部劇本　　POPULAR DRAMA (Cont.)

蜀山彈, 俗劇.
弋腔 高腔所用
劇本雖同崑曲但
唱法不同, 故暫列
之花部.

are, however, the same in most plays both classical and popular. The I-yang and Kao-yang plays use the same songs as in the classical drama, but the songs are sung in the I-yang (in Kiangsi) and Kao-yang (in Hopeh) airs. The classical drama is sung mostly in K'un Ch'iang or Soochow air.)

5714　弋腔, 高腔, 京腔 I-yang and Kao-yang Air Plays

5715　皮黃(京調) Hsi-p'i and Êrh-huang Air (used in Peking Operas

5716　秦腔(梆子調) Ch'in Ch'iang or P'ang-tzû (Northern high-pitch air plays prevailing in Hopeh, Shantung, Honan, Shansi, Shensi and Kansu)

其他各地俗劇
5717　嘴開戲, 魯劇, 諸劇, Other Local Plays (Subdivide by geographical
蘇劇, 灘黃, 漢調, 甬劇, 粵劇, 滇劇等入此. 依地理排, 用表二.　Table II)

5718-5719　話劇　　MODERN PROSE DRAMA

民初之文明戲及近日之
新劇入此.

(The plays to be classified in the previous two sections, whether classical or popular, are all musical drama or operas; whereas the modern drama introduced from the West is entirely in dialogues.)

5718　總集, 選刊　Collections and Selections

5719　專集　Collected Works of Individual Dramatists

5720-5730　其他戲曲文學 OTHER KINDS OF DRAMATIC LITERATURE

5720　概論　General Treatises

5721　傀儡劇　Puppet Shows; Pantomimes

5722　影戲劇本　Shadow Plays

5723-5724　電影脚本　Cinema; Photoplays

5725-5726　變文寶卷　Buddhist Song-tales
佛曲係宗教讚頌者　(Religious psalms are to be classified in
應入佛教儀規.　　1852 Buddhist Rituals)

5727　彈詞 木魚書.　Southern Song-tales (Secular)

5728　鼓詞 子弟書, 大鼓.　Northern Song-tales (Secular)

OTHER KINDS OF DRAMATIC LITERATURE (Cont.

5729-5730	俗曲,小調,歌謠 Popular Ballads and Folksongs
5729	目金彔,總集,選集 Bibliographies, Collections, Selections, etc.
5730	各地歌謠 Songs of Different Localities (Subdivide by Geographical Table II)

5731-5769	小說	**FICTION**
5731-5735	總錄	**GENERAL**
5731	期刊	Periodicals
5732	書目	Bibliographies
5733	歷史	History
5734	評論	Critiques
5735	作法	Technique of Writing Chinese Fiction

5736-5766	舊小說	**OLD STYLE FICTION**
5736-5749	筆記小說	(A) Short Stories in Literary Language
5736-5739	彙刊叢選	Collections and Selections
5736	歷代	Of All Periods
.2	漢三國	Han Dynasty and the Three Kingdoms (B.C. 206-265 A.D.)
.3	晉至隋	Chin Dynasty to Sui Dynasty (265-618)
.4	唐五代	T'ang and the Five Dynasties (618-960)
5737	宋元	Sung and Yüan Dynasties (960-1368)
5738	明	Ming Dynasty (1368-1644)
5739	清	Ch'ing Dynasty (1644-1912)
5740-5749	專集 依作品之時代分,用表三.	Works of Individual Authors (Subdivide chronologically by the dates of the works, using Table III)

| 5750 | 話本小說:短篇 平話,評話. | (B) Short Stories in Spoken Language (Hua-pên were manuscripts in outline form used by the story-tellers.) |
| 5750 | 彙刊,叢選 | Collections and Selections |

話本小說 (續) OLD STYLE FICTION (Cont.)

5750.5-.8	專箸	Individual Works
.5	宋	Sung Dynasty (960-1279)
.6	元	Yüan Dynasty (1280-1368)
.7	明	Ming Dynasty (1368-1644)
.8	清	Ch'ing Dynasty (1644-1912)

5751	話本小說：長篇	(C) Hua-pen Novels of Sung and Yüan Dynasties (960-1368)

5752-5766　章回小說　(D) Serial Novels

(Serial novels are mostly in colloquial language; only a few are in literary language. Some were developed out of copies used by the story-tellers in the Sung and Yüan Dynasties; others were original works by literary men.)

5752-5759	明	Ming Dynasty (1368-1644)
5752	水滸傳 施耐庵撰	Shui Hu Chuan by Shih Nai-an (cir.1290-1365)
5753	其他同時作品	Other Works of the Same Period
5754	三國志演義 羅貫中撰	San Kuo Chih Yen I by Lo Kuan-chung (cir. 1330-1400)
5755	其他同時作品	Other Works of the Same Period
5756	西遊記 吳承恩撰	Hsi Yu Chi by Wu Ch'êng-en (cir. 1500-1582)
5757	其他同時作品	Other Works of the Same Period
5758	金瓶梅 蘭陵笑笑生撰	Chin P'ing Mei by Lan-ling Hsiao-hsiao-shêng (cir. 1530-1600)
5759	其他同時作品	Other Works of the Same Period
5760-5765	清	Ch'ing Dynasty (1644-1912)
5761	儒林外史 吳敬梓撰	Ju Lin Wai Shih by Wu Ching-tzû (1701-1754)
5762	紅樓夢 曹霑撰	Hung Lou Mêng by Ts'ao Chan (? -1764)

章回小說 (續) OLD STYLE FICTION (Cont.)

5762.9	其他同時作品	Other Works of the Same Period
5763.1	野叟曝言 夏敬渠撰	Yeh Sou Pao Yen by Hsia Ching-ch'ü (fl. 1750)
.5	鏡花緣 李汝珍撰	Ching Hua Yüan by Li Ju-chên (1763-1830)
5764	兒女英雄傳 文康撰	Erh Nü Ying Hsiung Chuan by Wên-k'ang (fl. 1868)
.5	三俠五義 問竹主人撰	San Chieh Wu I by Wên-chu-chu-jên (fl. 1871)
5765	其他同時作者	Other Works of the Same Period
5766	民國	The Republic (1912-____)
5767-5769	新小說	MODERN FICTION (In modern fiction Hu style and the technique are introduced from the West)
5767-5768	短篇	Short Stories
5767	彙刊	Selections and Collections
5768	專集	Works of Individual Authors
5769	長篇	Novels
5770-5779	書牘 私書及公牘參見的委議.	LETTERS See also 4661-4664 Edicts and Memorials
5771	作法 軌範	Letter-writing: Technique and Models
5772	應用文程式	Official, Business and Social Forms
5773	書牘總集	General Collections
5774-5779	書牘專集	Collected Works of Individual Authors
5774		
5775	宋	Sung Dynasty (960-1279)
5776	元	Yüan Dynasty (1280-1368)
5777	明	Ming Dynasty (1368-1644)
5778	清	Ch'ing Dynasty (1644-1912)
5779	民國	The Republic (1912-____)

5780-5795	雜著	MISCELLANIES
5780-5783	制藝 八股文	Examination Essays
5780	作法,試律	Method of Writing; Style-books
5781	總集,叢選	Collections and Selections
5782-5783	專集	Collected Works of Individual Authors
5782	明	Ming Dynasty (1368-1644)
5783	清	Ch'ing Dynasty (1644-1912)
5784	日記文	Diaries
5785	演說	Orations
5786	迴文,詩鐘	Poetic Pastimes
5787	格言,恆言	Aphorisms, Maxims, Mottoes, etc.
5788	諺語	Proverbs
5789	楹聯,壽文,輓詞	Scrolls. Couplets for birthdays, funerals and other occasions
5790	寓言	Fables
5791	謎語	Riddles, etc.
5792	諷諧	Satire and Facetiae
5793	其他	Others
5796-5799	兒童文學	JUVENILE LITERATURE
5796	總類	General
5797	歷史讀物	Historical Readers
5798	科學讀物	Scientific Readers
5799	文藝讀物	Literature and Fiction

5800-5803　其他印度支那 OTHER INDO-CHINESE LANGUAGES AND LITERATURES
　　　　　　系各語文　　(Use Table F for form divisions in language and in
　　　　　　　　　　　　literature.)
　　　　　以下各語系語言文學文細分,用表已.

5800	泰系語文	TAI LANGUAGES AND LITERATURES
.1	概論	General Treatises
.2	獐語	The Chuang Group
.3	亞含姆語	Ahom
.4	甘姆蒂語	Kamti
.5	撣語	Shan
.6	暹羅語	Siamese
.7	牢語	Lao
.8	白泰,儂語	Tai Blanc, Nung, Tho
.9	黎語	Loi
5801	苗傜語文	MIAO-YAO LANGUAGES AND LITERATURES
.1	概論	General Treatises
5802	藏緬語文	TIBETAN-BURMAN LANGUAGES AND LITERATURES
.1	概論	General Treatises
.2	西藏語	Tibetan
.5	凱金語	Katchin
.6	緬甸語	Burmese
.8	玀玀語	Lolo
5803	憤安語文 南亞語文	MON-ANAM (AUSTRO-ASIATIC) LANGUAGES AND LITERATURES
.1	概論	General Treatises
.2	驃語	Mon (Pegu)
.4	扶南語 北孤語	Khmer
.6	安南語	Annamite
.8	捫達語	Munda

5804-5809	烏拉阿爾泰系 語文 以下各語系語言與文學之細分,用表己.	URAL-ALTAIC (SCYTHIAN, TURANIAN) LANGUAGES AND LITERATURES (Use Table F for form divisions in language and in literature.)
5804	總錄	GENERAL
5805	蒙古語文	MONGOLIAN LANGUAGES AND LITERATURES (Eastern Mongolian, Kalmuk, Buriat)
5806	通古斯語文 滿洲語等.	TUNGUSIC LANGUAGES AND LITERATURES (Tungus Proper, Lamut, Manchu)
5807	土耳其語文 韃靼,回鶻,突厥,等語.	TURKISH OR TATAR LANGUAGES AND LITERATURES
5808	撒摩耶語文	SAMOYED LANGUAGES AND LITERATURES
5809	烏拉語文 芬蘭,匈牙利等語.	UGRIAN, FINNO-HUNGARIAN, FINNO-UGRIC, OR URALIC LANGUAGES AND LITERATURES
5810-5859	日本語言文字學	JAPANESE LANGUAGE JAPANESE PHILOLOGY
5810	總錄	GENERAL
.1	期刊	Periodicals
.2	會社	Societies
.3	叢集	Collections
.3	大系,講座	Systemic Compilation
.34	諸家著作	General Collection
.37	個人著作	Individual Collection
.4	書目	Bibliographies
.5	教學	Study and Teaching
.6	語言學史	History of Language Studies
.8	語言史 依時代分,用表三.	History of Language (Divide by Period like Table III)
.9	通論	General Treatises
5811	音韻	PHONOLOGY
.4	五十音圖 論五十音圖不涉音韻者,入假名.	Syllabary　See also 5816
.5	音調	Accentuation
.7	古代語音	Ancient Phonology

日本語言文字學 JAPANESE LANGUAGE (Cont.)

5812-5826	文字及字母	GRAPHIC STUDIES. ORTHOGRAPHY
5812	概說	General Treatises
5814	漢字	Chinese Characters
.8	常用漢字	Characters in Common Use
.9	漢字限制論	Character Usage Limitation
5815	字音	Pronounciation of Characters
5816	假名. 伊呂波	Kana. Iroha See also 5811.4
5817	假名遣	Spelling
5818	國語假名遣	For Japanese Language
5819	字音假名遣	For Chinese Characters
.7	振假名	Furikana
5820	送假名	Okurikana
5821	假名專用論	Exclusive Use of Kana
5822	羅馬字	Romanization
5823	速記	Stenography
5826	國字問題	Other Problems
5827	語源	ETYMOLOGY, DERIVATION
5828-5845	辭書, 語釋	LEXICOGRAPHY, DICTIONARIES
5828	分類辭典	Dictionaries Compiled by Classified Subject
5829	部首引辭典	Dictionaries Compiled by Radicals
.3	難訓辭典	Dictionaries of Difficult Characters
.5	畫引辭典	Dictionaries Compiled by Number of Strokes
.8	四隅番化辭典	Dictionaries Compiled by Four-Corner Numbers
.9	伊呂波引辭典	Dictionaries Compiled by Iroha
5830	五十音引辭典	Dictionaries Compiled by Gojūon
.1	類語辭典	Dictionaries of Synonyms

日本語言文字學 JAPANESE LANGUAGE (Cont.)
（續）

5831.2	口語辭典	Dictionaries of Spoken Language
.4	雅言辭典，古語辭典	Dictionaries of Archaism
.7	熟語辭典	Dictionaries of Idioms and Phrases
	互譯辭典	Japanese-Foreign Dictionaries
5833	和漢辭典	Japanese-Chinese
.1	部首引	By Radicals
.5	五十音引	By Kana
.8	羅馬字引	By Romanization
.9	日文與中國方言辭典	Japanese-Chinese Dialects
5834	和鮮辭典	Japanese-Korean
5835	和滿辭典	Japanese-Manchu
5836	和蒙辭典	Japanese-Mongolian
5837	和藏辭典	Japanese-Tibetan
5838	和梵辭典	Japanese-Sanskrit
5840	和英辭典	Japanese-English
.9	英和辭典	English-Japanese
5841	和獨辭典	Japanese-German
.9	獨和辭典	German-Japanese
5842	和佛辭典	Japanese-French
.9	佛和辭典	French-Japanese
5843	和西辭典	Japanese-Spanish
.9	西和辭典	Spanish-Japanese
5844	和露辭典	Japanese-Russian
.9	露和辭典	Russian-Japanese
5845	其他	Japanese - Other Languages

為便宜起見日文解釋之西文辭典可置此下.

日本語言文字學 JAPANESE LANGUAGE (Cont.)
(續)

5846-5854	文法	GRAMMAR
5846.3	叢集	Collections
.8	歷史	History
.9	概論	General Treatises
5847	品詞論, 單語論	Parts of Speech
5847	名詞 代名詞	Nouns and Pronouns
5848	動詞 助動詞	Verbs and Their Auxiliaries
5849	形容詞 數詞	Adjectives and Numerals
5850	副詞 接續詞 感歎詞	Adverbs, Conjunctions and Interjections
5851	助詞 天爾遠波	Post-positions
5852	冠詞 枕詞等	Prefixes and Makurakotoba
5853	文章論	Syntax
.5	作文	Composition
.7	訓點法	Punctuation
5854	修辭學	Rhetoric
.7	敬語法	Honorific Expression
5855	解釋, 翻譯	INTERPRETATION AND TRANSLATION
.8	俗語, 俚諺	COLLOQUIALISM, SLANGS, ETC.
5856	方言	DIALECTS
.03	叢集	Collections
.06	辭書	Dictionaries
.08	概論	General Treatises
.09	特別研究	Special Studies
.1-.9	各地方言 依地理分, 用表二.	Regional Divisions (Subdivide geographically like Table II)
5857	外來語	FOREIGN WORDS AND PHRASES
5858	學習書	INSTRUCTION BOOKS

日本語文學習書 INSTRUCTION BOOKS

5858.3	讀本	Readers
.6	會話	Conversation Books
5860-5969	日本文學	<u>JAPANESE LITERATURE</u>
5861-5869	總錄	GENERAL
5861	期刊	Periodicals
.5	年刊	Yearbooks
5862	會社	Societies
	叢集	Collections
5863	講座大系等	Systematic Collections
.4	諸家論文集	Miscellaneous Collections of Different Authors
.7	一家論文集	Miscellaneous Collections of Same Authors
	文學作品集 見下總集及別集	Collections of Literary Works. See 5880-5889
5864	書目	Bibliographies
.9	索引	Indexes
5865	教學	Study and Teaching
5866	辭典	Dictionaries and Encyclopedia
5869	文學家合傳	Collective Literary Biographies
5870-5879	歷史及評論	HISTORY AND CRITICISM
5870.1-.9	專史	Special Treatises
5870.1	文學思想與文學精神	Literary Thought and Spirit
.2-.3	作者與作品	Special Classes of Writers
.5	文學批評	General Critiques
	時代史	By Periods
5871	上世 上代, 中古.	Ancient (Earliest to 1185 A.D.)

歷史及評論 (續) HISTORY AND CRITICISM (Cont.)

5872	大和時代 包括奈良時代.	Yamato Period (To 781 A.D.)
5873	平安時代	Heian Period (781-1185)
5874	中世 近古.	Medieval (1185-1600)
.5	鎌倉時代	Kamakura Period (1185-1333)
5875	室町時代 包括吉野,安土,桃山時代.	Muramachi Period (1333-1600)
5876	近世 江戸時代.	Modern (1600-1867)
5877	現代	Recent (1867 to date)
.1	明治	Meiji Period (1867-1912)
.3	大正	Taishō Period (1912-1925)
.5	昭和	Shōwa Period (1925 to date)
5879	地方史 依地理分,用表二.	By Localities (Subdivide geographically by Table II)
5880	文學總集	GENERAL COLLECTIONS OF LITERARY WORKS
.1	上世	Ancient Works (Earliest to 1185 A.D.)
.2	大和時代	Yamato Period (To 781 A.D.)
.3	平安時代	Heian Period (781-1185 A.D.)
.4	中世	Medieval Works (1185-1600)
.4	鎌倉時代	Kamakura Period (1185-1333)
.5	室町時代	Muramachi Period (1333-1600)
.6	近世	Modern Works (1600-1867)
.7	現代	Recent Works (1867 to date)
.9	地方文藝集 依地理分,用表二.	Local Collections of Literary Works (Subdivide by Table II)
5881	文學選集 必要時仿文學總集細分.	GENERAL ANTHOLOGIES OF CHOICE SELECTIONS (Subdivide like 5880 when necessary)

	文學別集	COLLECTED LITERARY WORKS OF INDIVIDUAL AUTHORS
5882	奈良時代	Nara Period (710-781)
5883	平安時代	Heian Period (781-1185)
5884	鎌倉時代	Kamakura Period (1185-1333)
5885	室町時代	Muramachi Period (1333-1600)
5886	江戸時代	Edo Period (1600-1867)
5887	明治時代	Meiji Period (1867-1912)
5888	現代	Contemporary (1912 to date)
5890-5909	詩歌	JAPANESE POETRY AND SONGS
5890	總錄 依體裁分賬一	<u>General</u> (Subdivide by form like Table I)
5891	和歌	<u>WAKA</u> (31 SYLLABLE ODES)
.8	史傳	History and Biography
.9	歌學,歌論	Theory and Method
	總集	Comprehensive General Collections
5892	附索引者	With Index
.2	無索引者	Without Index
.4	類纂總集	Classified Arrangement
	選集	Selections.　Anthologies
5892.5	類選	By Special Subjects
.8	雜選	General
5893	記紀の歌	Waka Extracted from <u>Kojiki</u> and <u>Nihon-shoki</u>
5894	萬葉集 二十卷	<u>Manyōshū</u>
.0	白文及古本	Text
.1	注釋書	Commentaries
.2	關係書	Relative Compilations
.21	類纂	Classified arrangement

233

詩歌 (續) JAPANESE POETRY AND SONGS (Cont.)

5894.22	別家	Author arrangement
.23	編年	Chronological arrangement
.26	羅馬字本	Transliteration
.27	譯解本 假去本入此.	Translation
.3	圖表大綱	Outline, Table, Illustration, etc.
.34	書目	Bibliographies
.36	辭典	Dictionaries
.37	索引	Indexes and Concordances
.4	研究書	Studies
.41	人物	Personal and Biographical
.42	年代	Chronological
.43	文學	Literary
.44	文法	Grammatical
.45	音義	Linguistic
.46	生物	Biological
.47	歷史	Historical
.48	地理	Geographical
.49	其他	Others
.5	評論書	General Treatises and Criticism
.6	傳習書	Study and Teaching
	選集	Selections
.7	鈔釋	Best Pieces
.8	選歌	Special Style or Subject
5895	敕撰歌集	COLLECTIONS COMPILED BY IMPERIAL ORDERS
.1	八代集	Hachi dai shū

敕撰歌集 (續) COLLECTIONS COMPILED BY IMPERIAL
　　　　　　　　　ORDERS (Cont.)

5895.2	三代集	Sandai shū
.3	古今和歌集 二十巻	Kokin wakashū
.4	後撰和歌集 二十巻	Gosen wakashū
.5	拾遺和歌集 二十巻	Shūi wakashū
.6	後拾遺和歌集 二十巻	Go shūi wakashū
.7	金葉和歌集 十巻	Kinyō wakashū
.8	詞花和歌集 十巻	Shika wakashū
.9	千載和歌集 二十巻	Senzai wakashū
5896.1	新古今和歌集 二十巻	Shin kokin wakashū
.2	十三代集	Jūsan dai shū
.3	新敕撰和歌集 二十巻	Shin chukusen wakashū
.4	續後撰和歌集 二十巻	Zoku gosen wakashū
.5	續古今和歌集 二十巻	Zoku kokin wakashū
.6	續拾遺和歌集 二十巻	Zoku shūi wakashū
.7	新後撰和歌集 二十巻	Shin gosen wakashū
.8	玉葉和歌集 二十巻	Gyokuyō wakashū
.9	續千載和歌集 二十巻	Zoku senzai wakashū
5897.1	續後拾遺和歌集 二十巻	Zoku go shūi wakashū
.3	風雅和歌集 二十巻	Fūga wakashū
.4	新千載和歌集 二十巻	Shin senzai wakashū
.5	新拾遺和歌集 二十巻	Shin shūi wakashū
.6	新後拾遺和歌集 二十巻	Shin go shūi wakashū
.7	新續古今和歌集 二十巻	Shin zoku kokin wakashū
.9	新葉和歌集 二十巻	Shin yō wakashū

宗良親王撰，准敕撰集．

| 5898.1-.9 | 私撰歌集 | COLLECTIONS PRIVATELY COMPILED |
| .2 | 平安時代 | Heian Period (781-1185) |

新撰萬葉集二巻.菅原道真		Shinsen manyōshū
新撰和歌集二巻.比賣之		Shinsen wakashū
古今和歌六帖十二巻.		Kokin waka rokujō
金玉集 藤原公任		Kingyoku shū
玄玄集 能因		Gengen shū
續詞花和歌集二十巻.藤原清輔		Shoku shika wakashū
後葉和歌集十八巻		Kōyō waka shū
月詣和歌集四巻.賀茂重保		(Getsukei) waka shū *Tsukimode*
三十六人集十六巻.藤原公任 歌仙家集・入家集		Sanjūroku nin shū
三十六人撰 藤原公任		Sanjuroku nin sen

| .3 | 鎌倉時代 | Kamakura Period (1185-1333) |

玄玉和歌集十二巻(存七巻)		Gen-gyoku waka shū
萬代和歌集二十巻		Mandai waka shū
東撰和歌六帖		Tōsen waka rokujō
現存和歌六帖		Gen-son waka rokujō
秋風抄三巻.小野春雄		Shūfū shō
雲葉和歌集十巻.		Unyō waka shū
新和歌集二十巻.藤原高氏 宇都都打閒新和歌集		Shin waka shu
風葉和歌集二十巻		Fūyō waka shū
續門葉和歌集十巻.伏冷家親覽		Shoku (zoku) monyō waka shū

| .4 | 夫木和歌集三十六巻.藤原長清 | Fuboku waka shū |
| .5 | 百人一首 藤原定家 小倉百人一首. | Ogura hyakunin isshu |

自讚歌		Jisan ka
柳風和歌抄五巻.		Ryūfū waka shō

私撰歌集 (續)　　COLLECTIONS PRIVATELY COMPILED (Cont.)

5898.6　室町時代　　　Muromachi Period (1333-1600)

續現葉和歌集 +巻　　Shoku genyō waka shū

臨永和歌集 +巻　　Rinei waka shū

菊葉和歌集 二+巻 二條師嗣 Kikuyō waka shū

藤葉和歌集 六巻　　Tōyō waka shū

風葉和歌集 二+巻 (存 +八巻) Fūyō waka shū

　.7　江戸時代　　　Edo Period (1600-1867)

慶長千首　　　　Keichō senshū

類題和歌集 三+巻 後水尾天皇 Ruidai wakashū (Class in 5892.4)

林葉累塵集 二+巻 下河邊長流 Rinyō ruijin shū

萍水和歌集 二+巻 下河邊長流 Heisui waka shū

和歌鳥の跡 五巻 戸田茂睡 Waka Tori no ato

和歌渚の松 九巻 松宮俊仍 Waka Nagisa no matsu

類題和歌怜野集 +巻 藤井高尚 Ruidai waka Reiya shū

類題草野集 +二巻 木村定良 Ruidai Kusano shū

類題和歌鰒玉集 五四巻 加納諸平 Ruidai waka Awabidama shū

類題和歌鴨川集 二巻 長澤伴雄 Ruidai waka Kamogawa shū

菅根集 二+五巻 清水濱臣 Sugene shū

清原集 三百五+巻 橘守部 Kiyohara shū

類題玉藻集 二巻 村上忠順 Ruidai Gyokusō shū

明倫歌集 +巻 鶴峯戊申等 Meiron kashū

　.8　明治及以後　　Since Meiji Period (1867-Date)

5899　家集　　　SPECIAL COLLECTIONS OF INDIVIDUAL AUTHORS
　　家集叢編入此,例如三+六人集,以及河西慶百首,等.

　.1　奈良時代　　　Nara Period (672-781)

山上憶良　　　　Yamanoue (no) Okura (660-733)

家集(續)　　　　INDIVIDUAL COLLECTIONS (Cont.)

5899.1	柿本人麿	Kakinomoto Hitomaro (662? - 710?)
	山部赤人	Yamabe Akihito (? - c.740)
	大伴家持	Ōtomono Yakamochi (718-785)
.2	平安時代	Heian Period (781-1185)
	遍照	Henjō (816-890)
	在原業平	Ariwara Narihira (827-880)
	小野小町	Onono Komachi (? - c.900)
	伊勢	Ise (? - c.900)
	紀友則	Kino Tomonori (845-905)
	素性	Sosei (? - c.906)
	凡河内躬恆	Oshikochi no Mitsune (859-907)
	藤原敏行	Fujiwara no Toshiyuki (? - 907)
	藤原興風	Fujiwara no Okikaze (? -911)
	坂上是則	Sakanoue no Korenori (? - c.925)
	藤原兼輔	Fujiwara no Kanesuke (878-933)
	源宗于	Minamoto no Muneyuki (? -939)
	紀貫之	Kino Tsurayuki (882-946)
	壬生忠岑	Mibu Todamine (? - c.950)
	清原元輔	Kiyohara Motosuke (908-990)
	源順	Minamoto no Shitago (911-983)
	平兼盛	Tairano Kanemori (? -990)
	大中臣能宣	Ōnakatomi Yoshinobu (922-991)
	中務	Naka tsukasa (? - c.992)
	檜垣嫗	Higaki no uba (- c.993)
	曽根好忠	Sone Yoshitada (? - c.994)
	大中臣輔親	Ōnakatomi Sukechika (954-1038)

家集（續）　　　INDIVIDUAL COLLECTIONS (Cont.)

5899.2	藤原公任	Fujiwarano Kinto (966-1041)
	源重之	Minamoto no Shigeyuki (? -1000)
	小大君	Koōigimi (? -c.1011)
	清少納言	Sei Shōnagon (? -c.1013)
	紫式部	Murasaki Shikibu (987-1015)
	和泉式部	Izumi Shikibu (? -c.1016)
	赤染衛門	Akazome Emon (? -c.1017)
	伊勢大輔	Ise no Ōsuke (? -c.1018)
	相模	Sagami (? -c.1040)
	藤原基俊	Fujiwara no Mototoshi (? -c.1138)
	源俊頼	Minamoto no Toshiyori (? -c.1140)
	藤原顯輔	Fujiwara no Akisuke (? -c.1154)
	源頼政	Minamoto no Yorimasa (1124-1180)
	平忠度	Tairano Tadanori (1144-1184)
.4	鎌倉時代	**Kamakura Period (1185-1333)**
	藤原俊成	Fujiwara no Toshinari (1114-1204)
	西行	Saigyō (1118-1190)
	俊惠	Shune (? -c.1190)
	寂蓮	Jakuren (? -c.1190)
	藤原隆信	Fujiwara no Takanobu (1138-1205)
	鴨長明	Kamono Chōmei (1153-1216)
	慈圓	Jien (1155-1225)
	藤原家隆	Fujiwara no Ietaka (1158-1237)
	待宵小侍從	Matsuyoi no Kojijū (? -c.1154)
	藤原伊利女	Fujiwarano Koretoshi no Jo
	藤原俊成女	Fujiwarano Toshinari no Jo
	藤原定家	Fujiwarano Sadaie (1162-1241)

家集（續） INDIVIDUAL COLLECTIONS (Cont.)

5899.4	藤原良經	Fujiwarano Yoshitsune (1169-1216)
	藤原雅經	Fujiwarano Masatsune (1170-1221)
	後鳥羽天皇	Go-Toba Tennō (1180-1239)
	源實朝	Minamotono Sanetomo (1192-1219)
	土御門天皇	Tsuchimikado Tennō (1195-1231)
	順德天皇	Juntoku Tennō (1197-1242)
	藤原為家	Fujiwara no Tameie (1197-1275)
	宗尊親王	Munetaka Shinō (1242-1274)
	冷泉為相	Reizei Tamesuke (1263-1328)
	藤原為兼	Fujiwarano Tamekane (1273-1332)
5899.5	室町時代	Muromachi Period (1333-1600)
	吉田兼好	Yoshida Kenkō (1283-1350)
	頓阿	Tona (1289-1372)
	嘉喜門院	Kakimonin (? -c.1381)
	藤原勝子	Fujiwarano Katsuko
	宗良親王	Munenaga Shinō (? -c.1381)
	正徹	Shōtetsu (1380-1458)
	東常緣	Tō Tsuneyori (1401-1494)
	飛鳥井雅親	Asukai Masachika (1417-1492)
	太田道灌	Ōta Dōkan (1432-1486)
	細川藤孝	Hosokawa Fujitaka (1534-1610)
	冷泉政為	Reizei Masatame (1445-1523)
	三條西實隆	Sanjōnishi Sanetaka (1455-1537)
	後柏原天皇	Go-Kashiwabara Tennō (1464-1526)
.6	江戶時代	Edo Period (1600-1867)
	木下長嘯子	Kinoshita Chōshōshi (1569-1649)

家集 (續)　　　　INDIVIDUAL COLLECTIONS (Cont.)

5899.6

松永貞德	Matsunaga Teitoku (1571-1653)
烏丸光廣	Karasumaru Mitsuhiru (1579-1638)
後水尾天皇	Go-Mizunoo Tennō (1594-1678)
烏丸資慶	Karasumaru Sukeyoshi (1623-1669)
下河邊長流	Shimokobe Nagaru (1624-1686)
德川光圀	Tokugawa Mitsukuni (1628-1700)
戶田茂睡	Toda Mosui (1629-1706)
契沖	Keichū (1640-1701)
梶子	Kajiko (? - c. 1710)
井上通女	Inoue Tsūjo (1660-1738)
荷田春滿	Koda (no) Azumamaro
似雲	Jiun (1673-1753)
油谷倭文子	Yuya Shizuko (1683-1752)
烏丸光榮	Karasumaru Mitsuhide (1689-1842)
加藤枝直	Katō Enao (1692-1785)
賀茂真淵	Kamo Mabuchi (1697-1769)
進藤茂子	Shindō Shigeko (? - c.1761)
石塚倉子	Ishizuka Kurako ( )
澄月	Chōgetsu (1714-1798)
田安宗武	Tayasu Munetake (1715-1771)
加藤竹里	Katō Chikuri (1720-1796)
加藤美樹	Katō Umaki (1721-1777)
荷田蒼生子	Kada (no) Tameko (1722-1786)
楫取魚彥	Katori Nahiko (1723-1765)
小澤蘆庵	Ozawa Roan (1723-1801)
橘千蔭	Tachibana Chikage (1725-1808)

家集（續）　　　INDIVIDUAL COLLECTIONS　(Cont.)

5899.6

鵜殿餘野子	Udono Yonoko (1729-1788)
本居宣長	Motoori Norinaga (1730-1801)
村田春海	Murata Harumi (1746-1811)
賀茂季鷹	Kamono Suetaka (1751-1842)
本居大平	Motoori Ōhira (1756-1833)
良寛	Ryōkan (1757-1831)
本居春庭	Motoori Haruniwa (1763-1828)
香川景樹	Kagawa Kageshige (1768-1843)
伴信友	Ban Nobutomo (1773-1846)
清水濱臣	Shimizu Hamaomi (1776-1824)
小林歌城	Kobayashi Utaki (1778-1862)
木下幸文	Kinoshita Sachibumi (1779-1821)
橘守部	Tachibana Moribe (1781-1849)
熊谷直好	Kumagai Naoyoshi (1782-1862)
松田真兄	Matsuda Naoe (1783-1854)
高畠志貴婦	Takabatake Shikibu (1785-1881)
石川依平	Ishikawa Yoshihira (1791-1859)
蓮月	Rengetsu (1791-1875)
中島廣足	Nakajima Hirotari (1792-1864)
大國隆正	Ōkuni Takamasa (1792-1871)
千種有功	Chikusa Arikoto (1797-1854)
大隈言道	Ōkuma Kotomichi (1798-1868)
八田知紀	Hatta Tomonori (1799-1873)
平賀元義	Hiraga Motoyoshi (1800-1865)
井上文雄	Inoue Fumio (1800-1871)
加納諸平	Kanō Morohira (1806-1857)

家集 (續)　　　INDIVIDUAL COLLECTIONS (Cont.)

5899.6　　　野村望東　　　　Nomura Bōtō (1806-1907)

渡忠秋　　　　Watari Tadaaki (1811-1881)

橘曙覽　　　　Tachibana Akemi (1812-1868)

5899.8　　　明治及以後　　Since Meiji Period (1867-date)

神山魚貫　　　Kamiyama Natsura (1792-1882)

行誠　　　　　Gyūkai (1806-1888)

辨玉　　　　　Bengyoku (1818-1880)

加藤千浪　　　Katō Chinami (1820-1877)

稅所敦子　　　Saisho Atsuko (1825-1900)

佐佐木弘綱　　Sasaki Hirotsuna (1828-1891)

海上胤平　　　Unagami Tanehira (1829-1916)

黑田清綱　　　Kuroda Kiyotsuna (1830-1917)

小出粲　　　　Koide Tsubara (1833-1908)

高崎正風　　　Takasaki Masakaze (1836-1912)

中島歌子　　　Nakajima Utako (1841-1903)

昭憲皇太后　　Shōken Kōtaiko (1850-1914)

明治天皇　　　Meiji Tennō (1852-1912)

阪正臣　　　　Ban Masaomi (1855-1931)

落合直文　　　Ochiai Naobumi (1861-1903)

大口鯛二　　　Oguchi Chitaiji (1864-1920)

佐佐木信綱　　Sasaki Nobutsuna (1872-　)

與謝野寬 鐵幹　Yosano Hiroshi (1873-1935)

島木赤彥　　　Shimagi Akahiko (1876-1926)

金子薰園　　　Kaneko Kunen (1876-　)

與謝野晶子　　Yosano Akiko (1878-　)

若山牧水　　　Wakayama Bokusui (1885-1928)

石川啄木　　　Ishikawa Takuboku (1886-1912)

5900	歌合	<u>UTA AWASE (CAPPING VERSES)</u>
.1	歷史	History
.2	論説	Theory and prosody
.3	撰集	Collections
	家集	Individual authors
.4	平安時代	Heian period
.5	鎌倉時代	Kamakura period
.6	室町時代	Muromachi period
.7	江戸時代	Edo period
.8	現代	Present age
5901	狂歌	**KYOKA (SATIRICAL POEMS)**
.3	狂歌書	Prosody
.6	撰集	Collections
.7	家集	Individual authors
5902	新詩	<u>POETRY OF NEW STYLE</u>
.3	歷史	History
.4	詩學	Prosody
.5	總集	General collections
.6	家集合輯	Series of Individual collections
.7	家集	Individual authors
5903	連歌	<u>RENGA (POETIC DIALOGUES)</u>
.1	歷史	History
.2	歌學 連歌式目	Prosody
.6	撰集	Selections
.7	家集	Individual authors
5904	俳諧 俳句, 發句.	<u>HAIKAI HOKKU (17 SYLLABLE VERSE)</u>
.1	期刊	Periodicals

俳諧（續）　　　HAIKAI　　　　（Cont.）

5904 .2	叢書.大系	Series. Collections
.3	書目	Bibliographies
.35	辭典 解釋術語者.	Dictionaries of nomanclature
.4	傳記	Biographies
.42	系譜	Pedigrees
.43	人名辭典	Dictionaries
.47	歷史	History
.5	俳論俳話.作句法	Theory and vertification
.6	歲時記.李寄	Seasonal inspiration
.7	全集及索引 俳諧辭典入此.	General collections and indexes
.72	排字俳句總集	Lexicographic
.74	分類俳句總集	Classified
.75	類集	Collections of special subjects
.8	撰集	Selections and Compilations
.81	芭蕉前撰集	Before Basho (? - 1670)
.82	芭蕉七部集	Compilation by Basho
.83	冬の日 一名尾張五歌仙.	Fuyu no Hi
.84	春の目	Haru no Hi
.85	曠野	Arano
.86	瓢	Hisago
.87	猿蓑	Sarumino
.883	炭俵	Sumidawara
.885	續猿蓑	Zoku Sarumino
.887	初懷紙 一名鶴の步.	Hatsu Kaishi
.889	深川集	Fukagawa Shu
	別座敷	Betsu Zashiki
.89	芭蕉後撰集	After Basho (1670-　　)

245

俳諧 (續)　HAIKAI　　　(Cont.)

5904.9　　　家集　　　　Works of Individual Authors

松永貞德　Matsunaga Teitoku (1571-1653)

鵜冠井今德　Kaedei Ryōtoku (1591-1679)

野野口立圃　Nonoguchi Ryūho (1599-1669)

西山宗因　Nishiyama Sōin (1605-1681)

安原貞室　Yasuhara Teishitsu (1610-1673)

北村季吟　Kitamura Kigin (1624-1705)

井原西鶴　Ihara Saikaku (1642-1693)

山口素堂　Yamaguchi Sodō (1642-1716)

松尾芭蕉　Matsuo Bashō (1644-1694)

杉山杉風　Sugiyama Sampū (1647-1732)

池西言水　Ikenishi Gonsui (1648-1719)

服部嵐雪　Hattori Ransetsu (1654-1707)

森川許六　Morikawa Kyoroku (1656-1715)

越智越人　Ochi Etsujin (1656-1730)

榎本其角　Enomoto Kikaku (1661-1707)

岩田涼菟　Iwata Ryōto (1661-1717)

上島鬼貫　Kamishima Onitsura (1661-1738)

稲津祇空　Inazu Gikū (1663-1733)

志田野坡　Shida Yaha (1663-1740)

各務支考　Kagami Shikō (1665-1731)

横井也有　Yokoi Yayū (1702-1783)

大島蓼太　Ōshima Ryōta (1708-1787)

谷口蕪村　Taniguchi Buson (1716-1783)

安井大江丸　Yasui Ōemaru (1722-1805)

加藤暁臺　Katō Gyōdai (1732-1792)

加舎白雄　Kaya Shirao (1738-1791)

川村碩布　Kawamura Sekifu (1750-1843)

	俳諧(續)	HAIKAI-HOKKU (Cont.)
5904.95	家集(續)	Works of Individual Authors
	遠藤同人	Endō Etsujin (1758-1836)
	小林一茶	Kobayashi Issa (1763-1827)
.96	正岡子規	Masaoka Shiki (1867-1902)
	大野洒竹	Ōno Sachiku (1872-1913)
	佐佐政一	Sassa Masakazu (1872-1917)
.97	沿波瓊音	Nunami Keion (1877-1927)
5905.1	俳諧句合	Haikai Kuawase
.2	春興歳旦帖	New Year compositions
.3	雜俳	Zappai (Minor haikai styles)
	前句附	Maekuzuke
	笠附	Kasazuke
	五文字	Gomoji
	折句	Oriku
	高點附句集	Kōten zukeku shū
.4	冠句	Kamuriku
.5	狂句	Kyōku
.6	地口	Jiguchi
.7	俳文 俳諧紀行	Haibun, Travel records containing haikai
.9	川柳	Senryu
5906	歌謠	KAYO (SONGS AND BALLADS)
.1	大歌 平安朝	Outa
.11	神樂歌	Kagura
.12	催馬樂	Saibara
.13	東遊歌	Azumaasobi no uta
.14	風俗歌	Fuzoku uta
.15	東歌	Azuma uta

247

歌謡（續）　　**KAYO (SONGS ~~AND BALLADS~~)**

5906.16	倭舞歌	Yamatomai uta
17	歌垣	Utagaki
.18	踏歌	Tōka
19	其他	Others
2	朗詠	Rōei
3	佛教歌　和讃,聲明,等.	Buddhist songs (Wasan, Shōmyō, etc.)
.4	今樣　梁塵秘鈔入此	Imayō
.5	神事歌　大曲樣志太良歌等. 書究1948.15	Shintoist songs (Ōutasama, Shidara uta, etc.)
.6	平曲　平家琵琶.	Heikyoku (Heikebiwa)
.63	琵琶	Biwa uta
.65	琴曲　明清樂	Koto uta
71	組歌	Kumi uta
.72	箏　黄生語入6742 箏貝)	Sōkyoku
73	三味線唄	Samisen uta
.75	地唄　上方唄	Jiuta (kamigata uta)
76	長唄	Nagauta
.77	端歌	Hauta
78	歌澤	Utazawa
	小唄　入俗謠	Kouta (see 5908.4-5908.8)
.8	現代唱歌	Modern songs
.9	宴曲　鎌倉至吉野朝	Enkyoku
.91	白拍子	Shira byōshi
.95	曲舞	Kyokumai
.93	延年舞	Ennemmai
97	幸若舞　舞的本入此	Kowakamai
.98	其他	Others

李板俗曲

歌謡（續）

5907	謡曲		**YŌKYOKU (NŌ SONGS)**
.1	歷史		History
.2	田樂		Dengaku
.3	猿樂		Sarugaku
.4	作法		Technique
.5	總集		Collections
.6	田樂能		Dengaku no nō
.7	猿樂能		Sarugaku no nō
.8	別集		Individual works
5908	俗謡		**ZOKUYŌ (FOLKSONGS)**
.1	室町小歌	加揷小謡	Muramichi period, 1392-1573)
.3	安土桃山小歌		Azuchi - Momoyama period, 1573-1600)
.4	江戸小歌	加揷小唄	Edo period, 1600-1868)
.6	明治小唄		Meiji period, 1868-1912
.7	大正小唄		Taishō period, 1912-1925
.8	昭和小唄		Shōwa period, 1926-
5909	俚謡		**RIYŌ (SONGS OF DIFFERENT LOCALITIES)**
.1	分地歌集		Collection by locality
.2	季節歌		Seasonal songs
.3	勞作歌		Working songs
.32	田歌	田植歌	Farmers' Songs
.34	棹歌	舟歌	Boatmen's Songs
.36	門付歌	乞食歌	Beggar's Songs
.38	其他		Other Songs
.4	祭禮歌		Rital Songs
.5	祝儀歌		Celebrating Songs
.6	踊歌	舞踊歌	Dancing Songs

俚謡(續) RIYŌ (Cont.)

5909.62	踊口説	Odorikudoki
.63	念佛踊	Nembutsu odori
.64	風流踊	Fūryū odori
.65	伊勢踊	Ise odori
.66	盆踊	Bonodori
.69	踊音頭	Odori ondō
.7	雜歌	Miscellaneous
.8	新民謡	New Sata bi uta
.9	童謡	Juvenile Songs
.97	新童謡	New juvenile songs

5910-5919	戲曲	**JAPANESE DRAMA**
5910	總錄 依體裁分用表一	**GENERAL** (Subdivide by form, like Table I)
5911	淨瑠璃	**JŌRURI (BALLAD-PLAYS)**
.1	歷史	History
.13	古淨瑠璃	Ancient jōruri
.15	初期淨瑠璃	Primitive jōruri, ? ~ 1623
.2	江戸淨瑠璃	Edo jōruri
.3	上方淨瑠璃	Kyōto jōruri
.39	新淨瑠璃	Modern jōruri
.4	義太夫	Gidayū
.5	豊後	Bungo
.52	大和路	Yamatoji
.54	繁太夫	Shigedayū
.56	薗八	Sonohachi
.6	新内	Shinnai

淨瑠璃(續)　JAPANESE DRAMA (Cont.)

5911.69	源氏	Genji
.7	常磐津	Tokiwazu
.8	富本	Tomimoto
.85	清元	Kiyomoto
5911.9	理論及作法	Theory and Methodology
5912	總集	Collections and Selections
5913	別集	Works of Individual Authors
	小野阿通	Onono Otsū (? - 1631)
	伊勢島宮内	Isejima Kūnai (? - c.1651)
	薩摩淨雲	Satsuma Jōun (1595-1672)
	松本治太夫	Matsumoto Jidayū (? - c.1682)
	井上播摩掾	Inoue Harima no Jō (1632-1685)
	岡清兵衛	Oka Seibe (? - 1686)
	岡本文彌	Okamoto Bunya (1632? - 1692?)
	宇治加賀掾	Uji Kaga no jō (1635-1711)
	竹本筑後少掾	Takemoto Chikugo no Shōjō (1651-1714)
	薩摩掾外記	Satsuma no Jō Geki (1652-1716)
	錦文流	Nishiki Bunryū (? - 1721)
	近松門左衛門	Chikamatsu Monzaemon (1653-1724)
	都太夫一中	Miyakodayū Itchū (? - 1724)
	紀海音	Kino Kaion (1663 - 1742)
	西澤一風	Nishizawa Ippū (1665-1731)
	宮古路豐後掾	Miyakoji Bungono Jō (? - 1740)
	文耕堂	Bunkōdō (? - c.1741)
	豐竹越前少掾	Toyotake Echizenno Shōjō (1681-1764)
	十寸見河東	Masumi Katō (1684-1725)

251

淨瑠璃(續) JAPANESE DRAMA (Cont.)

5913

長谷川千四	Hasegawa Senshi (1689-1733)
竹田出雲	Takeda Izumo (1691-1756)
並木宗輔	Namiki Sōsuke (1695-1751)
爲永太郎兵衛	Tamenaga Tarobē (? - c.1752)
竹田小出雲	Takeda Koizumo (? - 1759?)
吉田冠子	Yoshida Kanshi (? - 1760)
淺田一鳥	Asada Itcho (? - c. 1763)
三好松洛	Miyoshi Shōraku (1696? - 1772?)
並木丈輔	Namiki Jōsuke (c.1710-c.1750)
若竹笛躬	Wakatake Fuemi (? - c.1770)
鶴賀新內	Tsuruga Shinnai (1714-1774)
富本豐前太夫	Tomimoto Buzendayū (1716-1764)
鶴賀若狹掾	Tsuruga Wakasano Jō (1717-1786)
近松半二	Chikamatsu Hanji (1725-1787)
富本延壽	Tomimoto Enju (1727-1802)
平賀源內	Hiraga Gennai (1728-1779)
菅專助	Suga Sensuke (1728-1779)
並木正三	Namiki Shōzō (1730-1773)
筒井半二	Tsutsui Hanji (? - c.1778)
荻江露友	Ogie Royū (? - 1787)
中村阿契	Nakamura Akei (? - c.1788)
紀上太郎	Kino Jōtarō (1747-1799)
近松柳	Chikamatsu Yanagi (? - c.1801)
中村魚眼	Nakamura Gyogan (? - c.1817)
清本延壽太夫	Kiyomoto Enjudayū (1777-1825)
近松梅枝軒	Chikamatsu Baishiken (1785? - 1840?)

5914	狂言	**KYŌGEN (FARCES)**
	能狂言	Nō Kyōgen (Nō farce)
	間狂言	Aikyōgen (Interludes)
	本狂言	Hon Kyōgen (Independent performances)
	壬生狂言	Mibu Kyōgen
	照葉狂言	Teriha Kyōgen
5915-5919	脚本	**KYAKUHON (DRAMA)**
5915	歌舞伎	Kabuki (Operatic drama: Classical school)
.2	歷史	History
.4	理論	Theory
.6	總集	General Collections
.8	別集	Works of Individual Dramatists
	杵屋勘五郎	Kineya Kangorō (1574-1643)
	猿若勘三郎	Saruwaka Kansaburō (1598-1658)
	都傳内	Miyako Dennai (1618-1680)
	富永平兵衛	Tominaga Heibe (? -c.1698)
	津打治兵衛	Tsuuchi Jibe (? -c.1703)
	市川團十郎	Ichikawa Danjūrō (1660-1704)
	津打治兵衛 二世	Tsuuchi Jibe (1683-1760)
	藤本斗文	Fujimoto Toban (c.1693-c.1770)
	壕越二三治	Horigoshi Nisoji (1714-1778)
	奈河龜助	Nakawa Kamesuke (? -c.1785)
	櫻田治助	Sakurada Jisuke (1734-1806)
	增山金八	Masuyama Kimpachi (? -c.1798)
	瀬川如皐	Segawa Jokō (1739-1794)
	並木翁輔	Namiki Ōsuke (? -c.1800)
	辰岡萬作	Tatsuoka Mansaku (1742-1809)
	近松門喬	Chikamatsu Monkyō (? -1802?)

脚本 (續)　　　**KYAKUHON (DRAMA) (Cont.)**

5915.8

河竹新七	Kawatake Shinshichi (1747-1795)
並木五瓶	Namiki Gohei (1747-1808)
金井由輔	Kanai Yūsuke (? -c.1805)
並木十輔	Namiki Jūsuke (c.1759-c.1790)
並木正三 二世	Namiki Shōzō (? -1807)
村岡幸次	Muraoka Kōji (? -c.1810)
木村圍夫	Kimura Empu (? -1810)
近松徳三	Chikamatsu Tokuzō (1751-1810)
奈河七五三助	Nakawa Shimesuke (1754-1814)
鶴屋南北 四世	Tsuruya Nampoku (1755-1829)
瀬川如皐 二世	Segawa Jokō (1757-1833)
市岡和七	Ichioka Washichi (? -c.1817)
奈河篤助	Nakawa Tokusuke (1764-1842)
福森久助	Fukumori Kyūsuke (1767-1818)
篠田金治	Shinoda Kinji (1768-1819)
金井由輔 二世	Kanazawa Yūsuke (? -c.1820)
本屋宗七	Honya Sōshichi (? -1825)
増山金八 二世	Masuyama Kimpachi (? -1826)
櫻田治助 二世	Sakurada Jisuke (1768-1829)
百村猪三郎	Hyakumura Isaburō (1774-1834)
奈河七五三助 二世	Nakawa Shimesuke (? -1835?)
金澤吾輔	Kanazawa Gosuke (? -c.1837)
金澤一洗	Kanazawa Issen (? -c.1840)
金澤龍玉	Kanazawa Ryūgyoku (1779-1838)
金澤龍玉 二世	Kanazawa Ryūgyoku (? -1842)
勝俵藏 二世	Katsu Hyōzō (1781-1830)
奈河晴助	Nakawa Harusuke (1781-1826)

脚本 (續)　　　**KYAKUHON (DRAMA)** (Cont.)

5915.8	勝兵助	Katsu Hyōsuke (1786-1828)
	並木五瓶 三世	Namiki Gohei (1789-1855)
	増山金八 三世	Masuyama Kimpachi (? -c.1855)
	西澤一鳳	Nishizawa Ippō (1802-1852)
	櫻田治助 三世	Sakurada Jisuke (1802-1877)
	瀬川如皐 三世	Segawa Jokō (1806-1881)
	古河默阿彌	Furukawa Mokuami (1816-1893)
	勝能進	Katsu Nōshin (1821-1886)
	河竹新七 三世	Kawatake Shinshichi (1842-1901)
	竹柴其水	Takeshiba Kisui (1847-1923)
5916	新派劇	Shimpa geki (Operatic drama: New school)
.2	歷史	History
.4	理論	Theory
.6	總集	General collections
.8	別集	Individual collections
5917	新樂劇	Modern musical drama
.2	歷史	History
.4	理論	Theory
.6	總集	General collections
.8	別集	Individual collections
5918	近代劇	Modern prose drama
.2	歷史	History
.4	理論	Theory
.6	總集	General collections
.8	別集	Individual collections
5919	翻譯劇	Western drama translated

5921	小説	JAPANESE FICTION
	總記	GENERAL
.1	期刊	Periodicals
.2	會社	Societies
.3	叢集, 雜錄	Miscellanies
.4	書目	Bibliographies
.5	教學	Study and teaching
.6	辭典	Dictionaries
.8	歷史	History
.9	概論	General treatises
5921.95	總集	GENERAL COLLECTIONS
5922	奈良時代小説	Nara Period (novels)
5923	平安時代小説	Heian Period (781-1185) (novels)
5924.1	竹取物語	Taketori monogatari
.2	伊勢物語 二卷	Ise monogatari
.25	平中物語	Heichū monogatari
.3	大和物語 二卷	Yamato monogatari
.4	宇津保物語 二十卷	Utsubo monogatari
.5	落窪物語 四卷	Ochikubo monogatari
.6	源氏物語 五十四卷	Genji monogatari
.7	狹衣物語 四卷	Sagoromo monogatari
.74	濱松中納言物語 四卷	Hamamatsu chūnagon monogatari
.79	三寶繪詞	Sambō ekotoba
.8	今昔物語 六十卷	Konjaku monogatari
.87	打聞集	Uchigiki shū
.9	堤中納言物語 二卷	Tsutsumi chūnagon monogatari
5925.1	江談抄 五卷	Gōdanshō

小説（續）　　　JAPANESE FICTION (Cont.)

5925.3	取替へばや物語 四巻	Torikaebaya monogatari
.4	今取替へばや物語	Ima torikaebaya monogatari
.6	唐物語	Kara monogatari
.8	松浦宮物語 二巻	Matsurano miya monogatari
5926	鎌倉時代小説	**Kamakura Period (1185-1333)**
.11	寶物集 六巻	Hōbutsu shū
.17	住吉物語 二巻	Sumiyoshi monogatari
.2	古事談 六巻	Koji dan
.21	續古事談 六巻	Zoku koji dan
.25	發心集 三巻	Hosshin shū
.26	四季物語	Shiki monogatari
.27	閑居友 二巻	Kankyō no tomo
.29	撰集抄 九巻	Senjū shō
.3	宇治拾遺物語 十五巻	Uji shūi monogatari
.35	秋津島物語 入歴史	Akitsushima monogatari
.4	石清水物語 二巻	Iwashimizu monogatari
	十訓抄 三巻 入個人倫理	Jikkin shō　(Class in 1681)
.5	古今著聞集 二十巻	Kokon cho mon jū
5926.55	今物語	Ima monogatari
.6	鳴門中將物語	Naruto chūjō monogatari
.7	苔の衣 二巻	Koke no koromo
.73	わが身にたどる姫君	Wagami ni tadoru himegimi
.75	山路の露	Yamaji no tsuyu
.8	風につれなき物語	Kaze ni tsurenaki monogatari
.81	繪師草紙	Eshi zōshi
.82	男衾三郎繪詞	Obusuma Saburō ekotaba
.83	地獄草紙	Jigoku sōshi

	小説 (續)	JAPANESE FICTION (Cont.)
5926.84	ぼろぼろの草紙	Boroboro no sōshi
.85	砂石集 +卷	Shaseki shū
.86	雜談集 +卷	Zodan shū
.87	松蔭中納言物語	Shōin chūnagon monogatari
.88	長谷雄物語	Haseo monogatari
.89	小夜衣	Sayogoromo
.9	兵部卿物語	Hyōbukyō monogatari
5927	室町時代小説	Muromachi Period (1333-1600)
	御伽草子	
.1	稚兒物	Homosexual
.2	戀愛物	Romantic
.3	孝行譚及祝儀物	Filial
.4	繼子物	Step-child
.47	英雄譚或人傳説,復仇譚	Heroic and revengeful
.48	義經記 八卷	Gigkei ki
.49	曾我物語 +二卷	Sōga monogatari
	太平記 四十卷 入歷史	Taiheiki (Class in 3356)
.5	其他	Others
.6	遁世物	Hermitic
	發心譚及懺悔譚	
.7	法談物及本地物	Buddhistic
	地獄極樂囲説話入此.	
.8	異類物	Personific
	擬人物.	
.9	怪異譚	Supernatural
5928.	江戸時代小説	Edo Period (1600-1867)
5929.1	假名草子	Kana zōshi
.2	浮世草子	Ukiyo zōshi
.3		
.4	草雙紙	Kusa zōshi
.5	行成表紙	Kōseibyōshi

小説（續）　JAPANESE FICTION (Cont.)

5929.55	赤小本	Akakohon
.57	雛豆本	Hinamamehon
.6	赤本	Akahon
.7	黑本	Kurohon
.8	青本	Aohon
.9	黄表紙	Kibyōshi
5930	合巻	Gōkan mono
5930.2	讀本	Yomihon
.3	軍記,實録	Gunki and Jitsuroku
.4	洒落本	Share bon
.5	人情本	Ninjō bon
.6	滑稽本	Kokkei bon
.7	狂言本	Kyōgen bon
.9	其他	Others
5931	現代	Modern Period (1867 - ?)
5932	總集	General collections
5933	別集	Individual authors
5937	講談	Kōdan
5938	童話 御伽噺.	Fairy tales. Otogibanashi
5941	散文	JAPANESE PROSE, ESSAYS, DIARIES
5942	大和時代	Yamato Period (Earliest to 781)

祝詞,壽詞,宣命入神道.　For norito, yogoto and semmyō
氏文入傳記.　see 1947; for ujibumi see 2280.5;
風土記入地理.　for fūdoki see 3408.2; for Kojiki
古事記, 日本書紀, 入歷史.　and Nihon shoki see 3325 and 3326.

散文(續)　　　JAPANESE PROSE, ESSAYS (Cont.)

5943	平安時代		Heian Period (781-1185)
.2	土佐日記	紀貫之	Tosa nikki
.3	蜻蛉日記	三卷 藤原道綱母	Kagerō nikki
.35	高光日記		Takamitsu nikki
.37	篁日記	即多武峯少将物語 小野篁	Takamura nikki
.4	枕草子	清少納言	Makura no sōshi
.5	紫式部日記	二卷	Murasaki shikibu nikki
.55	和泉式部日記		Izumi shikibu nikki
.56	いほ奴し	増基	Ionushi
.6	更科日記	菅原孝標女 栗級日記	Sarashina no nikki
.7	成尋阿闍梨母集		Jōjin azari haha no shū
.8	建春門院中納言日記		Kenshun monin chūnagon nikki
.9	讚岐典侍日記	二卷	Sanuki no suke no nikki
.97	其他		Others
5944	鎌倉時代		Kamakura Period (1185-1333)
.1	方丈記	鴨長明	Hojō ki
.2	海道記	二卷	Kaidō ki
.3	東關紀行		Tō kan ki kō
.33	信生法師日記		Shinjō hōshi nikki
.36	辨内侍日記	二卷	Ben no naishi nikki
.72	十六夜日記	阿佛尼	Izayoi nikki
.5	源家長日記		Minamoto Ienaga nikki
.6	中務内侍日記		Nakatsukasa naishi nikki
.7	轉寢記	阿佛尼	Utatane no ki
.9	其他		Others

散文（續）　　　JAPANESE PROSE, ESSAYS (Cont.)

5945	室町時代	Muromachi Period (1333-1600)
.1	徒然草 二巻 吉田兼好	Tsurezure gusa
.2	寝覺記	Nezame ki
	大神宮參宮記 坂土佛	Daijingū sangū ki (Class in 1945.094)
.25	竹むきの記	Takemuki no ki
.3	小島の口すさび 二條良基	Oshima no guchisusabi
.35	なぐさめ草 正徹	Nagusame gusa
.4	道行きぶり 今川了俊	Michiyuki buri
.45	廻國雜記 道興	Kaikoku zakki
.52	東齋隨筆 一條兼良	Tōsai zuihitsu
.53	小夜の寝覺 一條兼良	Sayo no nezame
.54	藤河の記 一條兼良	Fujikawa no ki
.55	文明一統記 一條兼良	Bummei ittō ki
.56	樵談治要 一條兼良	Shōdan jiyō
.6	榻鴫曉筆	Tōten gyōhitsu sho
.65	身のかたみ	Mi no katami
.7	夢庵記 里見肖功	Muan ki
.75	三愛記	San'ai ki
.8	我宿草 三巻 太田道灌	Waga yado gusa
.85	平安紀行	Heian kikō
.9	其他	Others
5946.1	江戸時代	Edo Period (1600-1867)
.3	總集	Collections
.5	別集	Individual authors
.7	現代	Present Age (1867 -)
.9	總集	Collections
5947	別集	Individual authors

5948	演説	JAPANESE ORATORY
.9	總集	Collections
5949	別集	Individual authors
5950	書牘 消息文, 往來人	JAPANESE LETTERS (Epistolary and Documentary Style)
5951	總集	General collections
5952.9	別集	Individual authors
5963	諷刺, 滑稽 參見狂歌, 雜俳, 川柳.	JAPANESE SATIRE AND HUMOR See also 5901, 5905.3, 5905.9.
5964	戲文, 狂文, 撰書	Gibun, ~~Nonense literature~~ *Nonsensical tales*
5965	笑話 噺本落語漫談	Jokes, humorous stories
5966	雜文學	JAPANESE MISCELLANY
5967	諺語, 格言.	Proverbs, Mottoes
5968	謎	Riddles
5969	漢詩文 宜入中國文學.	LITERAL WRITINGS IN PURE CHINESE (Class with Chinese Literature, see 5560)

5970.4	近於日語言文學	OTHER LANGUAGES AND LITERATURES ~~SIMILAR~~ *NEAR* TO JAPANESE
5970	琉球語言文學	Loochoo language and literature
5971	蝦夷語言文學	Aino language and literature
5973	朝鮮語言文學	Korean language and literature

5975-5995[3]	印歐語言文學	<u>INDO-EUROPEAN LANGUAGES AND LITERATURES</u>
5975-5976	印度系語言文學	Indic languages and literatures (Sanskrit, Pali, etc.)
5977-5979	伊蘭系語言文學	Iranic languages and literatures (Persian, etc.)
5980	希臘語言文學	Greek language and literature
5981	拉丁語言文學	Latin language and literature
5982	意大利語言文學	Italian language and literature
5983	法蘭西語言文學	French language and literature
5984	西班牙語言文學	Spanish language and literature
5985	葡萄牙語言文學	Portuguese language and literature
5986	其他羅馬語言文學	Other Romanic languages and literatures
5987	斯堪得那威語文	Gothic. Scandinavian languages and literatures
5988	英美語言文學	English language and literature (including U.S.A.)
5989	荷蘭語言文學	Dutch language and literature
5990	德意志語言文學	German language and literature
5991	其他日耳曼語語文學	Other Germanic languages and literatures
5992	俄羅斯語言文學	Russian language and literature
5993	其他斯拉夫語語文學	Other Slavic languages and literatures
5994-5	含塞語言文學	<u>HAMITO-SEMITIC LANGUAGES AND LITERATURES</u>
5994	含族系語言文學	Hamitic languages and literatures (Egyptian)
5995	塞姆系語言文學	Semitic languages and literatures (Hebrew, Arabic, etc.)
5996	班圖語言文學	<u>BANTU (AFRICAN) LANGUAGES AND LITERATURES</u>
5997	美洲土人語言	<u>AMERICAN LANGUAGES</u>
5998	馬來海洋洲語言文學	<u>MALAY-POLYNESIAN LANGUAGES AND LITERATURES</u> (Phillippine, Formosan, Malay, Javanese, etc.)
5999	杜拉維典及其他語言文學	<u>DRAVIDIAN AND OTHER MINOR LANGUAGES AND LITERATURES</u>

6000-6999 美術游藝類 FINE AND RECREATIVE ARTS

6000-6069 一般藝術 ART IN GENERAL

6000-6009 總錄 GENERAL (Subdivide by Table I)

6010-6019 美術館,藝術展覽 ART GALLERIES AND MUSEUMS, EXHIBITIONS
依體裁分,用表一 (Catalogues, Directories, etc.)

6010 國際 International

6011-2 中國 China

6011 中央 National

6012 地方 Local (Subdivide by Geographical
依地理分,用表二. Table II)

6013-4 日本 Japan

6013 中央 National

6014 地方 Local (Subdivide by Geographical
依地理分,用表二. Table II)

6015 其他亞洲諸國 Other Countries in Asia
依地理分,用表二. (Subdivide by Geographical Table II)

6016-9 其他世界各國 Other Countries in the World
(Subdivide by Geographical Table II)

6020-6029 美學,藝術概論 AESTHETICS

6030-6069 藝術史 HISTORY OF ART

6030-6039 中國 Chinese (Subdivide by periods like Table III)
依時代分,用表三

6040-6048 日本 Japanese (Subdivide by periods like Table III)
依時代分,用表三,或
仿藝史傳分.

6049.8 琉球 Loochoo (Ryūkyū)

6049.9 朝鮮 Korean (Chōsen)

6050-6059 其他亞洲民族 Other Asiatic Peoples
依地理分,用表二. (Subdivide by Geographical Table II)

6060-6069 西洋 Western Art

6060 概論 General

6061 初民時代 Primitive and Ancient

6062 古代 Classical (Greek and Roman)

歴史 (續)
西洋 (續)　　　HISTORY OF WESTERN ART (Cont.)

6063-4	中世	Medieval
6065-8	近世	Modern
6065	文藝復興時代	Renaissance
6066	十七及十八世紀	17th and 18th Centuries
6067	十九世紀	19th Century
6068	二十世紀	20th Century
6069	專國 依地理分,用表二.	Special Countries (Use Table II)

6070-6299 書畫 附文房　　CALLIGRAPHY AND PAINTING

6070-6189 中國書畫　　CHINESE CALLIGRAPHY AND PAINTING

6070-9	總錄 依體裁分,用表一.	General (Form subdivisions by Table I.)
6080-6109	史傳 依時代分,用表三.	History and Biography of Calligraphy and Painting (Divide chronologically like Table III)
6090-9	書史傳 依時代分,用表三.	Of Calligraphy (Divide chronologically like Table III)
6100-9	畫史傳 依時代分,用表三.	Of Painting (Divide chronologically like Table III)
6110-6125	宗派	Schools of Calligraphy and Painting
6128-6130	法式	Technique of Calligraphing and Painting
6129	書法	Of Calligraphing
6130	畫法	Of Painting
6133-6135	評論	Critique of Calligraphy and Painting
6134	書評	Of Calligraphy
6135	畫評	Of Painting
6137-6139	題識考證	Commentaries on and Identification of Calligraphs and Paintings
6138	書之題識考證	On Calligraphs
6139	畫之題識考證	On Paintings
6140-6149	目錄 依時代分,用表三.	Catalogues of Calligraphs and Paintings (Divide chronologically like Table III)

CHINESE CALLIGRAPHY AND PAINTING (Cont.)

6150-6159	書畫譜	Collections of Calligraphs and Paintings
6160-6169	書譜	Of Calligraphs
6170-6179	畫譜	Of Paintings
6180-6189	雜考,雜識	Miscellanies
6190-6289	日本書畫	JAPANESE CALLIGRAPHY AND PAINTING
6190-6199	總錄	General (Subdivide by form like Table I)
6200-6230	史傳	History and Biography
		(See also 6040-8 History of Japanese Art)
6200-6209	書史傳	Calligraphy
		(Divide by period like 6210-6219)
6210-6219	畫史傳	Drawing and Painting
6210.9	上古時代	Primitive period (Earliest to 552 A.D.)
6211	飛鳥時代	Asuka period (552-645)
6212	奈良時代	Nara Period (645-810)
.3	白鳳時代	Haku hō period (645-720)
.6	天平時代	Tempyō period (720-810)
6212.9	平安時代	Heian period (810-1185)
6213	貞觀時代	Jōgan period (810-980)
6214	藤原時代	Fujiwara period (980-1185)
6215	鎌倉時代	Kamakura period (1185-1333)
6216	室町時代	Muromachi period (1333-1568)
6217	桃山時代	Momoyama period (1568-1600)
6218	江戸時代	Edo period (1600-1868)
6219	現代	Present age (1868-date)
6220-6230	家派	Schools
6221	佛畫派	Buddhist school (Koze and Takuma)
6222	漢畫派 (北宗)	Old Chinese school (Kano; Kaihoku; Sesshū; Unkoku; Hasegawa; Soga)

266

日本書畫(繪)　JAPANESE CALLIGRAPHY AND PAINTING (Cont.)

6224	文人畫(南宗) 文晁派等	~~Literary~~ School *of literati* (Bunchō and others).
6225	寫生畫派 長崎畫派及圓山,四條,岸諸派	Naturalistic school (Nagasaki, Maruyama, Shijō and Kishi)
6226	大和繪 土佐,住吉,光悦,光琳諸派.	Yamatoe school (Tosa, Sumiyoshi, Kōetsu, and Kōrin)
6228	浮世繪 菱川,宮川,鳥居,勝川,北齋,歌 麿,歌川,廣重,諸派.	Ukiyoe school (Hishikawa, Miyakawa, Torii, Katsukawa, Hokusai, Utamaro, Utagawa, Hiroshige)
6230	近世畫派	Modern schools
6238-6240	法式	Technique
6239	書法	Calligraphy
6240	畫法	Drawing and painting
6243-6245	評論	Critique
6244	書法	Calligraphy
6245	畫法	Drawing and painting
6247-6249	考證題識	Identification and Commentaries
6248	書	Calligraphy
6249	畫	Drawing and painting
6250-6252	目錄	Catalogues
6251	書	Calligraphy
6252	畫	Drawing and painting
6260-6269	書畫集	Collections (Divide by period like 6210-6219)
6270-6279	書集 仿畫史傳分時代	Calligraphs (Divide by period like 6210-6219)
6280-6289	畫集	Drawings and paintings
6281	佛畫派	Buddhist school

日本書畫(續)　JAPANESE CALLIGRAPHY AND PAINTING (Cont.)

6282	漢畫派	Chinese school
6283	文人畫派	~~Literary~~ School of literati
6284	寫生畫派	Naturalistic school
6285	大和繪	Yamatoe school
6286	浮世繪	Ukiyoe school
6287	近世畫派	Modern schools
6288.1-.9	諸家畫集 仿畫史傳分時代	Individual artists (Divide by period like 6210-6219)
6289	專類畫集	Special subjects
.1	繪卷物	Emaki mono
.2	風俗畫歷史畫 參見浮世繪畫集.	Genre (See Ukiyoe, 6286)
.3	名所繪	Views
.4	山水繪	Landscapes
.5	人物肖像	Human figures and portraits
.6	動物花卉	Animals and birds
.7	靜物	Still life
.8	圖案	Design
.9	其他	Others
6290-6299	文房	MATERIALS AND INSTRUMENTS, FANCY STATIONERIES
6291	概論	General treatises
6292	通史	General history
6293	紙	Paper
6294	筆	Brush ~~pens~~
6295	墨	Ink (Indian)
6296	硯	Ink slabs
6298	石	Artistic stones

6300-6349	西洋畫	WESTERN DRAWING AND PAINTING
6300-9	總錄 依體裁分,用表一.	GENERAL (Form Divisions like Table I)
6310-9	派別	VARIOUS SCHOOLS OF OCCIDENTAL PAINTING
6320-9	種類	SPECIAL SUBJECTS OF OCCIDENTAL PAINTING
6330-9	素畫	DRAWING AND DESIGN
6340-9	彩畫	PAINTING (Water-colour and oil)

6350-6359	版畫 此處祇收散張版畫 或畫本版畫,各種刻 版術及其歷史見9400- 9499.	ENGRAVINGS; COLLECTIONS OF PRINTS. Here are classed only prints in sheets or in book-form. For works on the History and Technique of the various kinds of engraving see 9400-9499 Printing and Publishing.
6350.1-.9	總錄	GENERAL
6351-3	木版畫	WOOD ENGRAVINGS
6351	中國	CHINESE PRINTS
6352	日本	JAPANESE PRINTS
6353	西洋	WESTERN PRINTS
6354	銅版畫	COPPER ENGRAVINGS
6355	鋼版畫	STEEL ENGRAVINGS
6356	石印畫	LITHOGRAPHS
6357	鋅版畫	ZINCOGRAPHS
6358-9	其他機器版畫	PRINTS MADE BY OTHER MECHANICAL PROCESSES

6360-6399　攝影　　　　　　　PHOTOGRAPHY
　　　　　　　照相,寫真.

6360.1-.9　總錄　　　　　　GENERAL (Form subdivisions like Table I)
　　　　　　依體裁分,用表一.

6361　　　攝影光學　　　　　PHOTO-OPTICS (Better class with 7260)
　　　　　　宜入科學.

6362　　　攝影化學　　　　　PHOTO-CHEMISTRY (Better class with 7350)
　　　　　　宜入科學

6363-6369　器材　　　　　　APPARATUS AND MATERIALS

6370-6379　方法　　　　　　PROCESSES OF PHOTOGRAPHING

6371-6376　陰攝法　　　　　NEGATIVE PROCESSES

6377-6379　陽攝法　　　　　POSITIVE PROCESSES

6380-6389　特種攝影法　　　SPECIAL APPLICATIONS

6390-6399　攝影集　　　　　COLLECTION OF PHOTOGRAPHS

6400-6499　雕塑　　　　　　SCULPTURE

6400-6409　總錄　　　　　　GENERAL
　　　　　　依體裁分,用表一.

6410-6419　印璽　　　　　　SIGILLOGRAPHY
　　　　　　圖章

6410　　　叢集,書目　　　　Collections, Bibliographies

6411　　　史傳　　　　　　History and Biography

6412　　　刻法,用法,印泥　　Technique of Seal-engraving, of using
　　　　　　　　　　　　　　Seals, and of preparing ink-pads
　　　　　　　　　　　　　　for Seals

	印璽 (續)	SCULPTURE (Cont.)
6413-6418	譜錄	Catalogues
6413	通代	All periods
6414	宋	Sung Dynasty (960-1279)
6415	元	Yüan Dynasty (1280-1368)
6416	明	Ming Dynasty (1368-1644)
6417	清	Ch'ing Dynasty (1644-1912)
6418	民國	The Republic (1912- date)
6419	文字考證	Inscriptions and Identification
6420-6429	石刻 琢玉	STONE CARVING, GEMS.
6430-6439	金刻	METAL CARVING, BRONZES.
6440-6449	木刻	WOOD CARVING
6450-6459	竹刻	BAMBOO CARVING
6460-6469	牙彫, 骨彫	IVORY AND BONE CARVING
6470-6479	泥塑	PLASTER AND CLAY WORK
6480-6489	特種彫塑	SPECIAL FORMS OF SCULPTURE
6490-6499	材具	MATERIALS AND INSTRUMENTS

6500-6599	建築	<u>ARCHITECTURE</u>
6500-6509	總錄 依體裁分, 用表一.	GENERAL (Form subdivisions like Table I)
6510-6539	歷史 附史蹟.	HISTORY (Including Historical Monuments)
6510-6519	中國	China
6510	通論	General Treatises
6511-6518	歷代 依時代分, 用表三.	Of Different Historical Periods (Subdivide chronologically by Table III)
6519	地方 依地域分, 用表二.	Of Different Localities (Subdivide geographically by Table II)
6520-6529	日本 做中國分.	Japan (Subdivide like ''China'')
6530	高麗 做中國分, 用小數. .01-.09 分時代, .1-.9 分地方.	Korea (Subdivide like ''China'' by using decimal numbers .01-.09 for periods and .1-.9 for localities.)
6531	其他亞洲諸國 依地理分, 用表二.	Other Asiatic Countries (Subdivide by geographical Table II)
6532-6539	西洋	Western Countries
6532	通論	General Treatises
6533-6	歷代	Of Different Historical Periods
6533	古代	Ancient and Classical
6534	中世	Medieval
6535	近世	Modern
6536	現代	Recent (20th Century)
6537-9	各國 依地理分, 用表二.	Of Different Countries (Subdivide by geographical Table II)

6540-6549	建築設計	ARCHITECTURAL DESIGN (DRAWING AND DETAILS)
6541	圖樣	Plans, Drawings.
6543	模型	Models and Modeling
6545	驗聲	Architectural Acoustics
6547	法式	Orders of Architecture
6549	細則	Details, Motifs, etc.
6550-6559	建築裝飾	ARCHITECTURAL DECORATION
6551	漆繪	Painted Decoration
6552	彫塑	Sculptured Decoration
6554	鑲嵌	Tesselated Work (Mosaic)
6556	木工	Woodwork
6557	鐵工	Iron work
6559	裝修	Fixed Furniture. Miscellaneous Accessories.
6560-6579	各種建築	SPECIAL CLASSES OF BUILDINGS
6531-3	宗教建築物	Religious Architecture
	參見各宗教寺廟及美術.	(See also Temples, Religious Art under each Religion.)
6564-6	國家建築物	National Architecture: Palaces, Castles, City-walls and Memorial Monuments, etc.
	宮殿,城郭,牌樓,及其他公共紀念物等,參見地理類之名勝古蹟.	(See also 3041-3049. Scenery, Antiquities in Geography)
6567-9	行政建築物 官署衙門	Governmental Buildings
6570-3	教育與科學建築物 學校,圖書館,博物館,天文台,試驗所,醫院,等.	Educational and Scientific Buildings
6574-5	游藝建築物 戲園,體育館,等.	Recreative Buildings (Theatres, etc.)
6576-7	工商建築物 工場,倉庫,市場,車站,商店,等.	Commercial and Industrial Buildings
6578-9	住宅建築	Domestic Architecture (Dwelling houses)

6580-6599	風景建築 風景園藝	LANDSCAPE ARCHITECTURE (LANDSCAPE GARDENING)
6580	總錄 依體裁分, 冊表一.	General
6581	都市計畫 汎論入此, 某城 市之特別計畫入 政治.	City Planning (General works only. Works on Special Cities go with Municipal Government, 4743-4769, 4786.)
6583	道路	Walks, Boulevards.
6585	公場	Public Squares and Promenades
6586	公園	Public Parks and Gardens
6587	水道	Water: lakes, etc.
6589	天然風景	Natural Landscapes, Scenery.
6590	庭園	Private Gardens
6591	水景	Water (Ponds, streams, waterfalls, fountains, wells, waterbasins)
6592	橋島	Bridges and Islands
6593	疊石	Rocks and Stones
6594	籬柵	Bars and Fences
6595	路, 燈	Paths and Lanterns
6596	花草 宜入園藝.	Flowers and Grasses (Better class with 8152 Horticulture)
6597	樹木 宜入林業.	Trees (Better class with 8160 Forestry)
6598	盆景	Pots and Vases (with flowers, plants or goldfish)
6599	其他	Others

6600-6699	工藝美術	ART APPLIED TO INDUSTRY
6600-6609	總錄	GENERAL (Form subdivisions like Table I)
	依體裁分、用表一.	
6610-6615	工藝美術運動	ARTS AND CRAFTS MOVEMENT
6616-6619	工藝品圖案飾模樣	DESIGNS FOR DECORATION AND ORNAMENT
6616	中國	Chinese
6617	日本	Japanese
6618	其他亞洲諸國	Other Asiatic Peoples
6619	西洋	Western
6620-6629	室内裝飾	INTERIOR DECORATION
6621	漆畫	Decorative Painting
6622	家具	Furniture
6623	地壇	Rugs, Carpets.
6624	屏風	Screens
6625	掛錦	Tapestries
6626	壁軸	Upholstery, Wall-hangings, etc.
6627	裱紙	Wall-papers
6629	其他	Others (Lamps, etc.)
6630-6639	佩帶飾品	COSTUME ACCESSORIES AND GLYPTIC ARTS
6631	刀劍	Swords
6633	扇	Fans
6634	玉	Jades
6636	象牙	Ivories
6637	珠寶首飾	Gold and Silver Jewelry
6639	其他	Others

6640-6649	窰工 陶磁.	CERAMICS
6641	陶器	Earthenware
6643	石器	Stoneware
6644	磁器	Porcelain
6646	珐瑯 景泰藍.	Cloisonné
6647	琉璃	Glassware
6649	其他	Others

| 6650-6659 | 刺繡染織. | **NEEDLEWORK AND TEXTILE ARTS** |

| 6660-6669 | 竹木器 | **BAMBOO AND WOOD WORKS** |

| 6670-6679 | 漆器 | **LACQUER WARES** |

| 6680-6689 | 鐵器 | **METAL WORKS (Pewters, Iron Pictures, etc)** |

| 6690-6699 | 其他 如皮件,牛角,筆. | **OTHERS (Leather Works, Horn Wares, etc.)** |

6700-6799	音樂	**MUSIC**
6701-9	總錄 依體裁分,用表一.	GENERAL (Form subdivisions like Table I)
6710-6729	史傳	HISTORY AND BIOGRAPHY
6711-2	中國	China
6713-4	日本	Japan
6715-6	其他亞洲諸國 依地理分,用表二.	Other Asiatic Countries (Subdivide by Table II)
6717-29	西洋 依地理分,用表二.	Western Countries (Subdivide by Table II)
6730-6739	樂理樂律	THEORY AND COMPOSITION
6740-6749	聲樂	VOCAL MUSIC
6740	歌集	Collected songs
6741	發聲法,歌唱法	Art of singing
6742	民歌	Folk songs
6743	國歌	National airs
6744	節氣歌	Festival songs
6745	團體歌	Society songs
6746	學校歌	School and college songs
6747	幼童歌	Nursery songs
6748-6751	典禮樂,聖樂	RITUALISTIC MUSIC; SACRED MUSIC.
6748	中國	Chinese
6749	日本	Japanese
6749.9	朝鮮	Korean
6750	印度及其他亞洲諸國 依地理分,用表二.	Indian and other Asiatic Countries (Subdivide by Table II)
6751	西洋 依地理分,用表二.	Western Countries (Subdivide by Table II)

6752-6755	舞樂	DANCING MUSIC
6752	中國 古舞	Chinese
6753	日本 舞	Japanese
6754	其他亞洲諸國	Other Asiatic Countries (Subdivide by Table II)
	依地理分,用表二.	
6755	西洋 依地理分,用表二.	Western Countries (Subdivide by Table II)
6756-6759	劇樂	DRAMATIC MUSIC
6756	中國 曲譜入此,曲文入文學(5650),身段譜入演劇(6830).	Chinese
.2	崑曲	Kun Ch'u or Soochow Airs
.4	弋腔,高腔	I-yang and Kao-yang Airs
.5	京調 皮黄	Peking Airs (Hsi-p'i and Erh-huang)
.7	梆子調	P'ang-tzû or Northern high pitch Airs
.9	其他	Others
6757	日本 能樂,歌舞伎,新歌劇.	Japanese
6758	其他亞洲諸國 依地理分,用表二.	Other Asiatic Countries (Subdivide by Table II)
6759	西洋 依地理分,用表二.	Western Countries (Subdivide by Table II)
6760-6799	管絃樂	INSTRUMENTAL MUSIC AND INSTRUMENTS
6760-6769	管樂	Wind Instruments
6760	壎(塤),鴿鈴,等	Hsün, Ko-ling, etc. (Whistles)
6761	簫,尺八	Hsiao and Shakuhachi (Vertically blown pipes)
	排簫,篠笛,等	P'ai-hsiao and Shinobue, etc. (Pandean pipes)
6762	笛	Ti or Fue (Flutes or transversely blown pipes)
	神樂笛,狛笛	Kagurabue, Komabue.

278

	管樂 (續)	Wind Instruments (Cont.)
6763	簧	Kuan (Pipes with reeds)
	觱篥 (篳篥), 喇叭等	Pi-li (Hichiriki), La-pa, etc.
6764	笙	Shêng or Shô (Small hand-organ composed of bamboo pipes with free reeds)
6765	號角	Ho, Chiao and their family. (Horns and Tubes or cut-mouth pieces)
6766	其他東洋管樂器	Other Oriental Wind Instruments
6767-8	西洋管樂器	Western Wind Instruments
6769	風琴	Western Organs
6770-6779	絃樂	Stringed Instruments
6771	琴	Ch'in or Kin (Koto) (Horizontal Psalteries)
	和琴	Yamatogoto (Japanese Harp)
6772	瑟	Shê or Shitsu (Lyres)
	箏	Chêng or Sō (A smaller kind of Shê)
6773	月琴	Yüeh Ch'in (Chinese Moon-shaped Guitar)
	琵琶	P'i-p'a or Biwa (Guitars)
6774	絃子, 三絃, 三味線	Hsien-tzu, San Hsien, Samisen (Strings)
6775	胡琴, 鼓弓	Hu Ch'in or Kokyū (Violins)
6776	其他東洋絃樂器	Other Oriental Stringed Instruments
6777	凡亞林	Western Violins
6778	其他西洋絃樂器	Other Western Stringed Instruments
6779		Western Pianos

6780-6789	打擊及機械樂器	<u>Percussion and Mechanical Instruments</u>
6781	鼓	Ku (Drums)
6782	木魚	Mu Yü (Wood drums)
6783	板 拍子	Pan (Castanets)
6784	鈸	Po (Cymbals)
6785	鑼	Lo (Gongs)
6786	鐘鈴	Chung, Ling (Bells without or with Clappers)
6787	其他東洋打擊樂器	Other Oriental Percussion Instruments
6788	西洋打擊樂器	Western Percussion Instruments
6789	機械樂器	Mechanical Instruments
.1	音樂箱	Music box
.2	留聲機	Phonographs and records
.3		
.4		
.5		
.6		

6790-6799	樂團,隊樂	INSTRUMENTAL ENSEMBLE
6791	中國	Chinese Orchestral Music
6792	日本	Japanese Orchestral Music
6793	其他亞洲民族	Orchestral Music of other Asiatic Peoples
6794	西洋	Western Orchestral Music
6795	西洋附歌團樂	Western Orchestral Music with Voice
6796-8	軍樂	Brass band music
6799	室內音樂	Chamber Music

6800-6899	游藝,娛樂	<u>AMUSEMENTS AND GAMES</u>
6801-6809	總錄 依體裁分,用表一.	GENERAL (Form subdivisions like Table I)
6810-6825	跳舞	DANCING
6811-9	史傳	History and biography
6812-5	中國	China
6816-7	日本	Japan
6818	其他亞洲諸國	Other Asiatic Countries (Divide by Table II)
6819	西洋諸國	Western Countries (Divide by Table II)
6822	跳舞道德	Ethics of dancing
6823	跳舞會	Balls, parties, etc.
6824	跳舞法	Technique. Instruction.
6825	各式跳舞	Special Forms of Dancing
6826-6839	戲院,演劇 戲劇,舞台藝術	THEATER STAGE DRAMATIC ART
6826.1-.9	總錄 依體裁分,用表一.	General (Form subdivisions like Table I)
6827-6833	中國劇 文詞入文學. 樂譜入音樂.	Chinese Theater Words of Songs and texts of dialogues go with 5660 Dramatic Literature. Composition of Songs in notation go with 5756 Dramatic Music.
6827	總錄 史傳,評論,等入此.	General; Biographies, critique and anecdotes
6828	戲台,砌末,佈景	Stage, stage paraphernalia and scenery
6829	腳色	Roles and characters
6830	身段	Acting or bodily expression
6831	臉譜,髯口	Make-up and masks (Technique of painting faces and of wearing beards)
6832	行頭	Costumes and accessories (hats, caps, boots, shoes, etc.
6833	其他	Other miscellaneous

戲院演劇(續) DRAMATIC ART (cont.)

6834-6835	日本劇	Japanese Theater
6834	能 狂言	Nō-play ~~and Interlude~~
.1	歷史	History
.2	理論 及 技術	Theory and technique
.22	編作法	Dramati~~zation~~ _urgy_
.23	演出法	Production
.24	評判記	Criticism
.26	田樂	Dengaku [Ancient pantomine]
.27	幸若舞	Kōwaka-dance
.28	能仕舞	Nō-dance
.4	囃子, 拍子	Nō-rhythm, musical accompaniments
.5	能舞台	Nō-stage
.6	能具	Nō-paraphernalia
.61	能面	Masks
.63	能装束	Costumes
.64	作り物	Scenery
.65	小道具	Miscellaneous accessories
.7	流派	Various schools of Nō
.71	觀世流	Kanze-Ryū
.72	今春流	Komparu-Ryū
.74	金剛流	Kongō-Ryū
.75	喜多流	Kita-Ryū
.76	梅若流	Umewaka-Ryū
.8	狂言	Nō-farce
.9	其他	Others

戏院,演剧(续) DRAMATIC ART (cont.)

6835	歌舞伎	Kabuki
.1	歷史,年代記	History, Chronology
.11	理論及技術	Theory and technique
.12	編作法	Dramaturgy
.13	演出法	Production
.14	劇評 評判記	Criticism
.15	歌舞伎踊	Kabuki-dance
.16	阿國歌舞伎踊	Okuni kabuki
.17	女歌舞伎踊	Onna kabuki
.18	若衆歌舞伎踊	Wakashu kabuki
.19	脇踊,大踊	Waki odori, Ōodori
.2	役者	Actors
.23	創始期	Before 1684 A.D.
.24	元祿期 貞享至享保	1683–1716
.25	寶曆期 享保至天明	1716–1788
.26	近世期 寬政至明治	1789–1863
.27	明治以後	After 1868
.28	女形	Actors playing Feminine rôle (Oyama)
.29	芝居繪	Portraits and other pictures
.3	番附,筋書本,畫抜等	Programs, Synopsis, etc.
.4	囃子,下座樂,所作樂	Musical accompaniments
.5	劇場	Stages
.58	舞台裝置	Stage settings
.59	劇場圖	Plans and views
.6	道具	Stage paraphernalia
.62	道具方	Scene shifters

戲院 演劇 (續) DRAMATIC ART (cont.)

6835.63	道具立	Scenery
.65	小道具	Miscellaneous accessories
.67	衣裳	Costumes
.672	衣裳方	Costumers
.68	鬘 床山	Wigs
.69	扮装 隈取	Make-up
.7	慣習	Customs. Usages.
.8	新派劇	Plays of the new school
.81	壯士劇 書生芝居	Sōshi-play
.82	女優劇	Theatricals by actress
.83	喜劇	(Modern) comedies
.9	新劇	Modern drama
.94	文士劇	Theatricals by literary man
.95	自由劇場	~~Liberal~~ Independent theaters
.98	ブロレタリヤ演劇	Proletariat theaters
6836	西洋劇	Occidental Theaters
.1		
.2		
.3		
6837	傀儡劇	Puppet Shows; Pantomimes.
.1	傀儡, 人形	Puppets
.3	中國傀儡戲	Chinese
.4	日本操芝居	Japanese (Ayatsuri, Jōruri-plays)
	即淨瑠璃, 其腳本入文學	For Jōruri literature see 5911-5913.
.5-9	其他諸國傀儡戲	Other Countries
	依地理分, 用表一	(Divide geographically by Table II.)

戲院,演劇 (續)　DRAMATIC ART (cont.)

6838	影劇	Shadow-plays and Photo-plays
.1	中國影戲	Chinese shadow-plays
.2	其他東洋影戲	Other Oriental shadow-plays
.3	西洋影戲	Western shadow-plays
.4	電影	Kinema (Movies and talkies)
.5	攝影場	Studio Management
.6	導演及演員	Directors and actors
.7	電影劇本及編排	Scenario and continuity
.8	攝影及錄音	Photographing and Phonographing
.9	電影院	Kinema theaters
6839	無線電廣播劇	Radio entertainments
.1		
.2		
.3		

6840-6849	雜戲	VARIETY ENTERTAINMENTS
6841	說書,相聲	Story telling and comic talks
6842	走會,儀 寄席茶番狂言	Public fêtes, Pageantry, etc.
6843	奇技	Performances of skill
6844	戲法	Magic plays
6845	展觀,見世物	Panoramas and other shows
6846	動物戲	Trained animals. Animal fighting sports.
6847	大馬戲	Circuses
6848		
6849		

6850-6899	游戲	GAMES
6850	一般游戲	<u>Games in General</u>
6851-2	兒童游戲	<u>Children's Games</u>
6853-6874	機會與技巧游戲	<u>Games of Chance and Skill</u>
6853-6869	牌戲	Card games
6853	古博戲	Ancient Chinese chance games
6854	骰子	Dices
6855	牙牌	Ya-p'ai
6856	麻雀	Ma-chiang (Mahjong)
6857	葉子	Yeh-tzu
6858	花骨牌 花合	Hanagaruta
6859	雙陸	Shuang-lu or Sugoroku
6860	物合	Monoawase
6862	其他	Others
6863-9	西洋牌戲	Western card games (poker, etc.)
6870-3	棋	Chess games
6870	圍棋	Wei-ch'i or Igo
6871	象棋	Hsiang-ch'i
6871.8	將棋	Shōgi
6872	西洋棋	Western chess and checkers
6873	檯球 彈子戲,撞球,玉突	Billiards, Pool, etc.
6874	乒乓球 台球	Table-tennis (Ping-pong)
6874.9	其他技巧游戲	Other games of skill

游戲 (續)   **GAMES** (cont.)

6875-6879	審美游戲	<u>Artistic Games and Amusements</u>
6875	酒令	Wine games
6876	品茶, 茶道	Tea ceremony
6877	焚香, 香道	Incense burning
6878	供花, 華道	Flower arrangement
6879	其他	Others
6880-6889	動作游戲	<u>Moving Games</u>
6881-3	投壺	T'ou-hu or Tōko
6884	投扇興, 拳, 獨樂	Tōsenkyō, Ken (Mora), Koma
6889	其他	Others
6890-6896	文藝與智力游戲	<u>Literary and Intellectual Games</u>
6890	燈謎 入文學為宜.	Lantern Riddles (Better class with Literature)
6891	七巧圖	Chinese puzzle
6892	數理游戲	Mathematical games
6897-9	其他游戲	<u>Miscellaneous Games</u>
6900-6999	體育運動	<u>**PHYSICAL TRAINING AND SPORTS**</u>
6901-6909	總錄 依體裁分, 用表一.	GENERAL (Form subdivisions like Table D
6910-6919	體育通論	PHYSICAL EDUCATION: GENERAL TREATISES
6920-6929	柔軟及機械體操	GYMNASTICS AND CALLISTHENICS
6930-6969	競技運動	ATHLETIC SPORTS
6930	總錄	General treatises
6940	空中運動	Air sports

體育運動(續) PHYSICAL TRAINING AND SPORTS (cont.)

競技運動(續) ATHLETIC SPORTS (cont.)

6945	水中運動	Aquatic sports
6950	冰雪運動	Ice and snow sports
6953	球戲蹴鞠	Ball games
6960	脚踏車	Cycling
6963	汽車	Automobiling
6967	競走	Foot-racing, running
6968	投擲運動	Throwing games
6970-6979	武術	FIGHTING SPORTS
6973	拳術,柔道	Boxing, Jūdō or Jūjutsu
6975	蹟跤,相撲	Wrestling, Sumō
6976	劍棍	Fencing with swords or poles
6977	射箭	Archery
6978	決鬥	Dueling
6979	射鎗	Shooting
6980-4	畋獵,垂釣	HUNTING AND ANGLING
6981	放鷹	Hawking falconry
6982	打獵	Hunting
6983	釣魚	Angling
6984	其他	Others
6985-9	野外運動	OUTDOOR RECREATIONS
6985	登山	Mountaineering
6986	遠足	Hiking
6987	露營	Camping
6988	養雀,養鴿等	Outing with birds in hand
6989	其他	Others
6990-9	騎術,競馬	HORSE RACING
6991	馬球	Polo

7000-7999　自然科學類 NATURAL SCIENCES

7001-7019　科學總論　　　　GENERAL

7002　　期刊　　　　　　Periodicals

7004　　會社　　　　　　Societies

7006　　叢集　　　　　　Collections

7008　　書目　　　　　　Bibliography

7009　　博物館　　　　　Museums

7010　　科學教育　　　　Scientific education

7011　　旅行及探查　　　Voyages and expeditions

7012　　字典,辭書　　　　Dictionaries, encyclopedias

7013　　指南　　　　　　Pocketbooks, handbooks, *manuals*

7015　　儀器　　　　　　Instruments and apparatus

7016　　科學史傳　　　　History of Science.　Collective biography.

7017　　科學概論　　　　General treatises

7019　　科學原理,分類　　Philosophy.　Classification of sciences.

7020-7099　算學　　　　MATHEMATICS

7021-7029　總錄　　　　　GENERAL (Form subdivisions like Table I)
　　　　依體裁分,用表一.

7030-7039　中國算學史　　HISTORY OF CHINESE MATHEMATICAL
　　　　依時代分,用表三.　　TREATISES (Subdivide chronologically
　　　　　　　　　　　　　　by Table III)

算學(續)　　　MATHEMATICS (cont.)

| 7040.1-.9 | 日本算學史 | HISTORY OF JAPANESE MATHEMATICAL |

依時代分,用表三.　　TREATISES (Subdivide by periods like Table III)

| 7044 | 混合算學 | GENERAL MATHEMATICS |

| 7045-7047 | 算術 | ARITHMETIC |

| 7048 | 籌算 | CALCULATION BY TALLIES |

| 7049 | 珠算 | ABACUS |

| 7050-7059 | 代數 | ALGEBRA |

| 7060-7069 | 微積分 | ANALYSIS (CALCULUS, FUNCTIONS AND DIFFERENTIAL EQUATIONS) |

| 7070-7074 | 幾何 | GEOMETRY |

| 7075-7079 | 畫法幾何 | DESCRIPTIVE GEOMETRY |

| 7080-7085 | 三角 | TRIGONOMETRY |

| 7086-7089 | 解析幾何 | ANALYTIC GEOMETRY |

| 7090-7097 | 數理力學 | ANALYTIC MECHANICS |

| 7098-7099 | 其他算學問題 | MISCELLANEOUS MATH. SUBJECTS |

| 7100-7199 | 天文學 | ASTRONOMY |

| 7101-7109 | 總錄 | GENERAL (Form subdivisions like Table D |

依體裁分,用表一.

| 7110-7119 | 實測天文學 | PRACTICAL ASTRONOMY |

| 7120-7129 | 球面天文學 | SPHERICAL ASTRONOMY |

天文學 (續)　　ASTRONOMY (cont.)

7130-7139	理論天文學,天體力學	THEORETICAL ASTRONOMY. CELESTIAL MECHANICS.
7140-7149	敘述天文學,天象	DESCRIPTIVE ASTRONOMY. CELESTIAL PHENOMENA. ASTROPHYSICS.
7150-7169	地球,測地學,地圖學	EARTH GEODESY CARTOGRAPHY
7170-7179	航海天文學	NAUTICAL ASTRONOMY
7180-7199	曆學,曆法,曆書	CHRONOLOGY HOROLOGY CALENDARS
7180	通論	General
7183	曆法	Methods of finding the time
7186	曆器	Instruments for measuring time e.g. sun-dials, hour glasses
7187	曆書	Calendars in general
7188-7190	中國曆書	Chinese Calendars
7191	日本曆書	Japanese Calendars
7192	其他古東方曆書	Other Oriental Calendars
7193	回曆	Mohammedan Calendars
7194	儒畧曆	Julian Calendar ~~Calendar of Julius Caesar~~
7196	格勒哥里曆	Gregorian Calendar ~~Calendar of Gregory~~
7198	近代改良曆法考案	Modern projects for reform of calendar

7200-7299	物理學	PHYSICS
7201-7209	總錄	GENERAL (Form subdivisions like Table D
	依體裁分,用表一.	
7210-7219	權度	WEIGHTS AND MEASURES
7220-7229	試驗物理學	EXPERIMENTAL MECHANICS
7230-7239	物質說	CONSTITUTION AND PROPERTIES OF MATTER
7240-7249	聲學	SOUND　ACOUSTICS
7250-7259	熱學	HEAT
7260-7279	光學	LIGHT　OPTICS
7280-7289	磁電學	MAGNETISM AND ELECTRICITY
7290-7299	鐳錠	RADIUM
7300-7399	化學	CHEMISTRY
7301-7309	總錄	GENERAL (Form subdivisions like Table D
	依體裁分,用表一.	
7310-7319	分析化學	ANALYTICAL CHEMISTRY
7314	定性分析	QUALITATIVE ANALYSIS
7317	定量分析	QUANTITATIVE ANALYSIS
7320-7329	無機化學	INORGANIC CHEMISTRY
7330-7349	有機化學	ORGANIC CHEMISTRY
7350-7369	理論化學	PHYSICAL AND THEORETICAL CHEMISTRY
7370-7389	電氣化學	ELECTROLYSIS
7390-7399	結晶學	CRYSTALLOGRAPHY

7400-7499	地學	GEOLOGICAL SCIENCES
7401-9	總錄 依體裁分, 用表一.	GENERAL (Form subdivisions like Table I)
7410-7429	各國地質	GEOLOGY OF SPECIAL COUNTRIES
7411-2	中國	OF CHINA
7411	全國	General
7412	地方 依地理分, 用表二.	Regional (Subdivide by Table II)
7413-4	日本 仿中國分.	OF JAPAN (Divide like 7411-2)
7415-9	其他亞洲各國 依地理分, 用表二.	OF OTHER ASIATIC COUNTRIES (Subdivide by Table II)
7420-9	西洋各國	OF WESTERN COUNTRIES (Subdivide by Table II)
7430-9	地變學, 地震學	PHYSICAL AND DYNAMIC GEOLOGY SEISMOLOGY
7440-9	地文學, 自然地理學	PHYSIOGRAPHY
7450-9	氣象學	METEOROLOGY
7460-9	地層學, 地史學	STRATIGRAPHIC (HISTORICAL) GEOLOGY
7470-9	岩石學	PETROLOGY (LITHOLOGY) AND PETROGRAPHY
7480-9	礦物學 經濟地學入礦業.	MINERALOGY (ECONOMIC GEOLOGY see 8600-8699)
7490-9	古生物學	PALEONTOLOGY
7490.1-.9	總錄 依體裁分, 用表一.	GENERAL
7491-2	中國 仿中國地質分.	CHINA Divide like 7411-2
7493-4	日本 仿中國地質分.	JAPAN Divide like 7411-2

7500-7599	博物學	NATURAL HISTORY
7501-7509	總錄	GENERAL (Form subdivisions like Table I)
	依體裁分, 用表一.	
7510	旅行探查	VOYAGES AND EXPEDITIONS
7521	儀器	COLLECTING APPARATUS
7523	水族館	AQUARIUMS
7525	博物院	MUSEUMS
	地理分布	GEOGRAPHICAL DISTRIBUTION
7531	通論	GENERAL WORKS
7523	北極	ARCTIC REGIONS
7535	南極	ANTARCTIC REGIONS
7537	温帶	TEMPERATE REGIONS
7639	熱帶	TROPICAL REGIONS
	地性區分	PHYSIOGRAPHIC DIVISIONS
7541	陸	LAND
7546	水	WATER (GENERAL)
7547	海水	OCEAN
7549	淡水	FRESH WATER
7550-7559	地域區分	TOPOGRAPHICAL DIVISIONS (Subdivide by Table II)
	用表二.	
7560-7569	顯微鏡學	MICROSCOPY

7570-7599	普通生物學	GENERAL BIOLOGY
7571	總錄	GENERAL WORKS
7576	生物質	PROPERTIES OF LIVING MATTER
7581	進化論	THEORY OF DESCENT　EVOLUTION ORIGIN OF SPECIES
7586	優生學, 生殖論	GENETICS
7589	生物生理學	GENERAL PHYSIOLOGY
7591	生物生態學	GENERAL ECOLOGY
7596	細胞學	GENERAL CYTOLOGY
7600-7699	植物學	BOTANY
7601-7609	總錄 依體裁分, 用表一.	GENERAL (Form subdivisions like Table I
7610-7619	植物採集	COLLECTING AND PRESERVATION
7620-7629	植物分布 依地理分, 用表二.	TOPOGRAPHICAL DIVISIONS (FLORA) (Subdivide by Table II
7630-7639	種子植物	SPERMATOPHYTA
7640-7659	隱花植物	CRYPTOGAMIC BOTANY
7660-7669	植物形態學,胚胎學	MORPHOLOGY, ANATOMY AND EMBRYOLOGY
7670-7679	植物解剖學,組織學	ANATOMY AND HISTOLOGY
7680-7689	植物生理學	PLANT PHYSIOLOGY
7690-7699	植物生態學	ECOLOGY

7700-7799	動物學	ZOOLOGY
7701-7709	總錄 依體裁分,用表一、	GENERAL (Form subdivisions like Table I)
7710-7719	動物採集	COLLECTING AND PRESERVATION
7720-7729	動物分布 依地理分,用表二、	TOPOGRAPHICAL DIVISIONS (FAUNA) (Subdivide like Table II)
7730-7745	無脊椎動物	INVERTEBRATES
7730	通論	GENERAL
7731	原生動物	PROTOZOA
7732	海綿動物	PORIFERA (SPONGES)
7733	腔腸動物	COELENTERATA
7734	棘皮動物	ECHINODERMATA
7735	蠕形動物	ACOELOMATA (VERMES)
7736	腕足類	BRACHIOPODA
7737	苔蘚蟲類	POLYZOA OR BRYOZOA
7738	軟體動物	MOLLUSCA
7739-7745	節肢動物	ARTHROPODA (ARTICULATA)
7740	甲殼類	CRUSTACEA
7741	多足類	MYRIAPODA
7742	蜘蛛類	ARACHNIDA
7743-5	昆蟲類	INSECTA
7746-7769	脊椎動物	VERTEBRATES
7746	通論	GENERAL
7747	原索動物	PROCHORDATA
7748	魚類	ICHTHYOLOGY (FISHES)
7752	爬蟲類	REPTILIA, AMPHIBIA (BATRACHIA)
7755	鳥類	ORNITHOLOGY (BIRDS)
7761	哺乳類	MAMMALIA

動物學(續)　　ZOOLOGY　(cont)

7770-7779　動物生態學　　ETHOLOGY (HABITS, BEHAVIOR, ETC.)

7780-7789　動物解剖學　　ANATOMY

7790-7799　動物胚胎學發生學　EMBRYOLOGY

7800-7869　人類學　　ANTHROPOLOGY - PHYSICAL

生理方面者入此.　(Historical side of anthropology,
歷史方面者入民族學 see 2200-2249)

7801-7809　總錄　　GENERAL (Form subdivisions like Table D
依體裁分,用表一.

7810-7819　人類分布學,人類測　ANTHROPOGRAPHY, ANTHROPOMETRY.
量學　體

7820-7829　人體比較學,人類　SOMATOLOGY, ANTHROPOGENY.
起源學

7830-7849　人體解剖學　　HUMAN ANATOMY

7850-7869　人體生理學　　HUMAN PHYSIOLOGY

7870-7899　心理學　　PSYCHOLOGY

7870.1-.9　總錄　　GENERAL (Form divisions like Table D
依體裁分,用表一.

7871　普通心理學　GENERAL PSYCHOLOGY

7875　推論心理學　SPECULATIVE PSYCHOLOGY
(MIND AND BODY)

7880　生理及實驗心理學 PHYSIOLOGICAL AND EXPERIMENTAL
PSYCHOLOGY

7890　比較及發育心理學 COMPARATIVE AND GENETIC PSYCHOLOGY

7896　變態心理學　METAPSYCHOLOGY, PSYCHIC RESEARCH
PSYCHOLOGY OF THE UNCONSCIOUS, ETC.

7897　應用心理學　APPLIED PSYCHOLOGY

7900-7999	醫學	MEDICAL SCIENCE
7901-7909	總錄 依體裁分;用表一.	GENERAL (Form subdivisions like Table I)
7910-7911	醫經	ANCIENT MEDICAL CLASSICS
7910	中國	Chinese
7911	日本	Japanese
7911.9	西洋	Western
7912-7915	攝生 衛生.	HYGIEŃE
7916-7919	公共衛生	PUBLIC HEALTH
7920-7923	細菌學	BACTERIOLOGY
7924-7929	病理學	PATHOLOGY
7930-7939	內科	INTERNAL MEDICINE
7930	診斷, 脈學	DIAGNOSIS　PULSE
7931	內科總論	GENERAL TREATISES
7932	傷寒	GENERAL WORKS ON FEVERS
7933	循環系病	DISEASES OF CIRCULATORY SYSTEM
7934	呼吸系病	DISEASES OF RESPIRATORY SYSTEM
7935	消化系病	DISEASES OF DIGESTIVE SYSTEM
7936	腺及淋巴系病	DISEASES OF GLANDULAR AND LYMPATHIC SYSTEM
7937	運動系病	DISEASES OF LOCOMOTOR SYSTEM
7938	神經系病	DISEASES OF NERVOUS SYSTEM

内科 (續)　　　　　INTERNAL MEDICINE (cont.)

7939	全身病,寄生蟲病,傳染病(瘟疫)及其他內科雜病	CONSTITUTIONAL, PARASITICAL, INFECTIOUS AND OTHER GENERAL DISEASES
7940-7946	外科	SURGERY
7940	外科總論	GENERAL TREATISES
7941	損傷	WOUNDS, INJURIES, AND ACCIDENTS
7942	骨科	ORTHOPAEDIC SURGERY
7943	局部外科	REGIONAL SURGERY
7944	生殖及泌尿器科	GENITO-URINARY ~~DISEASES~~ SURGERY
7945	皮膚科	DERMATOLOGY
7946	花柳科	SYPHILOLOGY
7947-7949	眼科	OPHTHALMOLOGY
7950-7953	耳鼻喉科	OTOLOGY　RHINOLOGY　LARYNGOLOGY
7954	牙科 齒科	DENTISTRY
7955-7964	婦科,產科	GYNAECOLOGY AND OBSTETRICS
7965-7969	幼科 小兒科	PEDIATRICS
7970-7979	藥物學 本草,方劑	MATERIA MEDICA AND PHARMACY
7970	總錄	GENERAL
7971-2	本草 生藥	DRUGS. PHARMACEUTICAL SUBSTANCES

藥物學 (續) MATERIA MEDICA AND PHARMACY (cont.)

7976	處方學 方書,藥典.	DISPENSATORIES POSOLOGY PHARMACOPOEIAS
7978	藥局	DISPENSARIES APOTHECARIES
7979	毒物學	TOXICOLOGY POISONS
7980-7988	治療學	THERAPEUTICS
7980	總錄	GENERAL
7981	醫案 醫話入此.	CASE RECORDS (Excluding miscellaneous remedies and anecdotes)
7982	食物療法 斷食療法.	DIETARY CURE NESTOTHERAPY
7983	血清療法 化學療法.	VACCINOTHERAPY SERUMTHERAPY
7984	自然療法 氣候療法.	PHYSIOTHERAPY
7985	光熱療法	PHOTOTHERAPY THERMOTHERAPY
7986	電氣療法 太陽燈等.	ELECTROTHERAPY RÖNTOGENO-THERAPY RADIOTHERAPY
7987	精神療法 心理療法,信仰療法.	PSYCHOTHERAPY FAITH CURE
7988	急救療法	EMERGENCY TREATMENT
7989	鍼灸,按摩(推拿), 及其他雜術	ACUPUNCTURE, MOXIBUSTION, MASSAGE AND OTHER MISCEL-LANEOUS ARTS OF CURE
7990-7995	醫院管理	HOSPITAL MANAGEMENT
7996-7998	看護學	NURSING
7999	醫學雜錄	MEDICAL MISCELLANIES

8000-8999 農業工藝類 AGRICULTURE AND TECHNOLOGY

8020-8239 農業 AGRICULTURE

8021-8029	總錄 依體裁分, 用表一.	GENERAL (Form subdivisions like Table D
8031-8038	中國古農書 依時代分, 用表三.	OLD CHINESE TREATISES ON AGRICULTURE (Subdivide by periods like Table III)
8039	日本古農書	OLD JAPANESE TREATISES ON AGRICULTURE
8040-8056	農業行政	AGRICULTURAL ADMINISTRATION AND LEGISLATION
8040-8042	農業法令	Agricultural Legislation
8040	中國	China
8041	日本	Japan
8042	其他各國 依地理分, 用表二.	Other countries (Subdivide by Table II)
8043-8047	農業組織	Agricultural Organization and Administration
8043-8044	中國	China
8043	全國	National
8044	地方 依省縣分, 用表二.	Provincial and local (Subdivide by Table II)
8045-8046	日本	Japan
8045	全國	National
8046	地方 依地理分, 用表二.	District and local (Subdivide by Table II)
8047	其他各國 依地理分, 用表二.	Other countries (Subdivide by Table II)
8048-8050	農業試驗場	Experimental Stations
8048	中國 依地理分, 用表二.	China (Subdivide by Table II)
8049	日本 依地理分, 用表二.	Japan (Subdivide by Table II)
8050	其他各國 依地理分, 用表二.	Other countries (Subdivide by Table II)

301

	農業行政 (續)	AGRICULTURAL ADMINISTRATION AND LEGISLATION (cont.)
8051-8053	農業博物館	Agricultural Museums
8051	中國 依地方分, 用表二.	China (Subdivide by Table II)
8052	日本 依地方分, 用表二.	Japan (Subdivide by Table II)
8053	其他各國 依地理分, 用表二.	Other countries (Subdivide by Table II)
8054-8056	農業展覽	Expositions, fairs, etc.
8054	中國 依地方分, 用表二.	China (Subdivide by Table II)
8055	日本 依地方分, 用表二.	Japan (Subdivide by Table II)
8056	其他各國 依地理分, 用表二.	Other countries (Subdivide by Table II)
8057-8060	農業教育 亦可入職業教育.	AGRICULTURAL EDUCATION (May be classified also in 4985.)
8057	總錄	General
8058	中國	China
8059	日本	Japan
8060	其他各國 依地理分, 用表二.	Other countries (Subdivide by Table II)
8061-8064	農業統計	AGRICULTURAL STATISTICS
8061	世界	International
8062	中國	China
8063	日本	Japan
8064	其他各國 依地理分, 用表二.	Other countries (Subdivide by Table II)
8066-8074	農業史地及現狀	HISTORY AND GEOGRAPHY OF AGRICULTURE
8066-8067	總論	General
8068-8069	中國	China
8068	全國	National
8069	地方 依省縣分, 用表二.	Local (Subdivide by Table II)

農業史地及現狀 (續) HISTORY AND GEOGRAPHY OF AGRICULTURE (cont.)

8070-8071	日本	Japan
8070	全國	National
8071	地方 依地理分，用表二.	Local (Subdivide by Table II)
8072-8073	其他各國 依地理分，用表二. 農業史地及現狀，普通 亦可入經濟中之土地與農業.	Other countries (Subdivide by Table II) (Works relating to the history and geography of agriculture may be classified in 4380-4419 in general libraries.)
8075-8079	鄉村社會學 亦可入社會學.	RURAL SOCIOLOGY (May be classified in 4196 in general libraries)
8080-8099	農業經濟 或入經濟.	AGRICULTURAL ECONOMICS (May be classified in 4380-4419 in general libraries)
8080	通論	General treatises
8081	農業政策	Agricultural policy
8082	農地利用	Land utilization
8083	農業與他業之關係	Relation of agriculture to other industries
8084	農村問題 農村改良	Agrarian problems Reform movements
8085	農業救濟, 荒政社倉	Farm Relief Public Granaries
8086	田賦	Farm Taxation
8087	農業生產與消費	Agricultural production and consumption
8088	農場組織及管理	Farm organization and management
8089	農場經營, 記錄	Farm operation Farm records
8090	農工	Farm labor
8091	農業金融	Agricultural credit
8092	農業保險	Agricultural insurance
8093	農業合作	Agricultural coöperatives
8094	農產銷售	Agricultural marketing
8095	農產物價	Agricultural prices
8096	農田地價	Land values and prices
8097	租佃制度	Farm tenancy

8100-8109	農用自然科學	BASIC NATURAL SCIENCES IN AGRICULTURE
8101	農用氣象學	Agricultural meteorology
8102	農用微生物學	Agricultural micro-biology
8103	農用植物學	Agricultural botany
8104	農用動物學	Agricultural zoology
8105	農用物理學	Agricultural physics
8106	農用化學通論	Agricultural chemistry in general
8107	土壤學	Soils
8108	肥料	Fertilizer, manures.
8110-8114	農具,農場工程	FARM IMPLEMENTS AND MACHINERY AGRICULTURAL ENGINEERING
8115-8119	耕種	TILLAGE, FARM OPERATIONS
8120-8124	栽培,育種	PLANT CULTURE, BREEDING, SEEDS, ETC.
8125-8129	災害	PESTS AND DISEASES, PROTECTION OF PLANTS
8130-8151	作物學 各種作物	AGRONOMY. CULTIVATION OF SPECIAL CROPS.
8131	禾穀類	Cereal crops. Grains.
8132	豆菽類	Podded grains. Legumes.
8133	牧草類	Forage crops
8134	根菜類	Root crops
8135	糖料類	Sugar and starch plants
8136	纖維類	Textile and fiber plants
8137	刺激料類	Alcaloidal plants

	作物學 (續)	AGRONOMY.　CULTIVATION OF SPECIAL CROPS　(cont.)
8138	藥料類	Medicinal plants
8139	油漆類	Oil producing plants
8140	橡皮類	Rubber and resin plants
8141	染料類	Dye plants
8142	辛料類	Spices and condiments
8143	香料類	Perfume plants
8144	其他作物	Other crops
	作物 以地域分.	Field crops grouped geographically
8145	溫帶	Temperate zones
8146	寒帶	Arctic zones
8147	熱帶	Subtropic and tropic zones
8148	濕帶	Humid regions
8149	乾帶	Arid regions
8150	山地	Mountain regions
8151	作物	Field crops by topographical subdivisions (Subdivide by Table II)
8152-8159	園藝	HORTICULTURE.　GARDENING.
8152	總錄	General (Form subdivisions like Table I)
8153	通論 依體裁分.隊—	Horticulture in general
8154	果木	Fruit culture (Pomiculture, Pomology)
8155	蔬菜	Vegetable culture (Olericulture)
8156	花卉	Flower culture (Floriculture)
8157	用具.溫室	Garden tools, greenhouses, and greenhouse culture
8158		

8160-8169	森林，林業	FORESTRY　ABORICULTURE
8160	總錄	General (Form subdivisions like Table I
	依體裁分,用表一	
8161	林業用自然科學	Basic natural sciences in forestry
8162	造林	Silviculture
8163	森林保護	Forest protection
8164	森林技術	Forest technology
8165	森林利用,林產製造	Forest utilization, lumbering.
8166	森林工程	Forest engineering
8167	森林管理	Forest management
8168	森林經濟,政策,及法令	Forest economics policy and legislation.
8169	森林與農業之關係	Forest in relation to agriculture
8170-8199	畜牧	ANIMAL HUSBANDRY VETERINARY MEDICINE
8171-8174	通論	Animal culture in general
8175-8179	獸醫	Veterinary medicine
8180-8185	家畜	Livestock　Domestic animals
8186-8189	乳業	Dairy and dairy products
8190-8197	家禽	Aviculture　Domestic birds
8198-8199	蜂蠟	Apiculture　Bee-keeping
8200-8219	蠶桑，絲業	SERICULTURE
8200-8205	總錄	General
8200	叢集期刊	Collections and periodicals
8201	絲業經濟	Sericultural economics
8202	絲業政策	Sericultural policies
8203	絲業法規	Law and legislation
8204	絲業組織	Organization in silk industries
8205	絲業貿易	Commerce and trade

	蠶桑 (續)	SERICULTURE (cont.)
8206-8209	蠶體學	Natural History of Silkworm
8206	解剖學	Anatomy
8207	生理學	Physiology
8208	病理學	Pathology
8209	生態學	Ecology
8210-8211	蠶種	Silkworm Eggs
8212-8216	育蠶法	Silkworm Culture
8212	器具	Equipment and implements
8213	飼育	Feeding and rearing
8214	病害	Diseases and injuries
8215	保護	Methods of protection
8216	其他	Others
8217	桑業	Mulberry Culture
8218	繭及其利用	Cocoon and its uses
8219	生絲業 參見絲紡織業.	Silk-realing Industry (See also 8472 Silk Textile)
8220-8239	漁獵 水產業, 田獵.	AQUATIC AND HUNTING INDUSTRIES FISHERY AND GAME
8240-8289	家政學	<u>HOME ECONOMICS (DOMESTIC SCIENCE)</u>
8241-8249	家事 總錄 依體裁分, 用表一.	GENERAL (Form subdivisions like Table I)
8250-8259	家庭經濟及管理	HOUSEHOLD ECONOMICS AND ADMINISTRATION
8260-8264	住宅及家具	SHELTER: HOUSE, FURNITURE, DECORATION
8265-8274	衣服及其整理	CLOTHES: CLEANING, WASHING, ETC.

	家政學 (續)	HOME ECONOMICS (cont.)
8275-8279	美容術	TOILET ~~OR~~ AND PERSONAL BEAUTY ARTS
8280-8287	食物及烹飪	FOODS AND COOKERY (GASTRONOMY
8281	中國食譜 (料理)	Chinese Cookery
8282	日本料理	Japanese Cookery
8283	其他東方烹飪法	Other Oriental Cookery
8284	西洋烹飪法	Western Cookery
8288-8289	育嬰, 家庭醫學	NURSERY DOMESTIC MEDICINE
8290-8299	工藝總論	TECHNOLOGY IN GENERAL
8291	雜誌, 社刊	PERIODICALS, SOCIETIES
8292	叢集, 雜錄	COLLECTIONS, MISCELLANIES
8293	會聚, 展覽	CONGRESSES, EXHIBITIONS
8294	博物館	MUSEUMS
8295	教學, 書目	STUDY AND TEACHING; BIBLIOGRAPHIES
8296	字典, 辭書	DICTIONARIES, ENCYCLOPEDIAS
8297	通論, 撮要, 手冊	GENERAL TREATISES, COMPENDS, HANDBOOKS
8298	史傳	HISTORY AND BIOGRAPHY
8299	發明及特許權	INVENTION AND INDUSTRIAL PROPERTY (PATENTS, TRADEMARKS, ETC.)

8300-8399	手工業及各項手藝	HANDICRAFTS AND ARTISAN TRADES
	祗收技術方面著作各工藝 之營業法入營業技術.	(Technical treatises are classed here. Economic studies go in 4559)
8301-8309	總錄 依體裁分,用表一.	GENERAL (Form subdivisions like Table D
8310-8319	五金工	METAL-WORKING TRADES
8311	金銀業	Gold and silver smithing
8313	鐘表業	Watch repairing, etc.
8315	銅器業	Copper and brass smithing
8317	錫器業	Tinsmithing
8318	鋼鐵業	Blacksmithing
8320-8329	竹木工	WOOD-WORKING TRADES
8321	木器業	Carpentry
8323	家具業	Furniture-making
8325	製盒業	Box-making
8327	竹器業	Bamboo articles
8329	藤器業	Willow wares and vine articles
8330-8339	石泥工	MASONRY, PLASTERING AND PAINTING
8331	磚石業	Masonry work
8334	泥水業	Plastering
8337	油漆業	Painting, varnishing, etc.
8340-8349	紙料工	PAPER-WORKING TRADES
8341	裱糊業	Paper-hanging
8342	製傘業	Umbrella-making
8344	造花業	Artificial flowers
8346	冥衣業	Funeral paper articles

	手工業(續)	HANDICRAFTS AND ARTISAN TRADES (cont.)
8350-8359	皮骨工	LEATHER-AND BONE-WORKING TRADES
8352	鞍轡業	Harnesses and saddles
8354	靴鞋業	Boots and shoes
8356	箱籠業	Trunks and bags
8357	骨角象牙業	Articles of horn, bone and ivory
8360-8369	服裝工	DRESSMAKING TRADES
8361	裁縫業	Tailoring
8362	成衣業	Ready-made and second-hand clothes
8365	冠帽業	Millineries and haberdashers
8366	針織業	Knit goods (Embroidery, see 6650-9)
8370-8374	修飾工	CLEANING TRADES
8371	理髮業	Barbers and hair-dressers
8372	浴堂業	Bathing houses
8373	洗衣業	Laundries
8374	染洗業	Dry-cleaning and dyeing plants
8375-8379	玩具工	TOY-MAKING TRADES
8380-8389	旅行業	TRAVELERS' SERVICING TRADES
8381	客店旅館	Inns and hotels
8383	旅行社	Travelers' agencies
8385	酒菜館	Restaurants
8390-8399	其他行業 文具業入美術類文房 印刷業入圖書學	OTHER TRADES AND CRAFTS Stationery-making, see 6290-6299. Printing trades, see 9400-9499.
8391	碓坊磨坊	Rice and flour millers
8392	屠宰業	Butcheries

8410-8499	機製工業 製造. 技術方面著述入此, 關于經濟者入經濟.	MANUFACTURES (INDUSTRIES USING POWER MACHINES) (Technical treatises are classed here. Economic studies go in 4434-4449.)
8401-8409	總錄 依體裁分, 用表一.	GENERAL (Form subdivisions like Table I)
8410-8439	五金類	METAL MANUFACTURES
8440-8449	木材類	LUMBER AND WOODWORK INDUSTRIES
8450-8469	皮革類	LEATHER INDUSTRIES.　TANNING.
8460-8469	紙　類	PAPER MANUFACTURE AND TRADE
	印刷出版類 入圖書學.	PRINTING AND PUBLISHING see 9400-9499
8470-8489	紡織類	TEXTILE INDUSTRIES
8472	絲	Silk manufactures
8474	棉	Cotton manufactures
8476	紗	Linen manufactures
8478	毛	Woolen manufactures
8480	麻	Flax, Hemp, and Jute manufactures
8481	人造絲	Rayon manufactures
8482	氈	Carpet, rugs, etc.
8484	蓆	Mattings
8486	繡 花邊	Lace, embroidery.　(Handicraft, see 6650-9)
8488	繩 參見美術類剌繡染織.	Cordage
8490-8499	雜類	MISCELLANEOUS INDUSTRIES
8491	橡皮	India rubber industry
8492	煙葉	Tobacco industry
8493	麵粉	Flour-milling industry

	機製工業 (續)	MISCELLANEOUS INDUSTRIES (cont.)
8494	米	Rice-cleaning industry
8496	畜產品工業	Animal products industries
8497	肉	Meat-packing industry
8498	蛋	Egg-drying industry
8500-8599	化學工業 應用化學, 工藝化學.	CHEMICAL TECHNOLOGY
8501-8509	總錄 依體裁分, 用表一.	GENERAL (Form subdivisions like Table I)
8510-8516	化學藥品	CHEMICALS AND THEIR MANUFACTURE
8517-8519	電氣化學工藝	INDUSTRIAL ELECTROCHEMISTRY
8520-8529	爆炸品, 燃燒品	EXPLOSIVES AND PYROTECHNICS
8521	煙火	Fireworks
8522	火柴	Matches
8524	燃料	Fuel
8527	火藥	Gun powder
8530-8539	食品工業	FOODS
8531	糖	Sugar
8532	鹽	Salt
8533	調味品	Condiments and flavoring products
8534-5	罐頭業	Food-preservation industry.　Canning.
8536-7	冷藏, 製冰業	Refrigeration and ice-making
8540-8549	釀造工業, 飲料	FERMENTATION INDUSTRIES.　BEVERAGES.
8541	酒	Wine and Spirit.　Alcohol.
8542	茶	Tea

	醸造工業,飲料 (續)	FERMENTATION INDUSTRIES. BEVERAGES (cont.)
8543	咖啡	Coffee, chocolate.
8544	醋	Vinegar
8545	醤油	Soy-sauce
8546	汽水	Artificial mineral waters
8550-8559	油脂工業 照明工業.	FAT INDUSTRIES ILLUMINATING INDUSTRIES.
8551	植物油	Vegetable oils
8552	動物油	Animal oils and fats
8553	蠟	Waxes
8554-6	礦物油, 氣	Mineral oils, gases and waxes
8557	肥皂 石鹼.	Soaps
8558	蠟燭	Candles
8560-8569	窰器工業	CLAY INDUSTRIES SILICATE INDUSTRIES.
8561	陶器	Pottery Earthenwares
8563	磁器	Ceramics Porcelains
8664	琺瑯 塗磁器.	Enamel wares
8566	玻璃	Glass wares
8567	人造石	Artificial stones and gems
8569	水泥 洋灰.	Cement
8570-8579	顔料,油漆工業	DYES, PIGMENTS, PAINTS AND VARNISHES
8571	漂白品	Bleaching chemicals
8572	染色術	Dyeing
8573	顔料	Dyes
8574	墨水	Ink (India)
8575-6	油漆	Paints, varnishes, and lacquers

8580-8585	化粧品工業	PERFUMERIES AND COSMETICS
8581	香水	Perfumes
8582	香料	Incense
8586-8589	纖維素製品工業 如化學象牙等.	CELLULOSE AND PLASTICS
8590-8599	其他化學工業	OTHER CHEMICAL INDUSTRIES
8600-8699	礦業及礦冶工程	MINERAL INDUSTRIES AND MINING ENGINEERING
8601-8609	總錄 依體裁分,用表一.	GENERAL (Form subdivisions like Table I)
8610-8619	礦務法規	MINING LAWS AND LEGISLATION
8620-8639	各國礦藏 依地理分,用表二.	MINERAL RESOURCES OF VARIOUS COUNTRIES (Subdivide by geographical Table II)
8640-8659	探礦工程	MINING ENGINEERING
8660-8679	冶金學	METALLURGY AND ASSAYING
8680-8699	煤,石油及石料開採法	COAL, PETROLEUM, AND QUARRYING
8700-8899	工程	ENGINEERING
8700-8719	工程總論	ENGINEERING IN GENERAL
8720-8729	土木工程	CIVIL ENGINEERING
8730-8739	水利工程	HYDRAULIC ENGINEERING
8740-8749	衛生及市政工程	SANITARY AND MUNICIPAL ENGINEERING
8750-8759	道路工程	ROADS AND PAVEMENTS
8760-8779	鐵路工程	RAILROAD ENGINEERING AND OPERATION
8780-8789	橋梁工程	BRIDGE AND ROOF ENGINEERING
8790-8799	建築工程	BUILDING AND CONSTRUCTION ENGINEERING

	工程 (續)	ENGINEERING (cont.)
8800-8829	機械工程及工業	MECHANICAL ENGINEERING AND MACHINERY
8830-8849	電氣工程及工業	ELECTRICAL ENGINEERING AND INDUSTRIES
8850-8859	汽車工程及工業	MOTOR VEHICLES AND AUTOMOBILE INDUSTRIES
8860-8879	飛機工程及工業	AERONAUTICAL ENGINEERING. AERIAL NAVIGATION. AVIATION INDUSTRIES.
8880-8899	造船工程海事工程 航行術	SHIPBUILDING AND MARINE ENGINEERING. NAVIGATION.
8900-8999	軍事學	THE TECHNOLOGY OF WARFARE (MILITARY NAVAL AND AERIAL-COMBAT SCIENCES)
8901-8909	總錄 依體裁分, 用表一.	GENERAL (Form subdivisions like Table D
8910-8918	中國古兵書	Chinese Ancient Military Treatises
8919	日本古兵書	Japanese Ancient Military Treatises
8920-8929	海陸空軍合論	GENERAL -- ARMY, NAVY AND AIR FORCE
8920	概論	General Treatises
8921	國防, 戰爭哲學	National Defense. Philosophy of War.
8922	軍政	Organization and Administration
8923	兵制	Military Systems -- Conscription vs. Voluntary Enlistment
8924	訓練	Training and Education
8925	軍需, 給養, 軍人生活	Maintenance and Military Life
8926	器械, 兵工廠	Arms Ordnance Arsenals
8928	戰畧, 戰術. 兵法.	Tactics and Strategy
8930-8959	陸軍	ARMY
8931-8933	組織	Organization and Distribution
8934-8936	行政	Administration

	陸軍 (續)	ARMY (cont.)
8937-8939	軍需	Maintenance
8940-8942	運輸	Transport
8943-8945	步兵	Infantry
8946-8948	騎兵	Cavalry
8949-8951	礮兵	Artillery
8952-8954	工兵	Engineering Corps
8955	其他	Other Services
8956-8957	器械	Ordnance
8958-8959	演習及戰術	Maneuvers and Tactics
8960-8979	海軍	NAVY
8961-8963	組織	Organization and Distribution
8964-8966	行政	Administration
8967-8969	軍需	Maintenance
8970-8972	各科水兵	Special Branches of Service
8973-8975	戰艦	Warships (See also 8880-8899)
8976	器械	Ordnance
8977-8979	演習及戰術	Maneuvers and Tactics
8980-8999	空軍	AIR FORCE
8981-8983	組織	Organization and Distribution
8984-8989	行政及軍需	Administration and Maintenance
8990-8992	各科航空員	Special Branches of Service
8993-8995	軍用機	Military and Naval Airplanes (See also 8860-8879)
8996	器械	Ordnance
8997-8999	演習及戰術	Maneuvers and Tactics

9000-9999 **總錄書志類** GENERALIA AND BIBLIOGRAPHY

9100-9120 **中國普通叢書** CHINESE GENERAL SERIES OR COLLECTIONS
專門叢書宜依其性質分入各類. (TS'UNG-SHU) Collections of works on
惟内容繁雜者入此. special subjects go with those subjects.

9100 **彙刻叢書** OF A COMPOSITE NATURE

此類叢書在書架上及排
架目錄中,依叢書名前數 (In the shelflist a mechanical arrange-
字之四角號碼或畫數排, ment by the name of the ts'ung-shu is
故書碼須揀書名定之;但 preferable to a chronological arrange-
在分類目錄中,仍宜照彙 ment by the date of compilation, which
刻年代排列. should be adopted in the classified
subject catalogue.)

9101-9109 **特種叢書** OF A SPECIAL TYPE

9108 **輯佚** Of recovered fragments
排法同上. (Same arrangement as above)

9110 **地方叢書** OF A PARTICULAR LOCALITY
郡邑叢書.
先依地理分,用表二,次按 (First classify by geographical
書名之四角號碼或畫數排. Table II, and secondly arrange by
name of the ts'ung-shu.)

9111 **族姓叢書** OF A PARTICULAR FAMILY
排法同彙刻叢書. (Same arrangement as 9100)

9112-9120 **個人叢書** OF INDIVIDUAL AUTHORS
自著叢書.
先按著者時代分,同時代 (Under each period arrange by the
之名叢書 在排架目錄中依 name of the author in the shelflist
姓名之四角號碼或筆畫數排, but by the dates of the author in
但在分類目錄中依生卒年排. the classified subject catalogue.)

9112 **宋** Sung Dynasty (960-1279)

9114 **元** Yüan Dynasty (1280-1368)

9115 **明** Ming Dynasty (1368-1644)

9117-9 **清** Ch'ing Dynasty (1644-1912)

9117 **初葉** First Period (1644-1822)

9118 **中葉** Middle Period (1822-1861)

9119 **季葉** Last Period (1861-1912)

9120 **民國** The Republic

9130-9159	中國雜著隨筆	CHINESE INDIVIDUAL POLYGRAPHIC BOOKS (GENERAL COLLECTED ESSAYS)

普通論叢.
凡四庫雜家類之雜學,雜考,雜說,雜品,雜纂,雜編,
小說類之雜事,及近人所著之普通論文與講演集,
不能分入他類者,皆入此.

9132	古代	Ancient period (Earliest to 206 B.C.)
9133	漢	Han Dynasty (B.C. 206-220 A.D.)
9135	三國	The Three Kingdoms (220-280)
9139	晉	Chin Dynasty (265-420)
9141	南北朝	Epoch of Southern and Northern dynasties (420-589)
9145	隋	Sui Dynasty (569-618)
9146	唐	T'ang Dynasty (618-906)
9148	五代	Five Dynasties (907-960)
9150	宋	Sung Dynasty (960-1279)
9151	元	Yüan Dynasty (1280-1368)
9153	明	Ming Dynasty (1368-1644)
9155	清	Ch'ing Dynasty (1644-1912)
9159	民國	The Republic (1912-)

9160-9164	中國國學	SINOLOGY

支那學

9160	中國人著作	Works by Chinese authors
9161	日本人著作	Works by Japanese authors
9163	西洋人著作	Works by Western authors

9165-9179	日本普通叢書	JAPANESE COLLECTIONS OR SERIES (SŌSHO)

9165	彙刻叢書	GENERAL COMPOSITE SERIES

在排架目錄中,依書名排. (Arrange according to the titles of such series in the shelflist.)

9170	地方叢書	GENERAL LOCAL COLLECTIONS (Subdivide by Table II)

依地理分,用表一.

9171-9	個人叢書	COLLECTED WORKS OF INDIVIDUAL AUTHORS (Subdivide chronologically by dates of authors like Table III)

依著者時代分,用表三.

9180-9189	日本雜著隨筆	JAPANESE INDIVIDUAL POLYGRAPHIC WORKS
9180	總集	Collections
9181-8	家集 依著者時代分, 用表三.	Independent editions (Subdivide by dates of authors like Table III)
9189	日本國學 日本學, 和學. 見日本哲學.	JAPANOLOGY (See also 1449.)
9190-8	朝鮮普通叢書雜著	KOREAN COLLECTIVE SERIES AND INDI- VIDUAL POLYGRAPHIC WORKS
9199	其他各國叢書雜著	GENERAL COLLECTIONS OF OTHER COUNTRIES
9200-9229	普通期刊社刊	GENERAL PERIODICALS AND SOCIETY PUBLICATIONS
9200	中國期刊	Chinese periodicals
9205	中國會社刊物	Chinese society publications (China societies in China and elsewhere e.g. China Institute in America)
9210	日本期刊	Japanese periodicals
9215	日本會社刊物	Japanese society publications
9216-9219	東方他國期刊社刊 依地理分, 用表二.	General periodicals and society publications of other Asiatic countries (Table II)
9220-9229	西洋各國期刊社刊 依地理分, 用表二.	General periodicals and society publications of Western countries (Subdivide geographically by Table II)
9230-9239	普通會議及展覽	GENERAL CONGRESSES AND EXHIBITIONS
9231-9232	中國	China
9231	全國	National
9232	地方 依地理分, 用表二.	Local (Divide by Table II)
9233-9234	日本 仿中國分.	Japan (Divide like China)
9235	東方他國 依地理分, 用表二.	Other Countries of Asia (Table II)
9236-9	西洋各國 依地理分, 用表二.	Western Countries (Divide by Table II)

319

9240-9289	普通博物院	<u>GENERAL MUSEUMS</u>
9240	博物院管理法	MUSEUM MANAGEMENT
9241-9269	博物院學. 中國	CHINA (Museums in each province are to be arranged by their names)
9241-9243	國立博物院	<u>National Museums</u>
9244-9269	省立及地方博物院	<u>Provincial and Local Museums</u>
9244	各省博物院依院名排. 遼寧	Liaoning
9245	吉林	Kirin
9246	黑龍江	Heilungkiang
9247	河北	Hopei
9248	山東	Shantung
9249	河南	Honan
9250	山西	Shansi
9251	陝西	Shensi
9252	甘肅	Kansu
9253	西康	Hsikang
9254	四川	Szechuan
9255	湖北	Hupei
9256	湖南	Hunan
9257	江西	Kiangsi
9258	安徽	Anhwei
9259	江蘇	Kiangsu
9260	浙江	Chekiang
9261	福建	Fukien
9262	廣東	Kwangtung
9263	廣西	Kwangsi
9264	雲南	Yunnan

	普通博物院 (續)	GENERAL MUSEUMS (cont.)
9265	貴州	Kweichow
9266-7	蒙古	Mongolia
9268	新疆	Sinkiang (Chinese Turkestan)
9269	青海	Chinghai (Kokonor) and Tibet
9270-9279	日本	JAPAN
9270	帝室博物館	Imperial (Household) Museum
9271-8	地方博物館 依地理分, 用表二.	Local (Divide by Table II)
9279-9284	朝鮮	KOREA
9285	其他亞洲諸國 依地理分, 用表二.	OTHER COUNTRIES OF ASIA (Divide by Table II)
9286-9289	西洋各國 依地理分, 用表二.	WESTERN COUNTRIES (Divide by Table II)

9280-9339	普通百科全書及類書 專門類書宜各入其類. 如詩 文典故入文學, 博物入科 學, 姓名彙考入傳記, 餘可 類推. 其不能分入各類者, 入此.	GENERAL ENCYCLOPEDIAS AND REFERENCE WORKS (Specialized encyclopedias and reference works relating to special subjects go with those subjects; such as a book of literary allusions is to be clas- sified with literature and dictionaries of personal names with biography, etc.)
9290-9319	中國類書	CHINESE GENERAL ENCYCLOPEDIAS AND REFERENCE WORKS
9290	彙刊, 叢集 如九通等.	Collections of all periods
9296-9302	類編, 彙考 以編纂朝代分.	Those arranged by classified categories or groups (Classify by dates of compilation)
9296	唐, 五代	T'ang and the Five Dynasties (618-960)
9297	宋	Sung Dynasty (960-1279)
9298	元	Yüan Dynasty (1280-1368)
9299	明	Ming Dynasty (1368-1644)
9301	清	Ch'ing Dynasty (1644-1912)
9302	民國	The Republic (1912-)

	中國類書(續)	CHINESE GENERAL ENCYCLOPEDIAS AND REFERENCE WORKS (cont.)
9303-9307	韻編, 字編	Those arranged by rhymes or strokes of characters
9303	宋	Sung Dynasty (960-1279)
9304	元	Yüan Dynasty (1280-1368)
9305	明	Ming Dynasty (1368-1644)
9306	清	Ch'ing Dynasty (1644-1912)
9307	民國	The Republic (1912-)
9308-9310	雜編, 摘錦 如數攷, 蒙求, 等.	Those arranged for popular or children's use
9308	古代至明	Ancient period to Ming Dynasty (Earliest to 1644)
9309	清	Ch'ing Dynasty (1644-1912)
9310	民國	The Republic (1912-)
9311-9316	歲時, 年鑑	Almanacs Yearbooks
9311	五代以前	Ancient Period to the Five Dynasties (Earliest to 960)
9312	宋	Sung Dynasty (960-1279)
9313	元	Yüan Dynasty (1280-1368)
9314	明	Ming Dynasty (1368-1644)
9315	清	Ch'ing Dynasty (1644-1912)
9316	民國	The Republic (1912-)
9317	普通手冊	General Handbooks
9318-9319	機關一覽	General Directories
9318	全國 機關一覽, 電話簿, 等.	National
9319	各地 依地理分, 用表二.	Local (Divide by Table II)

9320-9329	日本類書	JAPANESE GENERAL ENCYCLOPEDIAS AND REFERENCE WORKS
9320-9328	百科事彙	Encyclopedias (Subdivide chronologically by Table III according to date of compilation)
9329	普通手冊	General Handbooks
9330-9332	普通年鑑	Yearbooks　Almanacs
9330	世界	World
9331	亞洲及中國	Asia and China
9332	日本	Japan Proper
9333	普通機關名簿	General Directories
9334	朝鮮類書	KOREAN GENERAL ENCYCLOPEDIAS AND REFERENCE WORKS
9335	其他東方文字類書	OF OTHER ASIATIC LANGUAGES
9336-9339	西洋文字類書	WESTERN GENERAL ENCYCLOPEDIAS AND REFERENCE WORKS
9336	英文	English
9337	德文	German
9338	法文	French
9339	其他	Other Western Languages

9400-9699 書志學　　　　　　　BIBLIOGRAPHY

校讎學,目錄學,文獻學.

9401-9409 總錄　　　　　　　　GENERAL (Form subdivisions like Table I)

依體裁分,用表一.

9410-9469 圖書學　　　　　　HISTORY OF BOOKS AND BOOK-MAKING.
　　　　　　　　　　　　　　　BIBLIOLOGY.

9411-9415 書寫　　　　　　　WRITING

9411-9417 專為印刷術及
目錄學特藏而設,普通圖
書館中不必使用.

(Except in a library devoted to printing or bibliography the following subdivisions, 9411-7, are not to be used in general libraries.)

[9411] 文字之起源　　　　Invention of Writing, see 5010, 5068, 5810.8.

[9412] 古文字學　　　　　Paleography, see 2082, 2161.6.

[9413] 書法　　　　　　　Calligraphy, Penmanship, see 6129, 6239.

[9414] 速記術　　　　　　Shorthand, see 5033, 5169, 5823.

[9415] 密碼術　　　　　　Cryptography, see 5033, 4525.

9416-9419 寫本　　　　　　BOOKS IN MANUSCRIPT

[9416.1] 石刻,沙文　　　　Inscriptions on Stones and Sand, see 2096, 2166.

[9416.3] 甲骨文　　　　　　Inscriptions on Bones and Shells, see 2986, 2162.

[9416.5] 瓦書　　　　　　　Inscriptions on Terra-cotta, see 2089, 2164.

金文　　　　　　　Inscriptions on Metal Pieces, see 2105, 2168.

[9417.1] 竹簡　　　　　　　Manuscripts of Bamboo-strips, see 2115, 2170.

[9417.5] 木簡　　　　　　　Manuscripts of Wood-strips, see 2115, 2170.

9418 帛卷　　　　　　　　Manuscripts of Silk-rolls.

9419 皮卷　　　　　　　　Manuscripts of Parchment-rolls.

9420-9459	印刷與刻版	PRINTING AND ENGRAVING
9420.1-.9	總錄 依體裁分, 用表一.	General (Form subdivisions like Table I)
9421-5	史傳	History and Biography
9421	通載	General
9422	中國	Chinese
9423	日本	Japanese
9424	其他東方諸國 依地理分, 用表二.	Other Asiatic Countries (Table II)
9425	西洋各國 依地理分, 用表二.	Western Countries (Table II)
9426-9429	孤本善本 通論,圖錄與書影. 善本書籍應按內容 分入各類,如欲合 藏一處者,可在排架 號前加一字表示之.	Incunabula and Fine Printing: General treatises and reproduced specimens (Actual works go with subjects. If it is desired to put rare books together in one collection, a letter may be prefixed to their call numbers.)
9426	通錄	General
9427	中國	Chinese
9428	日本	Japanese
9428.9	其他東方諸國 依地理分, 用表二.	Other Asiatic Countries (Table II)
9429	西洋各國 依地理分, 用表二.	Western Countries (Table II)
9430-9459	各種印刷術	Technical Processes of Printing
9430	通錄	General
9431-9498	凸版術	<u>Raised-surface or Relief Processes</u>
9431-9435	木版	Wood-block Engraving and Printing. Xylography
9431	通錄	General
9432	中國	Chinese
9433	日本	Japanese
9434	其他東方諸國 依地理分, 用表二.	Other Asiatic Countries (Table II)
9435	西洋各國 依地理分, 用表二.	Western Countries (Table II)

	印刷與刻版 (續)	PRINTING AND ENGRAVING (cont.)
	凸版術 (續)	Raised-surface or Relief Processes (cont.)
9436-9439	金屬版	Metal Engraving
9436	雕刻版	Line and Stipple
9437	腐蝕版	Mezzotint and Aquatint
9438-9	照相版	Photo-engraving　Zincography
9440-9448	活字版	Letterpress Printing.　Typography.
9440	通錄	General
9441	活字, 字體樣本	Type　Specimen Books
9442	澆字, 銅模	Type-founding　Matrices
9443	排版, 欵式	Composition　Style-manuals
.1	手工排字	Hand
.2	機器排字總論	Machine, general.
.3	一行鑄字機	Linotype and intertype
.4	單字鑄字機	Monotype
.5	其他鑄字機	Other mechanical methods
9444	觶版	Type-distributing
9445	校正, 對版	Correcting for press or ''Make-up'' Proofreading
9446	整版	Imposition and locking-up
9447	製版, 留版	Stereotyping; electrotyping.
9448	印刷手續	Presswork
9449-9453	平版術	Flat-surface or Planographic Processes
9449	通論	General
9450	石印術	Lithography
9451	膠質版等	Multilith, Lithoprint, Gelatine and liquid duplicating Processes
9452	橡皮版	Photo-offset Processes
9453	其他方法 影印, 曬印等	Other Processes (Photostat, Blueprint)

	印刷與刻版	PRINTING AND ENGRAVING (cont.)
9454-9457	凹版術	Sunken-surface or Intaglio Processes
9454	通論	General
9454.9	椎搨 搨印法.	Rubbing on carved stones
9455	金蝕版	Etching on metals
9456	珂羅版	Collotype or photogelatin Process
9457	照相版	Photogravure
9458	其他特殊印刷術	Other Special Processes of Printing and Duplicating
.1	謄寫版 油印機	Mimeograph Process
.3	漏皮版	Dermaprint Process
.5	迴轉排印機	Multigraph Process
9459	打字機	Typewriters
9460-9469	裝釘	BINDING BIBLIOPEGY
9460.1-.9	總錄 依體裁分, 用表一.	GENERAL (Form subdivisions like Table D
9461	書籍裝潢通論	BOOK DECORATION IN GENERAL (BUCHKUNST
9462-9465	漢和裝	CHINESE AND JAPANESE BINDINGS
9462	歷史	History
9463-9464	欵式	Styles
9463.1	簡式	Strips tied with cords or diptych binding
9463.3	軸式, 卷子	Rolls with rod in center
9463.4	摺式	Folded rolls
9463.6	蝴蝶裝	Butterfly binding
9463.7-.9	其他古裝	Other ancient styles
9464	線裝	Ordinary stitched bindings
9465	材具	Materials and tools

9466-9469	西洋裝	WESTERN BINDINGS
9466	史傳	History and Biography
9467	手冊,要覽	Handbooks
9468	材具	Machinery, materials, tools
9469	各國裝釘樣本與傳說	Specimens and accounts by countries (Subdivide by Table II)

9470-9489	書業 出版業,販書業.	BOOKSELLING AND PUBLISHING
9470.1-.9	總錄 依體裁分,用表一.	GENERAL (Form subdivisions like Table I)
9471-9472	中國	CHINA
9471	全國書業公會及名錄	National Organizations and Directories
9472	各地書業公會及名錄	Local - Directories and Individual Bookstores
9473-9474	日本	JAPAN
9473	全國書籍商組合及名簿	National Organizations and Directories
9474	各地書籍商組合及名簿	Local - Directories and Individual Bookstores
9475-9479	其他東方諸國 依地理分,用表二.	OTHER ASIATIC COUNTRIES (Subdivide by Table II)
9480-9489	西洋各國 依地理分,用表二.	WESTERN COUNTRIES (Subdivide by Table II)

9490-9499	版權與出版法	COPYRIGHT AND LAW OF THE PRESS
9490	總論 原則,道德及雜錄.	GENERAL: THEORY, ETHICS, MISCELLANEOUS
9491	國際版權	INTERNATIONAL COPYRIGHT

版權及出版法 (續) COPYRIGHT AND LAW OF THE PRESS　(cont.)

9492-9496	各國版權及出版法	LAWS OF VARIOUS COUNTRIES (Better class with 4892-3 LAW. The following numbers may be used for keeping works on copyright and press laws of different countries together with works on Publishing.)
	如非省便版權及出版法與書通關于出版著作置于一處者,宜入法律.	

[9492]	中國	China, see 4892.7
[9493]	日本	Japan, see 4892.7
[9494]	其他東方諸國	Other Asiatic Countries (Subdivide by Table II, see 4892.9)
[9495-6]	西洋各國	Western Countries (Subdivide by Table II, see 4892.9)

9497	言論自由	LIBERTY OF THE PRESS
9498	文字獄	LITERARY INQUISITION General works only, works about special countries go with histories of those countries.
	總論入此,各國史實入歷史.	
[9499]	出版法	PRESS LAW General works only. For particular countries, see 4892.

9500-9510	文獻及研究事務法	LITERARY METHODS AND RESEARCH AIDS
9500	總論	General
	編纂義例及治學方法.	
9501	書籍記述法	Art of describing a book technically (See also 9766 Cataloguing)
	參見編目法.	
9502	編校法	Art of proofreading and editing
9503	辨僞法	Art of detecting forgeries
9504	序跋法	Art of writing prefaces and colophons
9505	書評法	Art of book-reviewing
9506	劄記法	Art of abstracting
9507	索引法	Art of indexing
9508	剪裁法	Art of clipping articles

文獻及研究事務法 (續) LITERARY METHODS AND RESEARCH AIDS (cont.)

9509	論文編著法	Art of writing theses and papers
9510	參考書及圖書館利用法	Art of using reference books and libraries (See also 9770 Reference Work)

[9511-9519] 各科書目   SUBJECT BIBLIOGRAPHY

各科書目宜分入各類,如欲將所有書目集中一處者,得用下列大類號碼,更可加以細分.最好此種書能有兩部,一部入各類中,一部置此.

(Better class with the subjects distributed throughout the classification. If it is desired to put all bibliographies on special subjects together in one place, the following numbers may be used for the main divisions, and each main division may further be subdivided in the order of the whole classification scheme. The most satisfactory arrangement is to buy two copies of each subject bibliography-- place one copy here and one copy with the subject.)

[9511]	中國經學	CHINESE CLASSICS
[9512]	哲學宗教	PHILOSOPHY AND RELIGION
[9513]	歷史科學	HISTORICAL SCIENCES
[9514]	社會科學	SOCIAL SCIENCES
[9515]	語言文學	LANGUAGE AND LITERATURE
[9516]	美術游藝	FINE AND RECREATIVE ARTS
[9517]	自然科學	NATURAL SCIENCES
[9518]	農業工藝	AGRICULTURE AND TECHNOLOGY
[9519]	總錄書志	GENERALIA

各國書目   BIBLIOGRAPHIES OF VARIOUS COUNTRIES

9520-9639	中國書目	CHINESE BIBLIOGRAPHIES
9521-9529	彙刊書目	GENERAL AND COLLECTIVE
9522	書目叢刊	Collections of bibliographies
9523	書目之書目	Bibliography of bibliographies

	中國書目 (續)	CHINESE BIBLIOGRAPHIES (cont.)
	彙刊書目 (續)	GENERAL AND COLLECTIVE (cont.)
9524	叢書總目	Bibliography of T'sung-shu
9525	叢書子目	Indexes to contents of T'sung-shu
9530-9	歷代史志	BIBLIOGRAPHICAL SECTIONS IN DYNASTIC HISTORIES
9532	漢	Han dynasty (B.C. 206-A. D. 220)
9533	魏晉,六朝	Wei, Chin and the Six Dynasties (220-617)
9534	唐,五代	T'ang and the Five Dynasties (618-960)
9535	宋	Sung dynasty (960-1279)
9536	元	Yüan dynasty (1280-1368)
9537	明	Ming dynasty (1368-1644)
9538	清	Ch'ing dynasty (1644-1912)
9540-9	其他一般書目	OTHER GENERAL BIBLIOGRAPHIES
9550-7	治學書目 標準書目,名著書目.	READING LISTS AND "BEST BOOKS"
9558	羣書引得	UNION INDEXES TO BOOKS
9559	期刊引得 各科論文引得入各學科.	GENERAL PERIODICAL INDEXES
9560-9569	特種書目	SPECIAL BIBLIOGRAPHIES
9561	徵存,知見	Of books known to be existing in a certain location.
9562	引用	Of works consulted in certain books.
9563	闕佚	Of lost books and books whose where-abouts is uncertain.
9564	禁燬	Of condemned, prohibited and expurgated books.
9565	僞書	Of spurious and apocryphal books.
9566	善本	Of rare and fine editions.
9567	官修,敕撰	Of imperial and other official compilations.

	中國書目(續)	CHINESE BIBLIOGRAPHIES (cont.)
	特種書目(續)	SPECIAL BIBLIOGRAPHIES (cont.)
9568	未刊, 稿本	Of unpublished books or autographic manuscripts.
9569	叙錄叢刊	Of authors' own collected prefaces and synopses.
9570-9579	考證書目 群書題記及校勘. 依著有時代分, 用表三.	BIBLIOGRAPHIES OF CRITICAL REVIEWS AND OF TYPOGRAPHICAL OR TEXTUAL CORRECTIONS (Subdivide chronologically by authors like Table III)
9580-9589	地方書目 郡邑藝文志. 依地理分, 用表二.	LOCAL BIBLIOGRAPHIES (Subdivide geographically by Table II)
9590	族姓書目 依姓氏排.	FAMILY BIBLIOGRAPHIES (Arrange by the name of the family)
9591-9599	個人書目 依所指人之時代分, 用表三.	PERSONAL BIBLIOGRAPHIES. BIO-BIBLIOGRAPHIES. (Subdivide chronologically by biographees like Table III)
9600-9629	收藏書目	LIBRARY CATALOGUES
9601-9619	公藏	Public and Semi-public Libraries
9601-9608	上古至清 依時代分, 用表三.	Earliest to Ch'ing Dynasty (Subdivide chronologically like Table III)
9609-9619	民國	The Republic (1912-)
9611	國立圖書館	National libraries
9613	省立圖書館	Provincial libraries
9614	公立圖書館	Free public libraries
9616	學校圖書館	School and college libraries
9618	會社圖書館	Society and club libraries
9619	寺廟圖書館	Monastic libraries
9620-9629	私藏 依時代分, 用表三. 每時代中, 依名稱排.	Private and family libraries (Divide by periods like Table III and under each period by the names of the libraries.)

中國書目 (續)　　CHINESE BIBLIOGRAPHIES (cont.)

9630-9639	出版目錄	PUBLISHERS' CATALOGUES
9631-2	官刊 刊行書目	Government publications
9631	中央	Central Government
9632	各省	Provincial Governments
9633-4	私刊	Private printers' catalogues
9633	前代	Prior to 1912
9634	現代	Contemporary (1912 -)
9635-6	學術團體出版物	Learned societies' publications
9635	全國	National
9636	地方	Local
9637	書店出版物	Commercial publishers' catalogues
9638	聯合出版目錄	Publishers' union catalogues
9639	營業目錄 依書商名稱排.	TRADE OR DEALERS' CATALOGUES
9640-9684	日本書目	JAPANESE BIBLIOGRAPHIES
9641-9649	一般書目	GENERAL AND COLLECTIVE
9641	書目之書目	Bibliography of bibliographies
9642	書目叢編	Collections of bibliographies
9643-4	歷代文獻志	Bibliographies of different periods
9645	其他一般書目	Other general bibliographies
9646	治學書目	Reading lists and "best books"
9647	叢書書目 標準書目, 優良書目.	Bibliographies of Sōshū
9648	叢書索引	Union indexes to Sōshū
9649	雜誌索引	General periodical indexes
9650-9653	特種書目	SPECIAL BIBLIOGRAPHIES
9651	徵闕	Of lost and latent books
9652	禁燬	Of condemned, prohibited, and expurgated books
9653	善本	Of rare and fine editions

	日本書目(續)	JAPANESE BIBLIOGRAPHIES (cont.)
9654	解題書目	CRITICAL BIBLIOGRAPHIES
9654.9	族姓書目	FAMILY BIBLIOGRAPHIES
9655.1-.9	個人書目 依所指人時代分, 用表三.	PERSONAL BIBLIOGRAPHIES. BIO-BIBLIOGRAPHIES. (Subdivide by dates of biographees like Table III)
9656-9	地方書目	LOCAL BIBLIOGRAPHIES (Table II)
9660-9678	收藏書目	LIBRARY CATALOGUES
9660-9669	公藏	Public and Semi-public libraries
9660-4	前代	Earliest to 1868
9665-9	現代	Since Meiji Period (1868 - date)
9665	寺院圖書館	Monastic libraries
9666	政府圖書館	National libraries
9667	公立圖書館	Free-public libraries
9668	學校圖書館	School and college libraries
9669	會社圖書館	Society and club libraries
9672-9278	私藏 依時代分, 用表三.	Private and family libraries (Subdivide by periods like Table III)
9679-9684	出版目錄	PUBLISHERS' CATALOGUES
9679	官刊	Government publications
9680	私刊	Private printers' catalogues
9681	學術機關出版品	Learned institutions' publications
9682	書店出版品	Commercial publishers' catalogues
9683	出版總目錄	Publishers' union catalogues
9684	營業目錄 販賣目錄.	TRADE OR DEALERS' CATALOGUES
9685-9694	朝鮮書目 依表年細分.	KOREAN BIBLIOGRAPHIES (Subdivide like Table H
9695	其他亞洲諸國書目	BIBLIOGRAPHIES OF OTHER ASIATIC COUNTRIES
9696-9699	西洋各國書目 亞洲及西洋各國書目先 依地理分, 用表二, 再依 性質分, 用表辛.	BIBLIOGRAPHIES OF WESTERN COUNTRIES (9695 and 9696-9699 first subdivide by geographical Table II and under each country use Form Subdivision Table H)

9701-9929	圖書館學	LIBRARY SCIENCE OR LIBRARIANSHIP
9701-9709	總錄 依體裁分,用表一.	GENERAL (Form subdivisions like Table D
9710-9729	藏書掌故及歷史	BOOK-COLLECTING AND BEGINNING OF LIBRARIES (BIBLIOPHILY AND BIBLIOMANIA)
9711-9719	中國	China
9720-9728	日本	Japan
9729	其他各國 依地理分,用表二.	Other countries (Subdivide by Table II
9730-9739	圖書館通論 理論,效用及設立諸問題.	SCOPE, USEFULNESS AND FOUNDING OF LIBRARIES
9740-9749	建築及設備	ARCHITECTURE AND EQUIPMENT
9750-9759	行政	ADMINISTRATION
9751	組織章程	Constitution and by-laws
9753	董事會,委員會	Governing board
9755	館員	Staff　Personnel
9757	館規	Regulations　Rules
9760-9779	管理	MANAGEMENT
9761	總務	General affairs
9762	採訪	Acquisition
9763	購書	Ordering and receiving
9764	交換	Gifts and exchanges
9765	登錄	Accession
9766	編目	Cataloguing
9767	分類	Classification
9768	典藏	Shelf or Stack Department
9769	出納	Loan　Circulation
9770	參考	Reference work

	圖書館學	LIBRARY SCIENCE OR LIBRARIANSHIP (cont.)
	管理	MANAGEMENT (cont.)
9771	善本	Rare books and manuscripts
9772	檔案	Archives
9773	輿圖	Maps
9774	金石,版畫	Rubbings and prints
9775	樂譜	Music scores
9776	影片	Microfilms
9777	鈔寫,照相	Copying Photostating
9778	裝訂,修理	Binding and repair of books
9779	庶務	Building care and upkeep
9780-9789	特種圖書館	LIBRARIES FOR SPECIAL CLASSES OF PEOPLE
9781	通俗圖書館	Popular libraries
9782	巡迴圖書館	Circulating libraries
9783	鄉村圖書館	Rural libraries
9784	兒童圖書館	Children libraries
9785	學校圖書館	School libraries
9786	書院大學圖書館	College and university libraries
9787	會社圖書館	Society and club libraries
9788	寺院圖書館	Monastic libraries
9789	其他 如盲人圖書館,士兵圖書館等.	Others (e.g. for the blind and for soldiers and sailors, etc.)
9790-9800	專科圖書館	LIBRARIES ON SPECIAL SUBJECTS
9791	文哲	Philosophical and literary
9792	史地	Historical and geographical
9793	社會,教育	Sociological and educational
9794	金融,商業	Financial and commercial
9795	政法	Political and legal

336

圖書館學 (續)　LIBRARY SCIENCE OR LIBRARIANSHIP (cont.)

專科圖書館 (續)　LIBRARIES ON SPECIAL SUBJECTS (cont.)

9796	科學	Scientific
9797	醫學	Medical
9798	農業	Agricultural
9799	工程, 工業	Technical, engineering and industrial
9800	美術, 音樂	Artistic and Musical

各種圖書館各科圖書館細目, 乃為討論此類圖書館之書而設, 各圖書館之報告期刊概况等, 仍宜依地理照下表細分之.

(The foregoing subdivisions 9780-9789 and 9790-9800 are used for books discussing problems relating to those distinct classes of libraries. Reports, bulletins, surveys, etc. of individual libraries go with the following geographical divisions, 9800-9929.)

9801-9909	中國圖書館刊物	LIBRARY PUBLICATIONS OF CHINA
9801-9805	國立圖書館	NATIONAL LIBRARIES
	各省圖書館	LIBRARIES IN THE PROVINCES

除河北湖北江蘇外, 各省下皆仿遼寧細分. 又各地方之圖書館皆依館名排列.

(Under each province subdivide like Liaoning, 9806-9808, except Hopei, Hupei and Kiangsu, and under each locality arrange by the names of libraries.)

9806-9808	遼寧	LIAONING
9806	省立圖書館	Provincial library
9807	瀋陽各圖書館	Mukden libraries
9808	其他各圖書館	Other libraries
9809-9811	吉林	KIRIN
9812-9814	黑龍江	HEILUNGKIANG
9815-9818	河北	HOPEI
9815	省立圖書館	Provincial library
9816	北平各圖書館	Peiping (Peking) libraries
9817	天津各圖書館	Tientsin libraries
9818	其他各圖書館	Other libraries

中國圖書館刊物_(續)LIBRARY PUBLICATIONS IN CHINA （cont.）

9819-9821	山東	SHANGTUNG
9822-9824	河南	HONAN
9825-9827	山西	SHANSI
9828-9830	陝西	SHENSI
9831-9833	甘肅	KANSU
9834-9836	西康	HSIKANG
9837-9839	四川	SZECHUAN
9840-9844	湖北	HUPEI
9840	省立圖書館	Provincial library
9841	武昌各圖書館	Wuchang libraries
9842	漢口各圖書館	Hankow libraries
9843	其他各圖書館	Other libraries
9845-9847	湖南	HUNAN
9848-9850	江西	KIANGSI
9851-9853	安徽	ANHWEI
9854-9857	江蘇	KIANGSU
9854	省立圖書館	Provincial library
9855	南京各圖書館	Nanking libraries
9856	上海各圖書館	Shanghai libraries
9857	其他各圖書館	Other libraries
9858-9860	浙江	CHEKIANG
9861-9863	福建	FUKIEN
9864-9866	廣東	KWANGTUNG
9867-9869	廣西	KWANGSI
9870-9872	雲南	YÜNNAN
9873-9875	貴州	KWEICHOW

中國圖書館刊物(續) LIBRARY PUBLICATIONS OF CHINA (cont.)

9876-9899	邊疆諸省	OUTLYING REGIONS
9876-9878	熱河	Jehol
9879-9881	綏遠	Suiyuan
9882-9884	察哈爾	Charhar
9885-9887	寧夏	Ninghsia
9888-9890	外蒙古	Outer Mongolia
9891-9893	新疆	Sinkiang (Chinese Turkestan)
9894-9896	青海	Chinghai (Kokonor)
9897-9899	西藏	Tibet
9900-9909	日本圖書館刊物	LIBRARY PUBLICATIONS OF JAPAN
9900	帝國圖書館	Imperial Library
9901	關東圖書館	Kantō libraries
9902	奧羽圖書館	Ou libraries
9903	中部圖書館	Chūbu libraries
9904	近畿圖書館	Kinki libraries
9905	中國圖書館	Chūgoku libraries
9906	四國圖書館	Shikoku libraries
9907	九州圖書館	Kyūshū and Ryūkyū libraries
9908	北海道及樺太圖書館	Hokkaidō and Karafuto libraries
9909	臺灣圖書館	Taiwan (Formosa) libraries

9910-9924　朝鮮圖書館刊物　LIBRARY PUBLICATIONS OF KOREA

9925　其他東方諸國圖書館刊物 LIBRARY PUBLICATIONS OF OTHER ASIATIC
　　　　依地理分,用表二.　COUNTRIES (Subdivide by Table II)

9926-9929　西洋各國圖書館刊物 LIBRARY PUBLICATIONS OF WESTERN
　　　　依地理分,用表二.　COUNTRIES (Subdivide by Table II)

9930-9999	報學 新聞學	JOURNALISM
9930-9939	總錄 依體裁分,用表一.	GENERAL (Form subdivisions like Table I)
9940-9946	報學原理	THEORIES. RELATIONS TO OTHER PROFESSIONS.
9947-9949	開設與主管	OWNERSHIP AND CONTROL
9950-9959	營業部	BUSINESS MANAGEMENT
9960-9969	編輯部	EDITORIAL MANAGEMENT
9970-9979	報學史	HISTORY OF JOURNALISM
9970	通錄	GENERAL
9971-2	中國	CHINA
9973-4	日本	JAPAN
9975	其他東方諸國 依地理分,用表二.	OTHER ASIATIC COUNTRIES (Subdivide by Table II)
9976-9979	西洋各國 依地理分,用表二.	WESTERN COUNTRIES (Subdivide by Table II)
9980-9999	報紙 日報,新聞紙.	NEWSPAPERS
9980	索引,一覽,等	INDEXES, DIRECTORIES, ETC.
9981-9989	中國報紙	CHINA
9981-9983	各省 依地理分,用表二. 每省下依所在地名排列, 但下列各地除外.	Different Provinces (Subdivide by Table II, and under each province by the names of cities, except the following cities.)
9984	南京	Nanking
9985	上海	Shanghai
9986	北平,天津	Peiping and Tientsin
9987	漢口	Hankow
9988	廣州	Canton
9989	重慶	Chungking

報紙 (續)　　　　　NEWSPAPERS (cont.)

| 9990-9994 | 日本報紙 | JAPAN |
| 9990.1-9990.9 | 各縣 | Different Prefectures |

依地理分,用表二.
每縣下依所在地名排,但
下列各地除外.

(Subdivide by Table II, and under each prefecture by the names of cities, except the following cities.)

9991	東京	Tōkyō
9992	京都	Kyōto
9993	大阪	Ōsaka
9994	神戸	Kōbe

| 9995 | 其他東方諸國報紙 | OTHER ASIATIC COUNTRIES |

依地理分,用表二.

(Subdivide by Table II)

| 9996-9999 | 西洋各國報紙 | WESTERN COUNTRIES |

依地理分,用表二.

(Subdivide by Table II)

341

附表一　　　Appended Table I　　　體裁細分

FORM SUBDIVISIONS OF ANY CLASS OR SECTION

1　期刊
日刊,週刊,半月刊,月刊,季刊,半年刊,年鑑,等一切定期刊物入此.可包括會社出版之定期刊物.

Periodicals
Serial publications of Societies issued at regular intervals are placed here.

2　會社
凡公私機關及一切學術團體出版之報告,檔案,及會議展覽紀錄等入此.

Societies, Exhibitions, Congresses
Irregular documentary and ancillary materials, such as, reports, bulletins, circulars, photographs, etc. are placed here.

3　叢集, 雜錄
凡雜文,講演錄,節錄,叢書劄記等入此.

Collections, Miscellanies
Miscellaneous notes, extracts, speeches, collections, sets or series are placed here.

4　書目
凡選錄簡目或收藏目錄均入此.

Bibliographies (Books about the subject)
Selective lists and library catalogs relating to that subject are placed here.

5　教學
凡研究法,教授法,專科教育概况與組織,教科書,課程表等均入此.

Study and Teaching
Scope, Relations of the Subject; Education or Training in it; Profession of it, organization, etc.

6　類書
凡字典,辭典,事彙,索引,通檢,手冊,綱要,圖表,等專為學考之用者入此.

Reference Books
Dictionaries, Glossaries, Encyclopedias, Indexes, Concordances, Handbooks, Compends, Atlases, Diagrams, etc. are placed here.

7　傳記
各專類之合傳入此;個人別傳或年譜仍入歷史科學之傳記類.

Biographies
Only collective biographies relevant to the subject are placed here.

8　歷史與現狀
得用表二依國別細分之.

History and Conditions
May be subdivided by countries like Table II.

9　義例, 理論
凡討論本題之哲學原理,思想派別或總括概論等著述入此.

Theory, Philosophy, General Treatises
All works relating to the theoretical aspects of the subject are placed here.

Appended Table II: GEOGRAPHICAL LIST
附表二 地域細分
(To be used for subjects that are subdivided geographically)

05	亞洲	Asia
10-39	中國	China
10	全國	China as a whole
101	北部諸省	Northern Provinces
11	遼寧	Liaoning
12	吉林	Kirin
13	黑龍江	Heilungkiang
14	河北	Hopei
15	山東	Shantung
16	河南	Honan
17	山西	Shansi
18	陝西	Shensi
19	甘肅	Kansu
20	中部諸省	Central Provinces
22	西康	Hsikang
23	四川	Szechuan
24	湖北	Hupei
25	湖南	Hunan
26	江西	Kiangsi
27	安徽	Anhwei
28	江蘇	Kiangsu
29	浙江	Chekiang

地域細分(續) GEOGRAPHICAL LIST　(cont.)

中國(續)　　　　　China (cont.)

30	南部諸省	Southern Provinces
31	福建	Fukien
32	廣東	Kwangtung
33	廣西	Kwangsi
34	雲南	Yunnan
35	貴州	Kweichow
36	蒙古	Mongolia as a whole
361	內蒙	Inner Mongolia
362	熱河	Jehol
363	察哈爾	Charhar
364	綏遠	Suiyuan
365	寧夏	Ninghsia
366	外蒙	Outer Mongolia
37	新疆	Sinkiang (Chinese Turkestan)
38	青海	Chinghai (Kokonor)
39	西藏	Tibet
40-49	日本及朝鮮	Japan and Korea
40	全國	Japan as a whole
41	關東	Kantō
42	奧羽	Ou
43	中部	Chūbu
44	近畿	Kinki
45	中國,四國	Chūgoku, Shikoku
46	九州,琉球	Kyūshū, Ryūkyū
47	北海道,樺太	Hokkaidō, Karafuto (Saghalien)
48	臺灣	Taiwan (Formosa)

344

地域細分(續)GEOGRAPHICAL LIST （cont.）

49	朝鮮	Korea
50	西伯利亞	Siberia　Russian Asia
51	菲律賓 俄國亞洲之部.	Philippine Islands
52	東印度群島	East Indies Islands
53	馬來半島	Malay Peninsula
54	泰國(暹羅)越南	Thailand (Siam)　Indo-China
55	印度, 緬甸	India　Burma
56	阿富汗, 俾路芝	Afghanistan　Baluchistan　Nepal
57	伊蘭, 伊剌克	Iran　Iraq　(Persia)
58	阿剌伯	Arabia
59	小亞細亞 土耳其亞洲之部.	Asia Minor　(Turkey in Asia)
60	歐洲	Europe
61	土耳其	Turkey in Europe
62	布和利亞羅馬尼亞	Bulgaria　Rumania
63	希臘,阿爾巴尼亞	Greece　Albania
64	俄國	Russia
65	波蘭	Poland
66	波羅的諸國 立陶宛,拉特維亞,愛沙尼亞	Baltic States: Lithuania, Latvia, Esthonia
67	斯堪地那威 芬蘭,瑞典,挪威,丹麥 及氷島	Scandinavian countries: Finland, Sweden, Norway, Denmark (including Iceland)
68	捷克, 巨哥斯拉夫	Czechoslovakia　Yugoslavia
69	匈牙利	Hungary
70	奧地利	Austria
71	德國	Germany
72	瑞士, 盧森堡	Switzerland　Luxembourg
73	荷蘭, 比利時	Holland　Belgium
74	法國	France

地域細分 (續) GEOGRAPHICAL LIST (cont.)

75	意大利	Italy
76	西班牙	Spain
77	葡萄牙	Portugal
78	英國	Great Britain (British Empire)
79	愛爾蘭	Eire (Irish Free State)
80	北美洲	North America
81-82	坎拿大	Canada
83-84	美國	United States
85	墨西哥	Mexico
86	中美洲	Central America
87	西印度羣島	West Indies
88-89	南美洲	South America
881	哥倫比亞	Colombia
882	委内瑞拉	Venezuela
883	圭亞那	The Guianas
884	巴西	Brazil
885	玻利維亞	Bolivia
886	巴拉圭,烏拉圭	Paraguay Uruguay
887	阿根廷	Argentina
888	智利	Chile
889	秘魯,厄瓜多爾	Peru Ecuador
90	非洲	Africa
91	北非洲,埃及	North Africa Egypt
92	法屬非洲	French West and Equatorial Africa
93	中非洲	Central Africa
94	南非洲	South Africa

地域細分(續)GEOGRAPHICAL LIST　(cont.)

95	澳大利亞	Australia
96	新西蘭	New Zealand
97	大洋洲	Oceania
98	南極	Antarctic Regions
99	北極	Arctic Regions

附表三
時代細分　Appended Table III: CHRONOLOGICAL PERIODS

(a)　　中國　　Chinese Chronological Periods

1	太古至秦	Ancient Period (Earliest to B.C.206)
2	漢,三國	Han Dynasty and the Three Kingdoms (B.C.206-265 A.D.)
3	晋至隋	Chin Dynasty to Sui Dynasty (265-618)
4	唐,五代	T'ang and the Five Dynasties (618-960)
5	宋	Sung Dynasty (960-1279)
6	元	Yüan Dynasty (1280-1368)
7	明	Ming Dynasty (1368-1644)
8	清	Ch'ing Dynasty (1644-1912)
0	順治	Shun-chih (1644-1662)
1	康熙	K'ang-hsi (1662-1722)
2	雍正	Yung-chêng (1723-1735)
3	乾隆	Ch'ien-lung (1736-1795)
4	嘉慶	Chia-ch'ing (1796-1820)
5	道光	Tao-kuang (1821-1850)
6	咸豐	Hsien-fêng (1850-1861)
7	同治	T'ung-chih (1861-1874)
8	光緒	Kuang-hsü (1875-1908)
9	宣統	Hsüan-t'ung (1908-1912)

Chinese Chronological Periods (cont.)

9	民國	The Republic (1912 - date)	
1	革命時代及臨時政府	Revolution of 1911 and the Provisional Government at Nanking (1911-1912)	
2	袁氏當政	President Yüan Shih-k'ai (1912-1916)	
3	南北分裂	Division between the North and the South (1917-1927)	
4	國民政府	The Nationalist Government (1928-date)	
(b)	日本	Japanese Chronological Periods	
1	上古時代	Ancient Period (Earliest to 710 A.D.)	
2	奈良時代 大和時代	Nara Period	(710-781)
3	平安時代	Heian Period	(781-1185)
4	鎌倉時代	Kamakura Period	(1185-1333)
5	室町時代	Muromachi Period	(1333-1600)
6	江戸時代	Edo Period	(1600-1867)
7	明治時代	Meiji Period	(1868-1912)
8	現代	Contemporary Period	(1912-date)
(c)	西洋	Western Chronological Periods	
1	上古時代	Primitive and Ancient Period	
2	經典時代	Classical (Grecian and Roman Age)	
3	中世紀	Medieval, V - XV Centuries A.D.	
4	文藝復興	Renaissance, XIV - XVI Centuries	
5	近世	Modern (Since the middle of the XV Century)	
6	十七世紀	17th Century	
7	十八世紀	18th Century	
8	十九世紀	19th Century	
9	二十世紀	20th Century	

專類細分表甲至辛
SPECIAL TABLES A TO H FOR SUBDIVISION IN PARTICULAR CLASSES

表甲　　　　Table A: <u>Schedule for Arranging Works on</u>
經學類羣經專題研究細分　<u>Special Topics in Chinese Classics</u>

1	義例,哲理,天道,人倫	Theoretical, Philosophical, Cosmological and Ethical Studies
2	人物	Biographical Studies
3	史地	Historical and Geographical Studies
4	社會典制	Sociological and Institutional Topics
5	文字音義	Linguistic Studies
6	文藝	Literary Studies
7	藝術	Artistic Topics
8	科學名物	Scientific and Technological Topics
9	雜錄	Miscellaneous Studies (e.g. Indexes)

表乙　　　　Table B: <u>Schedule for Arranging Works</u>
個人哲學專著細分　　<u>of Individual Philosophers</u>

1	全書 先,白文,次有注釋者 依注釋者或編校者之 時代排列.	Complete Work (First plain text, then arrange text with annotations by annotator's or editor's date.)
2	節本 依編選者排.	Partial Edition. Selections (Arrange by compiler's date.)
3	單篇 依書名或篇名排.	Separate Books or Chapters (Arrange by title.)
4	偽書 先依書名排,相同之書 再依編校者年代排.	Spurious and Apocryphal Works (Arrange first by title and under each title by editor's date.)
5	傳記,書目 依作者時代排.	Biography and Bibliography (Arrange by date of the compiler.)

表乙 (續)　　　Table B　(cont.)

6　　評論　　　　　　Criticism and Interpretation
　　　　依著述者時代排列.　(Arrange by date of the author.)

7　　專題研究　　　Special Topics
　　　　先依内容分類.再依　(First arrange by subjects following
　　　　作者時代排列.　　the whole classification scheme and
　　　　　　　　　　　then by the author's date.)

8　　譯本　　　　　Translations

9　　其他同時作者　Other Contemporary Writers

表丙　　　　Table C: Schedule for Arranging Works on A
宗敎類各敎各宗派細分　　Particular Sect in Any Religion

1　　類書　　　　　Reference Books: Dictionaries, Glossaries,
　　　字典.辭典.事彙書目等.　Encyclopedias, Bibliographies, etc.

2　　概論　　　　　General Treatises

3　　敎典　　　　　Canons: Texts and Commentaries

4　　宗義專著　　　Doctrines: Interpretative Works
　　　白文及注釋.

5　　儀規　　　　　Rituals and Rules

6　　組織,敎會　　　Organization.　　Orders

7　　歷史　　　　　History

8　　傳記　　　　　Biography

9　　雜著　　　　　Miscellanies

表丁　　　Table D: Schedule for Arranging Works on Special
考古學各類器物體裁細分　　Classes of Archaeological Remains

1　　叢書.選集　　　Collections　　Selections

2　　目錄　　　　　Catalogues

3　　哲理.義例.通論　Theory.　Methodology.　General Treatises.

4　　史傳　　　　　History and Biography

表丁(續)　　Table D　(cont.)

5	考釋, 題跋	Identifications.　Commentaries
6	文字	Inscriptions.　Paleography
7	摹拓, 圖像	Reproductions.　Rubbings.　Illustrations
8	書目	Bibliography
9	雜錄	Miscellanies

表戊　　Table E: <u>Schedule for Form Subdivisions</u>
中國各代歷史體裁細分　　<u>in each period of Chinese History</u>

1	紀傳	Chi-chuan Style
2	編年	Annals
3	本末	Topical Records
4	史論	Historical Essays
5	考證, 書評	Critical Studies.　Book Reviews
6	史鈔, 課本	Historical Excerpts.　Textbooks
7	雜史, 史料	Miscellanies.　Sources
8	表譜, 地圖	Tables.　Charts.　Atlases.　Maps
9	書目, 索引	Bibliographies.　Indexes

表巳　　Table F: <u>Schedule for Form Subdivisions</u>
各種語文體裁細分　　<u>in Languages and Literatures</u>

語言　　<u>LANGUAGE</u>

.01	通論	General treatises
.02	文字	Orthography.　Inscriptions
.03	音韻	Phonology
.04	語源	Etymology
.05	字典, 辭書	Lexicography

表己 (續)　　Table F (cont.)

語言 (續)　　LANGUAGE (cont.)

.06	同義字,同音字	Synonyms. Homonyms
.07	文法	Grammar
.08	韻律,修辭	Prosody. Rhetoric
.09	俗語,方言	Idioms. Dialects
	文學	LITERATURE
.1	概論,通史	General Treatises. General History
.2	叢集	Anthologies. Collections
.3	詩歌	Poetry and songs
.4	戲劇	Drama
.5	小說	Fiction
.6	散文	Essays
.7	書牘	Letters
.8	雜著	Miscellanies
.9	兒童文藝	Children's literature

表庚　　Table G: Schedule for Arranging Literary Works of Individual Authors

文學家別集細分

1	全集	Complete Works
	依校注者時代排.	(Arrange by editor's or annotator's date.)
2	選集	Selections. Anthologies
	依選編者時代排.	(Arrange by compiler's date.)
3	詩集	Collection of Poems
	依校注者時代排.	(Arrange by editor's or annotator's date.)
4	文集	Prose and Essays
	依校注者時代排.	(Same as above.)

表庚(續)　　　Table G　(cont.)

5　　傳記, 書目　　Biography and Bibliography, including
　　　依編著者時代排.　diaries, journals and memoirs of the
　　　　　　　　　　author　(Arrange by compiler's date.)

6　　評論　　　　Interpretation and Criticism
　　　依編著者時代排.　(Arrange by author's date.)

7　　專題研究　　Special Topics
　　　先依內容分類, 再　(First arrange by subjects following
　　　依著者時代排.　the whole classification scheme and
　　　　　　　　　　then by author's date.)

8　　譯本　　　　Translations

9　　同時著者　　Other Contemporary Writers

表辛　　　Table H:　Schedule for Subdivisions
　　　　　　　　　in National Bibliography
各國書目細分

1　　叢刊, 總錄　　General and Collective

2　　歷代書目　　Bibliographies by Periods

3　　國學書目　　The Country as Subject

4　　特種書目　　Special Bibliographies
　　　以該國為研究對象之書目.

5　　地方書目　　Local Bibliographies

6　　個人書目　　Personal Bibliographies

7　　收藏書目　　Library Catalogs

8　　出版書目　　Publishers' Catalogs

9　　營業書目　　Trade Catalogs

THE ARRANGEMENT OF BOOKS ON THE SHELVES
AND OF CARDS IN THE SHELF-LIST

Books having the same class number must be differentiated from each other by some system. The number, which prevents confusion of different books on the same subject, is called the "book number." Perhaps the most common method is to arrange books within each class in the order of their arrival at the library. Either the accession number of the whole collection or that of each class is used to distinguish books from each other on the same subject. The chief difficulty of such a system is that books by the same author or different editions of the same work could not be kept together, because it is not likely that all would arrive at the library at the same time or in such close sequence that no other books on the same subject were received.

In order to avoid the above difficulty, tables of numbers for alphabeting authors' names or book-titles have been devised in the West.* In China and Japan because of the difficulty in arranging characters, such tables have not been successful. The author-table at its best is an indirect way of getting an arbitrary number. Much time is usually wasted in getting the desired number for a particular surname or book-title, because of the unsatisfactory and time-consuming method in which characters representing those names or titles are arranged.

Realizing the necessity of arranging Chinese and Japanese books on the same subject in some automatic "alphabetical" way, I devised a system of book-numbers for them, basing upon Wong's "Four-corner Numerical System of Arranging Chinese Characters" in the spring of 1927.** The complete version of that scheme in Chinese and also table of Wong's Four-corner System*** are reproduced on pages 356 and 357. The chief points may be rendered in English as follows:--

Author Numbers

1. For Chinese authors a number of three or four digits is used to distinguish one author from another within the same class. This number may be derived by taking the upper left corner stroke and the lower right corner stroke of the character for the author's surname. This gives two figures. The third figure will be the number which represents the upper left corner stroke of the first character for the author's given name (the forename or given name for a Chinese, man or woman, is usually in two characters, although more men have their forenames in one character than women). In small classes where books are not numerous, book-numbers consisting of three figures each will be sufficient. When necessary, a fourth figure representing the upper left corner stroke of the second character for the given name (or the lower right corner stroke

---

* In America the best known is "Cutter-Sanborn Author Table" and in England Brown's Biographical Table appended to his Subject Classification, 1914 is also well-known.
** Chiu, A. K.: "How to File Books in Chinese," Library Journal, Nov. 1, 1927.
*** Wong, Y. W.: The Revised Four-corner Numeral System of Arranging Chinese Character, 1st.ed.1928, Pocket edition, 1934; English edition, 1928; Shanghai, The Commercial Press; Japanese Translation by Fujio Mamiya, Osaka, Mamiya and Company, 1930.

of the first character, when the author's given name is only in one character) may be added. That is, when two authors have the same surname and forename, or although having different surnames or fore-names, when the two numbers, both in three figures, representing them are the same, then use a fourth figure for the second author.

2. For Japanese authors, Chinese authors with double surnames (i.e. sur-name in two characters), and societies or institutions serving as authors, a number of four figures is used, each figure being derived from the number representing the upper left corner stroke of each character.

3. For anonymous books, periodicals and general collective series (t'sung-shu) the book-number is to be derived from the first three or four char-acters of the title. The upper left corner of each character is taken and the resulting number in three or four digits (depending upon whether title is in three or more characters) is used as the book-number.

4. All book-numbers, whether in three or four figures, are to be arranged decimally like the Biographical Numbers in J. Duff Brown's Subject Classification, London, Grafton, 1914.

Title or Work Numbers
Different works of an author in the same class may be distinguished from one another by adding a number (one or two figures) representing the first character of the title to the author-mark after a point.

Edition Numbers
When a work has been commented or edited by different persons, which is usually the case with many Chinese and Japanese classics, the several editions may be differentiated from one another by adding the number repre-senting the commentator's or editor's surname (one or two figures) to the author-mark after a point.

Application of Wong's "Four-corner System"
In assigning numbers to represent a character, the strokes at the upper left and lower right corners are usually taken. When the lower or right half of the character has only one simple or complex stroke, it is always to be taken as the lower right corner and not to be regarded as zero (0).

The Result
By using the above system of book-numbers, all the works of an author or different editions of a word within any one class are kept together in a simple way, for the same author will always have the same author-mark or book-number in that class. Since the numbers can always be derived from the characters for authors' names or titles of books by those who know Wong's Four-corner System, it is not necessary to use any prepared table, and the time needed for getting a book-number for a Chinese or Japanese work is thus less than that necessary for obtaining a book-number for any Western book from an author-table.*

---

* For Western authors, "Cutter-Sanborn Author Table," "Merrill's Author Numbers," "Brown's Biographical Table" or any other alphabetic numbering scheme for authors may also be used with this Classification Scheme.

同類各書書碼編製法

一、同類各書，因分類號碼相同，普通以各書著者姓名編製各書書碼，其法如次：

二、中國著者取第一字左上右下二角，第二字左上一角及第三字左上一角，無第三字則取第二字右下角。

三、中國雙姓著者，日本著者，有漢譯姓名之西洋著者，及著者係社團或地域名時，取第一至第四字各字左上角。團體名冗長時僅取其中主要數字即足，如國立中央大學文學院，可取中央文學四字各左上角為書碼。

四、無名氏或著者不可考之書，依書名前四字左上角取書碼。

五、雜誌及彙集叢書，依雜誌或叢書名前四字左上角取書碼。

六、某書著者在分類表中已有固定號碼時，依著釋者或校訂者之姓名編製書碼。

七、年譜傳記之類，依被傳人姓名取書碼。

八、一書之各種注譯本，以注者或譯者姓名第一二字號碼，用小數點隔開，加於著者號碼之後。

九、同類同著者之書，號碼重複時，以各該書書名之第二字左上角號碼，以小數點隔開，加於著者號碼之後。

十、一書之各種版本，以出版年為次，或依入藏先後為次，用 a b c d 等字母分別，加於著者號碼之後。

十一、書碼普通以四位數為準，但書少之類，可用三位數。時以其一取三位數分別之，一律按小數十進法排列之。又同類中二著者號碼相同時，

十二、各字號碼皆照王雲五氏第二次改訂四角號碼檢字法採取，惟字之下部或右部祇有一筆或一複筆時，無論其在何地位，均作右下角而不作零（0）。

第一条　本法取字之四角，以号码代表之。其四角之定法如下：先定五种笔形。

号码	笔形	例	说明
0	头	一丶广宀	凡与丶及此四类之头，其角均作为0（4567896为号者皆然）
1	横	一一乚乙	一乚之横，与乚皆为横
2	垂	｜丿	凡垂与丿皆作之
3	点捺	丶乀	凡点与捺，均作3，亅于3
4	叉	十乂	凡手与十大之交，皆作4
5	插	扌手夫	一手通过两手以上作5
6	方	囗	圆方匚回田甲曰皆作6
7	角	厂丁乛乙刀乙	丁厂乛等各类交零皆作7
8	八	八丷人入	凡八丷人入分张之笔作8
9	小	小⺌⺍小忄	凡小形类此者均作9

第二条　每字取其四角之笔形，共四角。

其法顺序如下：

（一）左上角　（二）右上角　（三）左下角　（四）右下角

(例) 顛（…）載（…）

357

THE ARRANGEMENT OF THE CLASSIFIED SUBJECT CATALOG

In American libraries the subject catalog is with few exceptions* always in the Dictionary Form, that is, each card is labelled with an appropriate heading, and the cards are grouped together under the same subject headings in the catalog. The arrangement of headings and therefore of cards is purely mechanical or alphabetical from A to Z. Entirely unrelated headings are filed together simply because they happen to begin with the same letter of the alphabet. Thus, numismatics, nuns and nurseries (horticulture) are filed closely together, although they have entirely nothing to do with one another. The Oriental and, in many cases, the European finds this kind of subject catalog illogical and hard to understand.** On the continent of Europe, and especially in Germany, the subject catalog, like that in the Orient, is usually in the classified form, which the German calls "Systematischer katalog."*** In China and Japan the Classified Subject Catalog has a history of more than two thousand years. Although the systems of classification used in different dynasties and by different libraries in each dynasty have undergone changes, the Classified Form of Subject Catalog has never been questioned. As most Chinese encyclopedias are arranged by categories in some systematic classified scheme, the Chinese have found the Classified Subject Catalog logical and easy to use.

The Dictionary Form of Subject Catalog for Chinese and Japanese books is beset with two other difficulties: First, the lack of standardization in terms, scientific as well as ordinary ones, makes it difficult for librarians to choose proper characters as subject headings. It is true that in any classified catalog the different classes and subdivisions must also be designated by appropriate words, but here the classifier or the subject cataloger has the liberty of using short phrases or more than one alternative term to express the content of a class. Moreover, terms set in their proper places in a logical and definite system of classification are clear and intelligible; whereas, detached from proper context, they become indefinite and ambiguous. Such is the case with Western subject headings; it is even more so with Chinese and Japanese terms. Second, the difficult way or ways in which characters are arranged make the task of assigning subject headings in Chinese or Japanese by the cataloger and the use of the Dictionary Form of Subject Catalog by the public a slow and cumbersome business. For these reasons very few libraries in China (and only recently a few libraries in Japan) have adopted the Dictionary Form of Subject Catalog. The great majority of libraries in both China and Japan have the Classified Subject

---

* The outstanding exceptions are the well-known classed catalogs maintained at the John Crear Library, Chicago, the Carnegie Library of Pittsburgh and the Engineering Societies Library in New York.

** Even American librarians begin to feel that such a subject catalog is ill defined. Osborn, A. D.: "The Crisis in Cataloging," Library Quarterly, vol. XI, no. 4 (Oct. 1941) p. 409.

*** For a discussion of recent developments in subject cataloging in Germany, see an article by Sigismund Rune tr. by John J. Lund in the Library Quarterly, vol. XI, no. 1, Jan. 1941.

Catalog supplemented by the title and author catalogs. Hence American Far Eastern libraries may follow this practice with advantages of established usage and economy.

This Classification Scheme may be used for arranging the Classified Subject Catalog by any American Far Eastern library, in which books have been classified by some other system. In other words, it is feasible to treat the shelflist as a separate tool apart from the Classified Subject Catalog,* for the shelflist, whether on a fixed or relative location basis, is always a catalog of the location of books in the library and no catalog of locations could strictly follow a bibliographic classification or the classification of knowledge. For practical purposes, it is always desirable to arrange books on the shelves or cards in the shelflist in a mechanical way (i.e. alphabetical or other mnemonic way), so that people can find them easily. But in the Classified Subject Catalog the aim is to arrange subjects in a systematic way. Here mechanical devices and arbitrary arrangements must give way to the requirements of logic and evolutional development. Hence in the catalogs of most old Chinese and Japanese libraries, books are arranged in a chronological order within each class. This is true not only of scientific and technical books but also of works on history, literature and many other subjects on the ground that the last book on a subject is influenced by the knowledge contained in all works previous to it. The following two tables of rules -- one in Chinese and one in English -- are offered as a suggestive way to arrange cards in the Classified Subject Catalog. They may be cut out, framed and hung over the Subject Catalog Case.

---

* While travelling in Europe in 1930 I found that in many European libraries the arrangement of books on the shelves did not follow any classified order. Books have been arranged by sizes or in the order of their arrival at the library. Since a Systematic or Classified Subject Catalog is always available and the closed-shelf system is the rule, such an arbitrary shelf arrangement has not been a great hardship as it would be in America. Of Rune, op. cit. p. 50. In American libraries where open access to the shelves is being granted freely to readers, it is desirable, of course, to have the shelf arrangement roughly follow the order of the Classified Subject Catalog.

分類目錄排列法

一、本館中日文圖書分類目錄依類目號碼（即目片左上角
所記者上行為類號下行表示年代但取閱圖書時請用右
上角所記號碼）排列其大綱如後

二、同類之書舊籍照著者年代排列時人著作以其出版年
月為次

三、一類中同一著者之各書以成書年月為次

四、一書之各種注本以注釋者或編纂者之年代為次

五、同一書而版次不同者照版次先後排列

六、讀者如欲尋究專題請檢閱詳細分類表及其索引其法
先檢索引中類目得其號碼再按號碼在目錄中尋所欲閱
圖書之目片

ARRANGEMENT OF CARDS IN THE CLASSIFIED SUBJECT CATALOGUE

1. Both Chinese and Japanese Subject Catalogue cards are arranged by numbers on the upper left corner of each card. The upper number represents the class or subject, and the lower number the date. (But books should be called for by the shelf number or call number on the upper right corner.) The following is an Outline of the Classification Schedule.*

2. Books on the same subject have the same class number. Old books are further arranged by authors' dates, while works by living authors are filed by dates of publication under the same class number.

3. All the works of an author on the same subject bearing the same class number are sub-arranged by their dates of compilation.

4. When a book is edited or annotated by two persons, the two editions are treated as two different works, which are arranged by the dates of their editors or annotators.

5. Two editions, which have the same textual matter but show different typographical features, are arranged by their publication dates.

6. For any specific subject, please consult the Classification Scheme and its Index. To find what the Library has on any given subject, find from the Index the class number of that subject. Under this number in the Classified Subject Catalogue will be found all the books in individual editions as well as those in collections (Ts'ung-shu or Sōshū)

* The fullness of the Outline Scheme to be posted will depend upon the resources of each library.